The Golden Age of Louis-Ferdinand Céline

Nicholas Hewitt

The Golden Age of
Louis-Ferdinand Céline

Oswald Wolff Books
Berg Publishers
Leamington Spa / Hamburg / New York
Distributed exclusively in the US and Canada by
St. Martin's Press, *New York*

First published in 1987 by
Berg Publishers Limited
24 Binswood Avenue, Leamington Spa, CV32 5SQ, UK
Schenefelder Landstr. 14K, 2000 Hamburg 55, W.-Germany
175 Fifth Avenue/Room 400, New York, NY 10010, USA

British Library Cataloguing in Publication Data

Hewitt, Nicholas
The golden age of Louis-Ferdinand Céline.—
(Oswald Wolff books)
1. Céline, Louis-Ferdinand—Criticism
and interpretation
I. Title
843'.912   PQ2607.E834Z/
ISBN 0–85496–524–6

Library of Congress Cataloging-in-Publication Data

Hewitt, Nicholas.
The golden age of Louis-Ferdinand Céline.

"Oswald Wolff books."
Bibliography: p.
Includes index.
1. Céline, Louis-Ferdinand, 1894–1961—Criticism and
interpretation.   I. Title.
PQ2607.E834Z695   1987   843'.912   86–26852
ISBN 0–85496–524–6

Printed in Great Britain by Billings of Worcester

Contents

For Kim

Abbreviations

Works by Céline are referred to in the text under the following indications:

BD   *Les Beaux draps*, Nouvelles Editions Françaises, 1941
BM   *Bagatelles pour un massacre*, Denoël, 1937
CP   *Casse-pipe*, Gallimard, coll: 'Folio'
E   *L'Eglise*, Gallimard, 1952
EC   *L'Ecole des cadavres*, Denoël, 1938
GB1   *Guignol's Band*, I, Gallimard, coll. 'Folio'
GB2   *Guignol's Band*, II (*Le Pont de Londres*), Gallimard, coll. 'Folio'
MC   *Mort à crédit*, in *Romans*, I, Gallimard, coll: 'La Pléiade', 1981
Mea   *Mea culpa*, Denoël, 1936
V   *Voyage au bout de la nuit*, in *Romans*, I, Gallimard, coll: 'La Pléiade', 1981

BLFC   *Bulletin de la Bibliothèque L-F Céline* (Publications de la Bibliothèque de Littérature française contemporaine de l'université Paris 7)
CC   *Cahiers Céline*, Gallimard
HER   *Cahiers de l'Herne*

Preface

This study began as an attempt to fill a gap in work on Céline by exploring his role as a historian of French society and politics in the inter-war years. Research into this aspect of his work, however, began to show very rapidly that his relationship to the period in question and his entire historical perspective in the years 1920–44 were both more oblique and more complicated than was originally suggested. In fact, Céline's evocation of French society between the wars is remarkably fragmentary when considered in isolation, approaching even vagueness, and is confined to expression of fears of the encroachment of modern techniques of industrialisation and the threat of war, of which the meeting-point is his anti-Semitism, expressed in the pamphlets of the late 1930s. The real solid historical base of Céline's writing — fictional and non-fictional — of this period is to be found, not in the period itself, but in the preceeding age of the *belle époque*, which ended definitively with the October Revolution in Russia and the Versailles Peace Conference, and which constitutes, for the first half of Céline's literary production — up to the end of the Second World War — a Golden Age, to be evoked, to be explored for its significance both as an absolute value of social coherence and as an awesome omen of social and technological evolution, and, constantly, as a measure against which to set the inadequacies of the present. An analysis of Céline's use of history, therefore, must go beyond the direct confrontation of the author with his own historical period, and must take into account the fact that Céline as a writer belongs to two historical periods: the Edwardian age before the First World War, from which he draws so many of his cultural signposts and which he examines with coldness but also with increasing affection as the present becomes darker; and the world of the inter-war years itself, in which he is writing but from which he feels increasingly exiled. It is precisely from this sense of exile that Céline derives one of his most complex and enduring images, that of the *fantôme*, the ghost who is condemned to live in a world which is no longer his own, who represents a vestige of a life which is no more and who, quite literally, is there to haunt the present, as a reproach and as a sense of loss. From this process of interaction between the ghost and the Golden Age, of which he is a shadow and a product, emerges a different perspective on Céline's work of the inter-war years, which reveals an altogether more complex system of historical vision and writing from the very outset than that which is normally attributed to him. The concept of the Golden Age dictates, not merely the author's political and intellectual choices, but the procedures of the writing itself.

In preparing this study, I have benefited from the advice and help of a number of individuals and institutions to whom I would wish to record my warmest thanks: the University of Warwick, who generously granted me study leave and contributed towards the cost of research travel and attendance at conferences; the University of Warwick library; the British Library; the Bibliothèque Nationale; the Library of the Musée des Invalides, Paris; the Library of the Institut de l'Histoire du Temps Présent, Paris; the Library of the Musée des Arts et Traditions Populaires, Paris; the Bibliothéque de Littérature Française Contemporaine, at the Université de Paris VII. I should also like to thank M. Henri Godard, of the Université de Paris VII, for his interest and help on a number of problems, and M. Jean-Pierre Dauphin, of Editions Gallimard, who has been a constant help in the research and composition of this volume. Finally, my thanks are due to Dr Merlin Thomas, of New College, Oxford, who was one of the founding members of the Société des Etudes Céliniennes and who, by inviting me to give a paper for the first colloquium of the Society, in 1975, pushed my work on Céline into what has become this volume, and to the Société des Etudes Céliniennes itself which, since 1975, has continued, with often too little recognition, to make available indispensable research documents and to maintain a high level of Céline criticism in the form of its biennial conferences.

Introduction

Céline and Zola

The beginning of the twentieth century in France was characterised in many quarters by a sense of foreboding, by a millenarian belief that, in some way, with the disappearance of the nineteenth century, even if it was only Léon Daudet's *Stupide dix-neuvième siècle*,[1] an entire world had vanished, to be replaced by something immeasurably more frightening and sordid. Commentators differed as to where the barrier between the worlds was to be precisely located. Most, looking back from the vantage-point of the inter-war years, set the crucial date of transition at either 1914 or 1918, the beginning of the First World War which definitively transformed the map of the Western world, or its end, which saw the fate of that Western world pass into the hands of the United States. For Louis Guilloux, looking back from the 1970s, it was the Bolshevik Revolution of 1917 which ushered in the New Order,[2] whilst for Edouard Drumont, a contemporary observer of the close of the nineteenth century, the *belle époque* itself already constituted 'la Fin d'un monde'.[3] Wherever the precise demarcation line was drawn, there is no doubt that, for French writers after the First World War, there was the marked sense of a barrier — cultural, social, political, and economic — between the inter-war period of 1918 to 1940 and the first *entre-deux-guerres*, the *belle époque* of the 1890s and 1900s, which only assumed its title in the first place as an antidote to the growing bleakness of the 1920s and 1930s. This shift from the old world to the new, effected through the four-year trauma of the First World War, possessed precise political and economic implications for

1. Léon Daudet, *Le Stupide dix-neuvième siècle, exposé des insanités meurtrières qui se sont abattus sur la France depuis 130 ans, 1789–1919*, Paris, Nouvelles Editions de la Librairie Nationale, 1922.
2. Louis Guilloux, *Carnets 1921–1944*, Paris, Gallimard, 1978.
3. Edouard Drumont, *La Fin d'un monde*, Paris, Albert Savine, 1892.

[3]

France. In the first place, as Roger Magraw has admirably demonstrated, in spite of continuing political and social dissent from
within the nation, momentarily suspended by the war itself, 1914
saw 'the success of the Republican bourgeosie in consolidating its
hegemony over French society'.[4] Secondly, by the end of the war,
France was definitively moving from an economy based essentially
on the traditional peasantry and urban petite bourgeoisie, towards a
model of social organisation which derived from American techniques of industrialisation fostered by Taylor and Ford. In other
words, by 1918, France was noticeably on the verge of relinquishing
its traditional economic and social patterns and of entering that
world which, in its caricatural version, is Chaplin's *Modern Times*.

Céline himself is in no doubt as to which date best signifies
France's change of direction towards the modern world. In *Mort à
crédit*, the year 1900, with its Universal Exposition casts a long
shadow which not only darkens the lives of the narrator and his
family in the years prior to the First World War, but extends as far
as the mature narrator, reminiscing from the vantage-point of 1934.
The Exposition symbolised the consolidation of political and economic power by the industrial bourgeoisie and thus ushered in a
century to be dominated by that class and by the spirit of the
nouveau: the principle of the modern in industrial and social
organisation and, more specifically, *art nouveau* in the plastic and
visual arts. Yet one class was to be the definitive victim of this
passage to bourgeois hegemony and to the modernity principle: the
narrator's own social group, the Parisian artisanal petite bourgeoisie, squeezed out of the capital as Ferdinand's family are jostled
out of the Exposition itself.

It is Céline who is the great chronicler of this transition and the
modern poet of the lost world of the *belle époque*, just as Baudelaire
is the poet of the old Paris destroyed by Haussmann, and he
manipulates his chronicle and his awareness of a lost age in such a
way as to provide a despairing indictment of French society in the
inter-war years. Yet, in this manipulation, he is embarking on a
project which is highly complex. In one sense, much of Céline's
writing has its origins in the nineteenth century. Thus, Philippe
Muray has rightly drawn attention to his positivism and his equally
characteristic debt to its counterpart, nineteenth-century occultism,[5]
whilst Philippe Roussin, in an important article, explores Céline's

---

4. Roger Magraw, *France 1815–1914: The Bourgeois Century*, London, Fontana,
1983, p. 354.
5. See Philippe Muray, *Céline*, Paris, Le Seuil, coll. 'Tel quel', 1981; Muray, 'Mort
à credo. Céline, le positivisme et l'occultisme', BLFC 8, 95–116.

attempt to continue into the twentieth century the nineteenth-century writer's ambition to 'tout dire'.[6] This attempt to establish a significant foothold in the nineteenth century is surely at the origin of his adoption of his maternal grandmother's name for his pseudonym. Philippe Muray is undoubtedly correct in suggesting a psychoanalytical component to this choice which directs itself to the grandmother whilst deliberately excluding the mother,[7] yet it possesses a more obvious historical significance: by using the name of his grandmother, Céline Lesjean, who died in 1904, rather than that of his mother Margueritte Guillou, who died in 1945,[8] he has linked his destiny to someone whose entire life was lived before the definitive onset of the modern world and has established that perspective as one of the poles of his work.[9] This establishment of a nineteenth-century stance in Céline's work is not to imply, however, that he is undertaking a simple celebration of nineteenth-century society in order to criticise that of the twentieth. When Robert Poulet writes of a 'fond mal dissimulé de traditionnalisme vieille France',[10] this should not be taken as indicating a particularly positive affection for old French values as such. There is little, after all, in *Mort à crédit*, to justify such affection: the petit-bourgeois world, whether in decline or not, has little attractiveness in its tight moral standards borrowed from its own vulnerability and in its financial stringency and materialism. Nevertheless, there is sorrow at its passing in Céline's work and stronger admiration for less corrupted areas of *belle époque* society, such as the pre-war cavalry.[11]

In other words, Céline bases his writing of the inter-war years upon a complex relationship between the past, from which he has dredged his pseudonym but to which he feels little loyalty, and the present, which horrifies him and in which he feels an intruder. He is therefore caught between two ages, in neither of which he can believe with any degree of conviction, and which reflect each other in such a way that they negate; and, between the two ages lies the barrier of the cataclysmic war which threatens, in its turn, to repeat itself. It is from this precise historical situation, that of alienation

6. Philippe Roussin, 'Tout dire', BLFC 8, 117–32.

7. Muray, *Céline*, pp. 65–6.

8. See François Gibault, *Céline*, 1, *1894–1932, Le Temps des espérances*, Paris, Mercure de France, 1977, Annexe II.

9. It is interesting to note that the use of the *mother's* name as a pseudonym is by no means unusual, and two examples from the *belle époque* are the figures of Ravachol and Picasso.

10. Robert Poulet, *Entretiens familiers avec Louis-Ferdinand Céline*, Paris, Plon, coll. 'Tribune Libre', 1958, p. 66.

11. See, particularly, the fragments of *Casse-pipe* in HER 1.

from the modern present-day world of the inter-war years and only vestigial confidence in the values of the *belle époque*, that the concrete nature of Céline's pessimism emerges. It is a pessimism which falls into a different category from that of Malraux, Marcel Arland and the *nouveau mal du siècle*, although both are to some extent generational problems which derive from the inapplicable nature of traditional values in the context of the post-war world. It is very different, also, from the concept of the Absurd in the early writings of Sartre and Camus, which has as its source a purely abstract clash between philosophically irreconcilable values. The difference lies, primarily, in the fact that the *nouveau mal du siècle* and the Absurd are the product of intellectual crises which have much to do with the problems of writing and thinking but little to do with social situations: for that very reason, there is a hint of artificiality about the way in which they are constructed, as if they are problems which carry with them a built-in solution. Malraux's *La Tentation de l'Occident* and 'D'une jeunesse européenne' already look forward to *La Voie royale* and *Les Conquérants* because, in Malraux's 'system', the Absurd already presupposes action and adventurism as its antidote and it is, in some ways, the necessary clearing of the philosophical ground before the philosophically significant action can take place. Similarly, Camus uses the concept of the Absurd almost as Descartes uses systematic doubt, again in order to clear the ground of all vestiges of bad faith which may prevent the passage to authentic revolt.[12] Céline's pessimism, on the other hand, is not self-generated, but arises from a specific historical perception, and for that reason it is far less easily dispersed. In this respect, it is far closer to that of Bernanos, of the same generation as Céline, and who wages the same ultimately futile battle, 'la France contre les robots'.[13]

At the same time, it is Céline's particular historical perspective which is at the source of the 'modernity' of his writing. Yet, here again it is necessary to be precise. It is not a question, as Philippe Muray suggests, of Céline making a conscious effort in the direction of modernity in literature; rather, modernity is imposed upon him by the fact that, however much he fears and despises the present, he is unable to return to or sustain past modes of writing. The *art poétique* in *Guignol's Band*: 'Le Jazz a renversé la valse, l'Impressionisme a tué le "faux-jour", vous écrirez "télégraphique" ou

---

12. See: Albert Camus, *Carnets*, Paris, Gallimard, 1962.

13. Georges Bernanos, *La France contre les robots*, Rio de Janeiro, 1944; Paris, Laffont, 1947.

vous écrirez plus du tout!' (GB 1, 377), prescribes 'telegraphic' writing as a means of dealing with the *fait accompli* of changing artistic modes. Similarly, in his 1933 address, 'Hommage à Zola', Céline indicates that his own method of writing is not so much a revolution against the kind of traditional forms of fiction resumed in Naturalism, as a recognition that, in addition to losing the relative stability and meaning of French society in the *belle époque*, he and his generation had also lost any possibility of writing with confidence in the same style as their forebears. In other words, Céline is cut off, not merely from his historical base, but from a cultural context as well, a cultural context which he is then forced to reinvent.

The 'Hommage à Zola' is an interesting text which has often failed to receive adequate critical interest. Doubtless, Céline's famous comment in a letter to Eveline Pollet: 'Justes Cieux je n'aime pas du tout Zola' (HER 1, 101), has led readers to devalue the text as a whole, seeing Zola the Naturalist and Céline the Modernist as improbably assorted bedfellows. Yet as Merlin Thomas points out,[14] and as early reviewers of *Mort à crédit*[15] were quick to recognise, the association of Céline with Zola is by no means gratuitous and, indeed, is essential if we are to understand the complexity of Céline's project in the inter-war years. Both novelists manipulate a complicated and ambigous time-scale: Zola, writing in the early years of the Third Republic, is acting both as an observer and chronicler of the Second Empire and as a prophet, using the deficiencies of Louis-Napoleon's regime to castigate and warn his contemporaries; Céline adopts precisely the same technique in his juxtaposition of the *belle époque* and the *entre-deux-guerres*. Both Céline and Zola are hyperconscious of the role of a war in ending the society they are chronicling: Zola's Second Empire collapses spectacularly at Sedan and is buried in the blood and violence of the Commune; Céline's *belle époque* is finally killed off in August 1914, the date which sees the beginning of *Voyage au bout de la nuit* and which echoes throughout his work of the inter-war years. Similarly, there are few writers who have such a feeling for and perception of the operation of gold and money in modern societies at all levels, material and psychological, as Céline and Zola. Finally, both writers, Zola in his fiction, Céline predominantly in his non-fiction, adopt a scientific model for their observation and analysis, a model

14. See: Merlin Thomas, *Louis-Ferdinand Céline*, London, Faber and Faber, 1979, pp. 55–6.
15. See: Patrick Macarthy, *Céline*, London, Allen Lane, 1975, p. 105.

which in both cases dervies in large part from the example of Pasteur. As Céline sums up Zola's position in the modern world:

> L'oeuvre de Zola ressemble pour nous par certains côtés à l'oeuvre de Pasteur, si solide, si vivante encore, en deux ou trois points essentiels. Chez ces deux hommes transposés, nous retrouvons la même technique méticuleuse de création, le même souci de probité expérimentale et surtout le même formidable pouvoir de démonstration, chez Zola devenu épique. Ce serait beaucoup trop pour notre époque. (HER 1, 172)

Thus, whilst in *La Vie et l'oeuvre de Philippe-Ignace Semmelweis*, Céline invokes Pasteur as the scientist who unconsciously recuperates Semmelweis, and whilst, in the medical pamphlets of the 1920s and the anti-Semitic pamphlets of the 1930s, he adopts the perspective of the medical scientist observing the health of society, when he comes to fiction, the model of Pasteur is a tragic mockery, conveyed through the burlesque depiction of Parapine and the Institut Bioduret Joseph in *Voyage au bout de la nuit*, which, incidentally, establishes a link with *Germinal* through the child Bébert.

Céline's detailed exploitation of Zola, however, is best seen in the close relationship between *Mort à crédit* and *L'Assommoir*. In Zola's novel, gold appears as a central reference, the symbol of an entire scale of value and power from which the characters are rigorously excluded. It is ironic, yet fitting, that these characters should be confined to the area of Paris known as 'La Goutte d'or', and Zola is careful to establish through his depiction of the slum district an excremental use of gold which will permit the revenge of Nana, as *la Mouche d'or*, on Second Empire society, and which will be fully exploited by Céline in his writing of the inter-war years. In addition, the gold is present in *L'Assommoir* through the goldsmiths, the Lorilleux couple, in the same way that it is present in *Mort à crédit* in the persons of Gorloge and his wife. Nor is the common time element lacking: conveyed through the 'mort' component of Céline's title and operating through credit and the loss of the past, time is central to the operation of *Mort à crédit*, just as it is to that of *L'Assommoir*, which reflects the time-scale of the Second Empire itself, by running from 1850 to 1869, and which charts the irreversible process of the decline of Gervaise through constant references to her *pendule*, which she is ultimately obliged to pawn: the *horloge du crédit* itself, which will dominate *Mort à crédit* and will become personnified in Titus Van Claben in *Guignol's Band*, the pawnbroker of Greenwich. Thus, *Mort à crédit*, which in its Modernist concern with memory, the past and the passage of time, owes a considerable specific debt to Proust, also looks back to Zola's Naturalist evocation of the decline of the *petits métiers* under the Second Empire in *L'Assommoir*. His scene depicting the visit of Gervaise's wedding guests to the Louvre, in which they become literally and figuratively lost in the labyrinth of the museum, has the same status as that showing the visit of Ferdinand's family to the Universal Exposition in that both scenes emphasise the disorientation of the Parisian artisans in a context in which they do not belong and from which they are in the process of being excluded by a triumphant bourgeoisie. And the final link between *Mort à crédit* and *L'Assommoir* is the fact that Zola's novel, too, has its Auguste and its Clémence: Auguste Lantier, the former companion of Gervaise and the instrument of her later ruin, and Clémence, the employee of Gervaise in the more prosperous days of her laundry business.

In other words, as both Philippe Roussin and Philippe Muray have suggested, there is a strong Zolaesque side to Céline's literary production which, as with all his literary sources, operates in a far more detailed way than normally assumed. Yet he is prevented from mere repetition or continuation of the Naturalist tradition by the barriers of the 1900 Exposition and the First World War, which mean that he can no longer write like Zola even if he wished to. Culturally, Céline is separated from Naturalism in the same way that he is separated from the *belle époque* historically, and by the same obstacles. It is for this reason that he introduces his 'Hommage à Zola' with the words: 'En pensant à Zola, nous demeurons un peu gênés devant son oeuvre' (HER 1, 169). For: 'A l'exposition de 1900, nous étions encore bien jeune, mais nous avons gardé le souvenir quand même, bien vivace, que c'etait une énorme brutalité . . . La vie moderne commençait' (HER 1, 169). It is precisely for those, like Céline, who are condemned to live in the modern world ushered in by the Exposition, that the old project of Naturalism is impossible: 'Aujourd'hui, le naturalisme de Zola, avec les moyens que nous possédons pour nous renseigner, devient presque impossible' (HER 1, 169). It is impossible, both because the project is no longer credible, and because the response of society would be too repressive. Henceforth, the creative writer must take refuge in 'les symboles et les rêves! Tous les transferts que la loi n'atteint pas, n'atteint pas encore! Car enfin c'est dans les symboles et les rêves que nous passons les neuf-dixièmes de notre vie, puisque les neuf-dixièmes de notre existence, c'est-à-dire du plaisir vivant, nous sont inconnus ou interdits' (HER 1, 169–70).

The 'Hommage à Zola' was clearly written at the height of

Freud's influence upon Céline, an influence which contributed to rendering his concept of the practise of literature immeasurably more complex than the Naturalist model. It is in part for this reason that '[il] n'est plus question de l'imiter ou de le suivre' (HER, 1, 172). For the Freudian model ultimately subverts and destroys the optimism which is, in spite of everything, inherent in Zola's Naturalism. In the first place, the 'Hommage à Zola' conveys an embryonic version of that general social and political pessimism which emerges clearly in *Mea culpa* four years later: 'Nous voici parvenus au bout de vingt siècles de haute civilisation et cependant aucun régime ne résisterait à deux mois de vérité. Je veux dire la société marxiste aussi bien que nos sociétés bourgeoises ou fascistes' (HER 1, 170). Secondly, following Freud, and, in particular, *Civilisation and its Discontents*, Céline is convinced that the 'instinct de mort chez l'Homme' (HER 1, 170) is immeasurably stronger than the pleasure principle which the 'symboles et les rêves' are originally designed to explore and translate, and that the death instinct is propelling the world towards another World War. In the shadow of an imminent renewed conflict, the optimism of a Zola is misplaced and unobtainable.

It is perhaps for that very reason that it possesses a dignity, a grandeur and a courage which are redundant in 'la vie moderne': 'Il fallait beaucoup de libéralisme pour supporter l'Affaire Dreyfus. Nous sommes loin de ces temps, malgré tout, académiques' (HER 1, 172). In comparison with the epic quality of Zola's project, the inter-war years appear petty and sordid. The problem is that, whilst the results of Zola's analyses remain true for the 1930s, as for the 1880s, the will to deal with their implications has evaporated: 'Nous n'avons évidemment ni le don, ni la force, ni la foi qui créent les grands mouvements d'âme' (HER 1, 172). It is this which constitutes the tragedy of the French artist of the inter-war years: the crusading power of words is no longer possible or credible. As Céline concludes:

Si notre musique tourne au tragique c'est qu'elle a ses raisons. Les mots d'aujourd'hui comme notre musique vont plus loin qu'au temps de Zola. Nous travaillons à présent par la sensibilité et non plus par l'analyse, en somme 'du dedans'. Nos mots vont jusqu'aux instincts et les touchent parfois, mais en même temps, nous avons appris que là s'arrêtait, et pour toujours, notre pouvoir (HER 1, 171).

There are not many definitions of Modernism which emphasise so clearly the movement's technical innovation and subtlety at the same time as its political impotence. Céline stands yet again, however, in a kind of no man's land in which the Naturalist ambition for committed and effective language, fulfilled ultimately in his own work in the anti-Semitic pamphlets, stands alongside the Modernist recognition of political redundancy.

This ambiguous situation, in which the validity of the Naturalist vision is still accepted, but where it is subverted by the impossibility of its implementation, has profound implications for Céline's work of the inter-war years. As a social and political analyst, he retains many of the same preoccupations as Zola and the Naturalists. Thus, from the medical writings of the 1920s emerge some of the classic Naturalist social themes: housing conditions and working conditions as determining factors in human development, the curse of alcoholism, all fostered by government and bourgeois neglect. Similarly, the pacifism implicit in all the volumes of *Les Rougon-Macquart*, with the looming shadow of 1870, dominates Céline's own work, which is bounded in the inter-war years by the traumatic memory of August 1914 and the certainty of June 1940. More ambiguously, Céline shares with Zola a similar fear of violence in all forms, particularly that violence which springs from the collective responses of a group who, individually, may be perfectly peaceable. The crowd has the same threatening status for both Céline and Zola: the rampaging crowd of striking miners in *Germinal*, likened, in the imagery of Shakespeare's history plays, to the force of an unleashed flood, looks forward to the potential *brutalité* of the crowds at the 1900 Exposition and the actual destructive power of the crowds who sack the offices of Courtial's *Le Génitron* in *Mort à crédit* and will, ultimately, wreck Céline's own apartment in Montmartre in 1944.

In the case of Zola, however, the fear of the crowd, built upon memories of the Commune, serves only to modify his own political significance and to shift it a notch towards the centre: the self-professed revolutionary is far more the mouthpiece of Clemenceau's Radicals than he may care to recognise. For Céline, however, the basic agreement with the Naturalist diagnosis and his similar distrust of violence and the crowd have a more complicated effect, for the precise reason that the fundamental social optimism which motivates Zola's work, in common with that of all nineteenth-century scientists, is now no longer possible. Céline is in the position of being forced to observe the appalling social conditions of urban France in the inter-war years and to contemplate a repetition of 1914 without the slightest conviction that the process can be mitigated or reversed. It is for this reason that his attitude to history is subtly different from that of Zola. The Naturalists chose as their historical space the period of the Second Empire, because they were politically opposed to it, because, in its twenty-year span, it offered possibilities of a biological metaphor of growth and decline, and because, by virtue of its position in the very recent collective memory of the French, it could be invoked as a potent lesson for the early years of the Third Republic. For Céline, however, writing in the inter-war years, when the Third Republic had established itself, largely through the First World War, as the unchallenged vehicle of bourgeois rule, the past no longer has the status of a lesson able to change the present: he is living in the irremediable and the past is there both as an explanation of the irreversible process which has led to the present and as the tantalisingly close image of a world which is no longer attainable. It is for this reason that, in common with other writers of the inter-war years, his historical references go further into the past than the immediately preceeding regime: there is a strong Napoleonic element in Céline's work which, like the evocation of the Emperor by Malraux and the writers of the *nouveau mal du siècle*, serves to underline the pettiness of the present; similarly, like Drieu la Rochelle or Bernanos, the Middle Ages appear in his work as a lost Golden Age of action and faith. In other words, whereas Zola and the Naturalists still retain some faith in historical progression, Céline increasingly perceives himself as caught in a cycle of historical repetition, in which the present is despicable, the future frightening, and the past lost. His whole fictional output of the inter-war years, characterised by its depiction of miscarriages and abortions, constitutes a powerful anti-*Germinal*.

In this context, whereas Zola's fear of the crowd and his underlying psychological obsessions serve to act as a break on his revolutionary, progressive ambitions, and push him towards a position of bourgeois liberalism, in the case of Céline, the same elements, coupled with his historical pessimism, make him downright reactionary. With no future to look forward to and no past to which to return, Céline simply lashes out at the present. In one of the most curious paradoxes of modern intellectual history, the man who, in 1933, recognised that '[il] fallait beaucoup de libéralisme pour supporter l'Affaire Dreyfus', had, by 1937, deprived of that 'libéralisme', become the author of *Bagatelles pour un massacre*. Yet it is precisely because of the dislocation of the Naturalist faith in history that Céline is apparently so hesitant and so contradictory in his political stances: the contradictory views on Ford and 'Fordism' in the medical writings of the 1920s and the Detroit episode of *Voyage au bout de la nuit*; the mockery of racism and nationalism in the opening sequence of that novel and the adoption of the very same principles five years later in the anti-Semitic pamphlets; the modest, tentative faith in Communism up to 1936, and the rabidly anti-Soviet writing after the journey to Russia. In this context, Céline is more than usually representative of the political and ideological confusion in France in the inter-war years.

It is precisely on this point of confusion, however, that Céline departs most radically from the Naturalist model, and not simply in terms of content. Zola's fiction may present ambiguities and complexities of which even he was unaware, but his polemical writing remains crystal clear: there is no possible doubt, in a reading of *J'accuse*, as to the commitment of the author or the identity of his enemies. In the case of Céline, however, the message is inextricably coded. In the anti-Semitic pamphlets, *Bagatelles pour un massacre*, *L'Ecole des cadavres* and *Les Beaux draps*, there is a conscious removal of the barrier between fiction and non-fiction, with the constant presence of the narrator of *Mort à crédit*, Ferdinand, the three ballets in *Bagatelles pour un massacre*, and the story of the vanished patient which concludes *Les Beaux draps*. Similarly, Céline is at pains to deploy contradiction, inconsistency and confusion, both within the polemical texts themselves and in their relationship to each other and the works of fiction, as a means of apparently subverting the ostensibly polemical purpose. To a certain extent, in the medical pamphlets of the 1920s and in the anti-Semitic pamphlets of the 1930s, this is due to a procedure of camouflage and self-preservation, but, more importantly, it translates Modernist features of literature — difficulty, self-consciousness, self-reflectiveness — into polemical writing itself. At the same time, however difficult Céline makes his polemical writing, there remains one underlying constant: the loathing of the present and the fear of the future.

Yet, if the enforced departure from Naturalist principles has important implications for the polemical writings of the inter-war years, it possesses enormous significance for the fictional production. A comparison of *Mort à crédit* with *L'Assommoir* already shows more areas of similarity between Céline and the Naturalist novelists than the normally acknowledged lack of compromise stylistically. Even more influential, however, is the historical situation in which Céline finds himself between the wars. Ambiguous as Céline's view of the *belle époque* undoubtedly is, it remains the only historical constant of his work and, as such, has a dominating position, analogous to that of the same period in *A la Recherche du temps perdu*. This domination of the past is conveyed in an expressly psychoanalytical form, through the role of the father-figure, explicit in *Mort à crédit* and thereafter, apart from a number of passing references, implicit, who is given by Céline clear sexual, economic and political connotations. At the same time, since for Céline the *real* world existed only prior to 1900 or, at the very latest, 1914, and since the world after the First World War has all the unreality of a pale reflection and a hallucinatory foreboding, his fiction of the inter-war years is a fiction of ghosts: the ghosts of the past, invoked to castigate the present; the ghosts of the past who, like the all-pervading presence of the father, dominate and stifle the present and must be exorcised; and, finally, the narrator himself who figuratively died in the war and has no place in the world of the inter-war years: that narrator who, because of his pliability and insubstantiality, is often confused with the picaresque hero but who, in reality, is no more than a ghost.

Thus it is possible to view Céline's production of the inter-war years as a body of work dominated by a nexus of ghostly presences, in which the *belle époque* is constantly the implicit point of reference, the tarnished Golden Age of Céline's literary world. It is this reflection on the world before 1914 which dominates his writing, from his thesis on Semmelweis in 1924 to the second volume of *Guignol's Band* composed twenty years later, and which dictates not merely highly complicated fictional and polemical manoeuvres, but also the deployment of a framework of references, psychological, historical, economic and, above all, literary, which is immeasurably more extensive than normally allowed. With this body of material, Céline embarks upon a complicated attempt to explore and criticise his own epoch through its interaction with the Golden Age, the period before the war which remains a constant point of reference for all his work of the inter-war years and the Occupation until it is finally exorcised in the final volume of *Guignol's Band*, to be replaced in the final phase of Céline's writing by the experience of the Second World War. It is a project which is at the centre of his work even before he takes on the significant pseudonym of Céline: the medical pamphlets published under the name of Dr Destouches on Ford and medical insurance constitute the first shots in a long battle, fought out in fiction and non-fiction and often blurring the distinctions between the two, and which will be waged right up until the end of the Occupation.

[1]

Semmelweis *and the Ghost of Bourgeois Medicine*

The interest shown in Céline's medical doctoral thesis of 1924, *La Vie et l'oeuvre de Philippe-Ignace Semmelweis (1818–1865)*, has tended to obscure the fact that the thesis itself forms only part of a considerable body of writing produced by Céline prior to the publication of *Voyage au bout de la nuit* in 1932. This writing covers an unusually broad range, extending from the two scientific research papers resulting from Céline's stay at the Marine Zoology Laboratory at Roscoff in 1920[1] to the pharmaceutical publicity written after the publication of the first novel in 1933,[2] and encompassing writing as diverse as *Semmelweis* itself, the long treatise on quinine,[3] a whole series of polemical essays on medicine and social hygiene, and the two plays of 1926–7, *Progrès (Périclès)* and *L'E-glise*. On one level, much of this writing confirms a dilettante interest in scientific research, as opposed to medical practice, which remains with Céline throughout the inter-war years and which he transposes ironically through the Institut Bioduret Joseph in *Voyage au bout de la nuit* and, even, through the character of Courtial des Pereires in *Mort à crédit*. As André Lwoff comments on the two Roscoff papers:

L'une et l'autre publication portent témoignage d'une certaine hâte et d'une naïveté non moins certaine dans la pensée et dans l'expression. L'ensemble correspond assez bien à cette image du chercheur que l'écrivain, sans ménagement, tracera dans le *Voyage* et qui, paradoxale-

---

1. 'Observations physiologiques sur *Convoluta roscoffensis*' (1920), CC 3, 242–4; 'Prolongation de la vie chez les *Galleria mellonella*' (1921), CC 3, 245–6.
2. 'Les Hémorragies minimes des gencives en clientèle' (1933), CC 3, 246–8; 'La Basedowine' (1933), CC 3, 248–52.
3. *La Quinine en thérapeutique*, in *Oeuvres de Louis-Ferdinand Céline*, I, Paris, Balland, 1966, pp. 623–708.

ment, est sa propre image . . . Nul ne regrettera qu'il ait sacrifié le métier
de chercheur à celui d'écrivain. Sa contribution à la science eût difficile-
ment pu égaler en valeur et en originalité son apport aux lettres, qui est
considérable.[4]

Yet Professor Lwoff misses the essential point: the defects of
Céline's research papers are due, not so much to his failings or
inexperience as a scientist, as to an unjustified haste to publish. In
other words, the often touching precociousness in Céline's non-
fictional writing of the 1920s is the result of an inordinate desire to
see his name and writings in print as quickly as possible. It is surely
this which explains his presumption in delivering two scientific
papers on the basis of the most cursory of visits to Roscoff — a
cursoriness which prefigures that of his visit to the Ford plant in
Detroit in 1925 which, in its turn, gives rise to a falsely authoritative
piece of writing — and with no background or qualification in
biological research. More important, it throws light on Céline's
constant urge in the 1920s to capitalise on any experience which
could be transformed into publication. The article taken from his
thesis on Semmelweis and which appeared in *La Presse Médicale*
only seven weeks after the *soutenance* is a case in point.[5] The
publication, at his own expense, of *La Quinine en thérapeutique*,
which Jean-Pierre Dauphin and Jacques Boudillet describe as a
'lointain prolongement de la thèse que l'un de ses grands-oncles
avait consacrée à la quinquina',[6] is another. The quite manifest
ambition which propels the young Destouches from the Mission
Rockefeller to the League of Nations in Geneva, through a tight net
of patronage in which Selsar Gunn is a central figure, is by no means
exclusively medical, or even bureaucratic. Rather, this ambition is
essentially literary in nature: Céline becomes and remains a doctor
who writes, a man who attempts to make his name, not through the
practice of medicine, and certainly not initially through the practice
of general medicine, but through the manipulation of the written
word. The prophetic last entry in the *Carnet du cuirassier Destouches*, 'en un mot je suis orgueilleux est-ce un défaut je ne le crois
et il me créera des déboires ou peut-être la *Réussite*' (CC 2, 11),
concluding a self-consciously literary and overwritten text, leaves
little doubt as to the direction in which success will lie.

4. André Lwoff, *Le Figaro Littéraire*, 7–13 April 1969. Quoted in CC 3, 242.
5. The *soutenance* of the thesis was on the 1 May 1924; Céline's article, 'Les
Derniers jours de Semmelweis', appeared in *La Presse Médicale* on 25 June 1924.
6. Jean-Pierre Dauphin and Jacques Boudillet, *Album Céline*, Paris, Gallimard,
coll. 'La Pléïade', 1977, p. 81.

Within this broad body of writing in the 1920s, however, there is a central core which is of particular significance for the whole development of Céline's work in the inter-war years, and that concerns his writing on hygiene. From 1925 to 1933, Céline produced a number of articles and confidential reports for the League of Nations on social medicine and the role of the doctor in a world rapidly being affected by innovations in industry and organisation which came from the New World. As such, they introduce a social, moral and political stance which will be maintained in the novels and pamphlets of the 1930s and which is based upon a complex and ambiguous perception of French society following the First World War. At the same time, the published material, as opposed to the League of Nations reports, constitutes a first incursion for Céline into the realm of polemic, a genre which he learns to manipulate with an ambiguity which mirrors his perception of the post-war world and which announces the complex task of reading the trilogy of pamphlets, *Bagatelles pour un massacre*, *L'Ecole des cadavres* and *Les Beaux draps*. These early polemical writings, therefore, published under the name of Dr Destouches, constitute an essential preliminary to a study of the novels and the pamphlets of the 1930s, in that they contain in embryo not merely much of the thematic substance of the later works but, more importantly, their ambiguities of historical perspective and their complexities of persuasion. In this respect, *Semmelweis* is an essential component in this core of writing. Its subject-matter — the search for the causes of puerpereal fever — clearly labels it as a work concerned with hygiene, and, indeed, Céline returns to the subject in an article of 1929.[7] Moreover, as a chronicle of the irreducible brutal imbecility of man when faced with a beneficial discovery, the thesis is essentially a polemical work, presumably designed to play its part in the campaign for better conditions of health amongst the urban French population. What makes the work so interesting, however, is that it is not only a polemical work in its own right, but has as its subject the career and fate of a medical polemicist and, indeed, the limits and effectiveness of polemic in general. With this dual function, Céline is able to both make his specific point in the battle for hygiene and against professional pettiness and to broaden the scope of his work so that it becomes a general reflection on the possibilities of persuasion in a very broad historical context indeed. When both Céline's own early practice of polemic in his medical writings of the 1920s and his study of a major failed polemicist of the nineteenth century are

7. 'L'Infection puerpérale et les antivirus' (1929), CC 3, 97–8.

explored, the way is then open to a more accurate appreciation of the succeeding works: not just the novels, *Voyage au bout de la nuit* and *Mort à crédit*, but the anti-Semitic pamphlets as well.

Social Insurance and the Practice of Polemic

In their introduction to the third volume of the *Cahiers Céline*, Jean-Pierre Dauphin and Henri Godard underline the importance of Céline's writings on the question of social medicine, emphasising that: 'leur mérite tient à ce qu'on peut les situer au carrefour des romans et des pamphlets' (CC 3, 8). Thus, the social reality depicted in the essays on the Ford plant at Detroit and on the introduction of a social security system is the same as that described in *Voyage au bout de la nuit* and *Mort à crédit*, whilst the themes of the essays, notably the author's preoccupation with hygiene, look forward to the social concerns and metaphorical structure of the anti-Semitic pamphlets. At the same time, the authors recognise that these texts constitute a problem for the reader. Dauphin and Godard can only explain the contradictions within the essays themselves by resorting to a concept of 'instabilité idéologique' on the part of the author (CC 3, 10). In the same way, Philippe Alméras, noting the striking discrepancy between the ostensible conclusions of Dr Destouches on the Ford factory and the harsh implied criticism of Bardamu in *Voyage au bout de la nuit*, concludes that the writer is 'moins humain' in his medical writings than in his fiction and that 'Louis-Ferdinand Céline semble-t-il ridiculiser ce que loue le docteur Destouches'.[8] The same discrepancy is clearly visible between the pessimistic remark in *Mea culpa*, that 'tous les Ford se ressemblent, soviétiques ou non' (*Mea*, 15), and the apparent enthusiasm of Céline for the Ford system in his lecture to the Société de Médecine in 1928.

Clearly, it is unsatisfactory that these contradictions, both within individual texts themselves and between individual texts, should go unresolved, and some attempt may be made towards a resolution by examining more closely the historical context in which Céline's writings on social medicine were produced and by examining in some detail the functioning of the polemic itself. The two key texts are the lecture that Céline gave to the Société de Médecine de Paris in May 1928, 'A propos du service sanitaire des usines Ford à

8. Philippe Alméras, 'L'Amérique femelle ou les enfants de Colomb', *Australian Journal of French Studies*, XIII, 1–2, 1976, p. 104.

Détroit' (CC 3, 140–52), and an article which appeared in *La Presse Médicale* on 24 November 1928, 'Les Assurances sociales et une politique économique de la santé publique' (CC 3, 156–67). However, against these ostensibly reactionary and pro-American texts, it is necessary to set three others: two unpublished reports to the League of Nations, 'Note sur l'organisation sanitaire des usines Ford' (CC 3, 119–30), of 1925, and the 'Mémoire pour le cours des hautes études' (CC 3, 178–214), of 1932; and the article 'La Santé publique en France', which appeared in the March 1930 issue of the left-wing review *Monde*, edited by Henri Barbusse.

These writings, contradictory as they appear, must be read in the specific historical context of the debate in France during the last half of the 1920s on the introduction of a law providing for a compulsory social security scheme, designed to replace the old system of private insurances and friendly societies, the *Mutuelles*, which operated under the aegis of the employers, by a system run by the state which would automatically provide sickness, maternity and invalidity benefit, as well as ensuring old-age pensions. In addition to this specific context, however, Céline's medical writings of the 1920s are related to a less well-known crisis which affected the role and function of the general practitioner and, ultimately, the entire philosophy behind general medicine. As Theodore Zeldin points out in his history of France from 1848 to 1945, contrary to general belief, the career of a general practitioner in France, and particularly in Paris, was far from assured.[9] This was due in part to competition from the paramedical professions of nurses, midwives and pharmacists, but also to the unequal distribution of doctors throughout the country. Thus, in 1931, whilst France as a whole came only seventeenth in a world order of density of doctors per head of the population, Paris had more doctors than any other city in Europe.[10] Hence, whilst the financial position of provincial doctors was often difficult, in Paris the situation became dramatically worse, threatened even more by the effects of inflation during the 1930s on the costs of medical treatment. Jeanne Singer-Kérel shows that the cost of a consultation in Paris rose from 20 francs in 1930 to 30 francs in 1938 and that a house-call, which was 30 francs in 1936, had risen to 35 or 40 francs by 1938.[11] In this situation, it is hardly surprising that the battle for fees, both against professional rivals and recalcitrant

9. Theodore Zeldin, *France 1848–1945*, 1, *Ambition, Love and Politics*, London, Oxford University Press, 1973, chap. 2, 'Doctors'.
10. Ibid., p. 37.
11. Jeanne Singer-Kérel, *Le Coût de la vie à Paris de 1840 à 1954*, Paris, Armand Colin, 1961, p. 409.

patients, should have been a major feature of Parisian medical life, and that many Parisian doctors quite literally faced bankruptcy. In this context, the failure of Céline's own private practice in Clichy in 1928 and the rapid impoverishment of Bardamu in La Garenne-Rancy are merely symptomatic of a general crisis in the profession. Similarly, Céline's post at the *dispensaire* in Clichy and Bardamu's flight to the *asile* in Vigny-sur-Seine are also symptomatic: if private practice failed, the only solution was a semi-official post in a *dispensaire*, a mental hospital or as a prison doctor. It was this crisis, which informs so much of *Voyage au bout de la nuit* and *Mort à crédit*, that led to a call for the introduction of a national health service, with doctors who would receive a state salary — a line of argument which complements but often confuses the demand for a reorganisation of the health insurance system.

Dissatisfaction with a system which was simply unable to guarantee its doctors a living often, in the period of the inter-war years, became combined with a reaction against the commercialisation of medicine and its increasing reliance on drugs, in favour of a return to more natural remedies. In this context, Céline's attack on the proliferation of new commercially-produced drugs in the 'Avant-propos' to *La Quinine en thérapeutique* is again symptomatic.[12] However, this rejection of the modern in medicine had precise political connotations, be it in terms of a devotion to hygiene, to homoeopathy or nature cures: as Zeldin comments on the 'Neo-Hippocratism': 'Just as in politics the Action Française revealed reaction towards traditionalism in the period between the two world wars, so at the same time there was a similar return to the past in medical doctrines'.[13] In other words, Céline's espousal of the *natural* values of quinine is connected to his complex relationship with French society before the First World War and his no less complex distrust of the society which followed it.

It is in this general context of an embattled medical profession that the long debate on health insurance must properly be seen. The introduction of such a system had been one of the demands in the programme of the Confédération Générale du Travail (CGT) as it came out of the war and the proposal had been readily adopted by the 'Chambre bleu-horizon', which drafted a bill in 1921 and passed it into law in 1924. This law, however, was not enacted, due to the monetary crisis of the mid-1920s, and it was not until 1928 and the stabilisation of the franc under Poincaré that the Chamber sent the

12. *La Quinine en thérapeutique*, p. 625.
13. Zeldin, *France 1848–1945*, 1, pp. 28–9.

law for ratification to the Senate. It was this move and the subsequent Senate vote which provoked the bitter debate in which Céline's two interventions figure. Eventually, the law was modified to meet some of the objections from the medical profession, and was finally put in to effect by the Tardieu government on 24 April 1930. Thus was passed a law which, to say the least, was highly ambiguous: a law which had been the object of constant opposition from the Right and, particularly, the employers; a law which, nevertheless, was rapidly adopted in 1921 by an ultra-conservative Chamber and was consistently taken up by successive governments throughout the 1920s, culminating in that headed by Tardieu, one of the few admirers in French political circles of American approaches to industrial organisation. The suspicion on the Left, held particularly by the Confédération Générale du Travail Unitaire (CGTU), was that successive governments had adopted the policy recommended by Céline in 'Les Assurances sociales' of making minimal concessions in order to defuse a potentially dangerous issue.

Nevertheless, the law of 24 April 1930 marked an advance in French social legislation in that it recognised the responsibility of society as a whole towards the health of its members and was careful to distance itself from a corporatist tradition of medical legislation. What makes the interpretation of Céline's medical writings so difficult is that the field of social medicine is a meeting-point of ideologies of the Left and the Right. Whereas the state control of the medical profession was exclusively an argument of the Left, the arguments in favour of hygiene and industrial medicine, which appeared progressive, were in fact traditionally the prerogative of the Right. This reactionary connotation of most aspects of social medicine goes back to the origins of public health in France in the early years of the nineteenth century. In 1826, the Société Industrielle de Mulhouse instituted a system of sickness benefit for its employees which, in spite of its progressive appearance, was in fact designed to ward off more extreme demands by the workforce.[14] This system of *caisses de secours mutuels* proliferated to such an extent that, in 1852, a law was passed creating an officially directed system of such schemes throughout the country. This had the effect of allowing the state to infiltrate, even surreptitiously to direct, the acts of workers' organisations and of guaranteeing for the employers a docile and productive work-force. In this context of state

14. See: Olivier Targowla, *Les Médecins aux mains sales*, Paris, Belfond, coll. 'L'Echappée', 1976, p. 24.

control of the work-force for economic ends, the apparently neutral concept of hygiene plays an increasingly conservative function. As G. Thuillier remarks, on the return to neo-Hippocratism: 'Les anciens "traités" donnaient de l'hygiène une conception très extensive, et en faisaient presque un probléme de morale et de politique',[15] and Oliver Targowla spells out precisely what those moral and political connotations were:

> Améliorer la condition hygiénique de l'ouvrier, c'est augmenter la production. Un état fort a besoin d'hygiénistes. La pensée médicale prend ses sources dans une réflexion générale sur le pouvoir. La médecine sociale, et par là même la médecine du travail, est avant tout un projet politique. A l'origine de la maladie, il y a le désordre, le taudis, l'insolubrité, le danger permanent. Il faut introduire l'ordre et la règle.[16]

For the specialist in hygiene, the worker only exists in relation to his industrial production, a production which must be strenuously maintained. For this reason, 'le XIXe siècle voit se constituer une véritable police médicale et sanitaire',[17] and 'de l'hygiène publique à la médecine sociale, se forge tout un savoir, une raison destinée à asseoir la force du travail'.[18] The corollary of this repressive tendency in social and industrial medicine is an inevitable dehumanisation of the individual worker, contained in Taylorism and amplified in the workings of the Ford system. In his *Principles of Scientific Management*, of 1911, Taylor, in a famous phrase (as quoted by Targowla), defines this dehumanisation:

> L'une des premières caractéristiques d'un homme capable de faire le métier de manutentionnaire de gueuses de fonte, c'est qu'il est si peu intelligent et si paresseux qu'on peut le comparer, en ce qui concerne son aptitude mentale, à un boeuf plutôt qu'à autre chose. L'homme qui a un esprit vif et intelligent est totalement inapte à ce metier,[19]

a comment which looks forward strikingly to Céline's report on his visit to Detroit, in which the company doctor reflects: 'l'employé rêvé pour nous, l'ouvrier rêvé c'est le chimpanzée . . .' (CC 3, 123), a phrase transposed in its turn into *Voyage au bout de la nuit* (V, 225). This dehumanisation of the worker gives rise to a certain

---

15. G. Thuillier, 'Hygiène corporelle aux XIXe et XXe siècles', *Annales de Démographie Historique*, 1975, p. 124.
16. Targowla, *Les Médecins aux mains sales*, p. 30.
17. Ibid., p. 44.
18. Ibid.
19. Quoted in ibid., pp. 84–5.

distrust amongst doctors of industrial diseases and injuries, a distrust which veers rapidly to contempt. Targowla cites two articles which appeared in medical journals at the beginning of the century which show that the essential criterion for industrial doctors was not the well-being of the patient, but his ability to fulfil the tasks demanded of him. Thus, in *Le Journal* of 21 May 1909, Dr Petitjean, a medical adviser to insurance companies and Senator for the Department of the Nièvre, writes:

> Voici les lésions inventées, les douleurs incontrôlables, les lumbagos étrangement persistants; il est si facile d'enlever un pansement, d'introduire dans la plaie un bout de bois ou une arête de poisson ... Enfin, quand bien même la lésion a existé, qu'elle a pris un caractère permanent, cela veut-il dire toujours que celui qui en est atteint a subi un réel dommage? Ce manoeuvre perdu un bout de doigt, cet ajusteur a un pied un peu raide; très probablement, leur capacité de travail n'en est pas modifiée, leur salaire reste le même,[20]

and Dr Rémy, a Professor of Medicine at Paris, comments:

> Une oreille fendue, une joue balafrée, un nez écrasé, une cicatrice étendue sur le dos ou sur une certaine région des membres constituent des difformités et parfois des infirmités, mais ne diminuent pas la valeur industrielle de l'individu ... Quand ces lésions ne nuisent à la victime qu'au point de vue esthétique, si désobligeantes ou désagréables qu'elles soient, elles doivent être non avenues, au regard de la loi de 1898.[21]

From which Targowla concludes: 'Ainsi, l'objectif de la médecine du travail . . . n'est pas la santé, mais une sorte de santé à minima qui suffit pour tourner les machines':[22] the entire philosophy of hygiene has the aim of creating and maintaining a strong industrial state in which the health of the individual is automatically transformed into an easy metaphor for the strength of the nation. There is therefore no coincidence in the fact that it was the Vichy regime, in a circular of 28 July 1942, which encouraged the setting-up of medical services in factories: the precise context of the republication of Céline's article on Ford and the interview he gave to *Le Concours Médical* on 'la médecine standard'.[23]

The debate in the medical profession on the introduction of a

20. Quoted in ibid., p. 100.
21. Quoted in ibid., p. 102.
22. Ibid., p. 121.
23. 'Les Idées de L-F Céline sur "la médecine standard"', *Le Concours Médical*, 7, 15 February 1942.

national health insurance scheme produced few arguments which differed from the positions adopted at the end of the nineteenth century. An examination of one of the most important medical journals, *La Presse Médicale*, from 1927 to 1929, shows that French doctors were largely split into three groups: those who wished to maintain the status quo, in terms of the strictly personal relationships between doctors and clients; those who, with some reservations, were willing to opt for those modifications provided for by the new law; and those who sought to subvert this apparently socialist legislation by seeking a radical extension of industrial medicine and hygiene, in order to bring the medical profession into the framework of an embryonic corporatist state.

Whilst recognising that the whole question of health insurance was 'un fameux nid de discordes',[24] *La Presse Médicale* was not uniformly hostile to the new law. Professor Balthazard, representing the medical unions at a hearing of the Commission d'Assurance et de Prévoyance Sociales of the Chambre des Députés, noted that doctors already operated as system of *tiers payant* with the various friendly societies, and stated that they were willing to act within the new law, providing that the government accepted the continuation of freedom of choice of patients concerning their doctor and the payment of fees.[25] At the same time, there was general agreement on the Right and the Left in condemning the parliamentary and electoral opportunism inherent in the new law, this 'vote à visées électorales',[26] this 'concession aux exigences des partis extrêmes, socialistes ou communistes'.[27] On the Left, writers expressed doubts about the sufficiency of the budget earmarked for the operation of the new system. Eugène Briau, in two highly perceptive articles, one on tuberculosis and the other on syphilis, calculated that the budget forecast of 560 million francs would be exceeded on expenditure on these two illnesses alone.[28] He regretted that 'dans sa hâte de bien faire, le législateur court le risque d'aboutir à une immense faillite qui retardera indéfiniment l'avènement du régime vraiment social qui s'impose'.[29] At the same

24. P. Desfosses, 'Quelques réflexions sur les Assurances Sociales', *La Presse Médicale*, 87, 29 October 1927, p. 1325.
25. 'Congrès de syndicats médicaux', *La Presse Médicale*, 11, 8 February 1928, p. 172.
26. 'Les Assurances Sociales', *La Presse Médicale*, 94, 24 November 1928, p. 1497.
27. E. Ory, 'Courtes réflexions d'un solitaire sur les Assurances Sociales', *La Presse Médicale*, 11, 8 February, 1928, p. 17.
28. Eugene Briau, 'Assurances sociales et tuberculose', *La Presse Médicale*, 3, 11 January 1928, p. 44; 'Assurances sociales et syphilis', *La Presse Médicale*, 11, 8 February 1928, pp. 171–2.

time, both progressives and conservatives united in condemning the medical system in a society in which successive governments did nothing to combat major social problems, such as poverty, poor housing conditions and alcoholism. Hence, Dr Specklin, in a speech at Bordeaux, declared: 'Faute de combattre efficacement le taudis et l'alcoolisme, faute de surveiller égouts et eaux potables, faute d'agir contre la dépopulation des campagnes favorisée par les lois sur l'héritage, l'Etat crée cet énorme et dispendieux appareil d'assurance-maladie pour soigner les tuberculeux et les typhiques, victimes de son incurie'.[30] Nevertheless, it was the conservative arguments which dominated the debate in La Presse Médicale, and these were grouped around the traditional distrust of bourgeois medical practitioners regarding the illnesses of the poor: 'Les indigents aiment les medicaments chers, surtout quand ils n'ont pas a les payer',[31] 'qui ne paie pas abuse',[32] 'dans la majorité des cas, c'est le malade qui abuse des soins'.[33] Jules Romains's play Knock, to which Céline himself appears to allude in his preface to Semmelweis (CC 3, 17–18), is invoked to prove that the introduction of a free medical service will lead to a mass exploitation of the facilities by the poor 'qui auront desormais à coeur d'avoir des consultations, fussent-elles inutiles, *pour leur argent*'.[34] This exploitation is assumed by conservative doctors to lead automatically to a general moral degeneration which will paralyse the entire nation. Thus, in order to escape a health insurance scheme at any cost, the Right tends to take refuge in a series of more or less chimerical schemes, such as 'l'épargne individuelle obligatoire'.[35]

The main lines of the debate in La Presse Médicale, therefore, tended to converge upon a position which was strongly anti-republican and which was based upon a defence of the traditional,

---

29. Briau, 'Assurances sociales et syphilis', p. 172.

30. Dr P. Specklin, 'Les Répercussions des Assurances Sociales sur l'exercice de la médecine', *La Presse Médicale*, 5, 16 January 1929, p. 79. See also: 'Les Méfaits des Assurances Sociales et les moyens d'y remédier. D'après Ervin Lick (de Dantzig)', *La Presse Médicale*, 94, 24 November 1928, pp. 1498–9. Céline's depiction, in *Voyage au bout de la nuit*, of the death of Bébert, of typhoid, in the suburb of La Garenne-Rancy, clearly falls into this category of social criticism.

31. Desfosses, 'Quelques réflexions sur les Assurances Sociales', p. 1325.

32. F. Jayle, 'Le Congrès des Syndicats Médicaux de France', *La Presse Médicale*, 94, 23 November 1927, p. 1435.

33. Ibid., p. 1435.

34. P. Desfosses, 'La Question des Assurances Sociales', *La Presse Médicale*, 3, 11 January 1928, p. 43.

35. P. Specklin, 'Considérations critiques sur les Assurances Sociales. Une solution nouvelle: l'épargne individuelle obligatoire', *La Presse Médicale*, 19, 6 March 1929, pp. 305–10.

paying relationship between doctor and patient and an implicit distrust of the poor. Often, protagonists translated their political realism into an acceptance of the worst: the state control of medicine and the public employment of doctors, in order to head off a wholesale socialisation of the medical system. This was the view propounded by Dr Lick, a doctor from Leipzig, whose account of his own experiences in a state-run system appeared in the same issue of *La Presse Médicale* as Céline's article on 'les assurances sociales'.[36]

Both Céline's lecture to the Société de Médecine on Ford and his article on 'les assurances sociales' recommend the immediate adoption of a system of industrial medicine and argue strongly against a social insurance scheme. In so doing, he draws clearly upon the reactionary tradition of Taylorism and *médecine du travail* in France, and seems to fit snugly into the context of right-wing medical thought in the 1920s. In other words, on the political level, the *thematic* substance of his medical polemic, like that of his later anti-Semitic pamphlets, presents no ambiguity whatsoever. At the same time, however, the significance of these medical writings in the context of Céline's work as a whole and, indeed, the polemical procedures which they adopt, are far from simple. In the first place, it is by no means certain that the reader to whom Céline directed his medical arguments in the 1920s was entirely convinced by the apparent simplicity of the ideas they contained. The editors of *La Presse Médicale*, in adding a warning to Céline's article on 'les assurances sociales', to the effect that 'ces idées paraîtront peut-être à certains un peu théoriques et aventureuses' (CC 3, 155), do not merely exhibit the embarassment of the professional at the precocious outpourings of the amateur outlined earlier, they also look forward to the disorientation of a reader such as Gide, reviewing *Bagatelles pour un massacre*,[37] or, for that matter, the vague feeling of the Fascist *Je suis partout* team, after reading *L'Ecole des cadavres*, that they were being mocked.[38] In other words, even for the contemporary reader, the medical texts are far more opaque than they seem. In addition, a synthesis of Céline's arguments on public medicine is impossible. Not only is his enthusiasm for a Ford-like system of industrial medicine, expressed in the lecture on Ford and the article on 'les assurances sociales', at total variance with the reactions of Bardamu in Detroit and Céline himself in his journey to

36. *La Presse Médicale*, 94, 24 November 1928.
37. André Gide, 'Céline, les Juifs et Maritain', *Nouvelle Revue Française*, April 1938, p. 634.
38. See Lucien Rebatet, HER 1, 45.

the Soviet Union, recounted in *Mea culpa*, it conflicts also with the conclusions of the other texts on social medicine: the 'Note sur l'organisation sanitaire des usines Ford', written as an internal report for the League of Nations after Céline's visit to the United States in 1925, the 'Mémoire pour le cours des hautes études', written in 1932 and similarly destined for private consumption at the League of Nations, and finally, the *Monde* article of 1930, 'La Santé publique en France'.

What is striking about the internal report in Céline's Ford visit, as opposed to the 1928 lecture, is its unemotional and objective tone. In the report, he attempts to see the Detroit factories in the context of Ford's career and then proceeds to list scrupulously the most striking characteristics of the system. In spite of a certain vestigial positive element in his observation: 'Cet état de chose à tout prendre au point de vue sanitaire, et même humain, n'est nullement désastreux quant au présent . . .' (CC 3, 129), the report is overshadowed by Céline's amazement at the 'cour des miracles'[39] that is constituted by the Ford plant in Detroit. Here, following Taylor's description, the workforce has become, not 'boeufs', but 'chimpanzées'.[40] Hence, the essentially *strange* experience of the Ford factory corresponds in no way to Céline's preconceptions of industrial medicine or the role of hygiene. In this context, the report contains an important *non sequitur*: 'Nous sommes venus à Détroit avec l'intention de savoir si l'hygiène appliquée, à l'industrie augmentait le rendement de cette industrie, la chose nous est apparue prouvée par l'expérience de la maison Westinghouse à Pittsburgh' (CC 3, 130). It is the Westinghouse plant, with its more traditional work system and its humane medical scheme, which corresponds to Céline's own intellectual and moral positions, positions which are, in contrast, violently challenged and inverted by Ford: 'Chez Ford la santé de l'ouvrier est sans importance, c'est la machine qui lui fait la charité d'avoir encore besoin de lui, les facteurs sont inversés' (CC 3, 130).

Yet it is in the transition from this unpublished text of 1925 to the lecture to the Société de Médecine of 1928 that the entire problem of Céline's polemical procedure becomes apparent, a problem which will by no means have disappeared by 1937, with the appearance of the anti-Semitic texts. As Jean-Pierre Dauphin and Henri Godard point out, Céline's favourite technique in his medical pamphlets is 'le renversement spectaculaire des positions' (CC 3, 9), an inversion

---

39. Alméras, 'L'Amérique femelle et les enfants de Colomb', p. 104.
40. Quoted in Targowla, *Les Médecins aux mains Sales*, pp. 84–5.

which mirrors exactly the inversion of values embodied in the Ford system. Hence, in his lecture, Céline retains all of the purely descriptive material on the Ford plant, material which is unequivocably damning, only to develop in the second part of his speech an enthusiastic and contradictory argument which counsels the immediate institution of this barbaric system in France itself.

The same disconcerting discrepancy is found between the published article on 'les assurances sociales' and the 1932 memorandum on the 'cours des hautes études'. Similarly, the same internal contradictions are present in the article as appear in the 1928 lecture. The article begins with a sharp warning of Communist infiltration into all levels of French society. In order to block this slow and insidious revolution, the article recommends Disraeli's policy of safeguarding the structure of British society by applying progressive measures before more radical policies are imposed by the force of revolution. Thus, Céline advises his readers to adopt the example of the Ford system and to implement it by placing all medical and social questions on a purely economic basis. In this way, Céline argues, the demands of the socialists, whose aim is to destroy the capitalist system, will be suddenly and perplexingly reintegrated into the very heart of the system against which they are directed. This allows him to look forward enthusiastically to a completely industrialised world in which the sick person will be sought out and treated as a criminal, tracked down by the 'police médicale' referred to by Targowla, or as a conscript, eternally mobilised in the economic struggle.

In contrast to this bleak vision of the future, the memorandum of 1932, in spite of some structural and stylistic defects, presents a perfectly coherent argument which attempts to lead the reader in precisely the opposite direction. In this memorandum, the main target is the inadequacy of the medical profession and, behind that, the workings of the entire economic system which blocks any measure designed to effect a genuine improvement in social medicine. Thus, Céline attacks the outdated rhetoric of the hygienists, 'toutes ces gentillesses alliées à la tartufferie monstrueuse des gros intérêts économiques' (CC 3, 186), and demands not a logical extension of the capitalist system, as he does in the 1928 article, but its immediate destruction: 'Il faudrait que cette société s'écroulât pour qu'on puisse parler véritablement d'hygiène généralisée qui ne s'accorde bien qu'avec une formule socialiste ou communiste d'Etat' (CC 3, 188). This last reference to a socialist or Communist state as sole guarantor of a truly workable system of hygiene coincides precisely with Céline's article 'La Santé publique en France', which appeared in Barbusse's *Monde* in 1930. Here, Céline is arguing clearly against the positions adopted in his Ford lecture and his article on the 'assurances sociales': in these essays, the introduction of a law on 'assurances sociales' is seen as, at best, a liberal, traditionalist piece of legislation, woefully inadequate compared with the example proferred by the New World or, in more sinister fashion, as the Trojan horse of Communist infiltration. Yet here, in 1930, Céline writes in favour of the law he has castigated two years earlier: 'les Assurances sociales possèdent une qualite essentielle, elles créent un ordre, une règle, des repères dans la médecine d'un pays. Elles viennent gêner beaucoup d'intérêts particuliers au profit de l'intérêt commun' (BLFC 2, 45) and: 'Avant les Assurances sociales, tout ce qui concerne les organisations sanitaires d'un pays est laissé à l'initiative incohérente, vélléitaire de formations officielles ou officieuses, ignorantes et disparates; après les Assurances sociales, ces situations se régularisent automatiquement ou bien disparaissent, ce qui le plus souvent est un bien' (BLFC 2, 46). Whilst pleading for a reorganisation of the medical system in France from the grass roots upwards and whilst evidently sharing some of the doubts expressed by the editors of *Monde*[41] concerning the effectiveness of the newly created post of Ministre de la Santé Publique, Céline clearly sees the national insurance scheme as a step in the right direction in the battle against France's high mortality rate, the appalling living conditions of its working class and the evils of tuberculosis, syphilis and, especially, alcoholism, all of which were the stock-in-trade of the *dispensaires*.

The contradictions between these five texts of Céline on the question of social medicine lead to two provisional conclusions. It is important to recall that is the two ostensibly pro-Ford articles which are deeply ambiguous internally, whilst the two unpublished memoranda and the pro-'Assurances' *Monde* article are totally coherent. In other words, it is the two overtly polemical works which are self-contradictory and at variance with the two private memoranda, in which Céline has no motive for dissemblance, and the *Monde* article, which is marked by an extreme low key in its expression. This variance raises in its turn two possibilities: either Céline, at an early stage in his career, is exhibiting already those chameleon qualities which make interpretation of his work of the 1930s so difficult, or it is the coherent, unified writings which must be considered as the authentic expression of his social thought at

41. 'On vient de créer un ministère de la Santé Publique. Nous doutons qu'il améliore la situation sanitaire de la France, dont l'article ci-dessus donne une vue saisissante et précise' (BLFC 2, 37).

this time, and not the lecture on Ford and the article in *La Presse Médicale*. This early left-wing stance, with its references to the socialist/Communist guarantee of a fair health system, has at least the merit of explaining why Céline's return from Soviet Russia was followed by *Mea culpa*, the title of which, without this prior enthusiasm for the Left, appears gratuitous. The problem persists, however, of what Céline was doing in his lecture and article, and whether there is any possibility of integrating them into a broad synthetic interpretation of the medical writings as a whole. It is here that the difficulties become remarkably similar to those presented by a reading of the anti-Semitic texts, and they centre upon the procedures which Céline adopts in order to manipulate his polemic.

All Céline's writing on the question of social medicine, however contradictory it becomes, starts from a broad common base. All five texts recognise the fact of the impossible state of French society under the Third Republic, a society dominated by money and where the power of the capitalist system remains an insurmountable barrier to social progress. The production of wealth is effected at the expense of an entire class, the proletariat (CC 3, 210–11) or 'classes laborieuses' (BLFC 2, 39), and implies the division of society along the lines of Disraeli's 'Two Nations', which reflects that between the *Maîtres* and the *miteux* which dominates *Voyage au bout de la nuit*. Nevertheless, this already corrupt society is threatened by a much more dangerous system: the very apotheosis of capitalism embodied in the Ford philosophy. In this context, it is important to note that Céline, in his lecture on Ford, uses a procedure which recurs in the anti-Semitic writings: the falsification of statistics and shameless exaggeration, which have the effect of creating a powerful symbolism but also of changing the direction of the argument.[42] The importance of Ford for Céline is that it foreshadows the imminent Americanisation of France as a whole: 'Il y a peu de chances que nous échappions à cette évolution' (CC 3, 146). In this inescapable situation, the old artisanal France will be swept away definitively, to make way for a totally mechanised society in which man will be reduced to the state of a slave, not merely of other men, as in *Voyage au bout de la nuit*, but of machines themselves. Céline's vision is analogous to that of the German Expressionist dramatists and film-makers and to that of Chaplin in *Modern Times*, and is by no means without echoes of late nineteenth-century and early twentieth-century science fiction, such as that of

42. See: Jean-Pierre Dauphin and Henri Godard, 'Avant-propos' (CC 3); Kim Saunders, 'Images of the Foreign in Céline's Early Fiction', MA dissertation, University of Warwick, 1976.

Jules Verne and H.G. Wells, who finds a much more precise echo in *Mort à crédit*.

Faced with this double threat — the indifference of the bourgeois regime to the suffering of the poor and the inevitability of the adoption of an American attitude to industrial work — Céline recognises the inadequacy of the traditional humanist responses. The medical profession takes refuge in an outmoded rhetoric yet, for Céline, 'notre humanisme aussi est désuet et nuisible, il n'a que faire dans la societé où fonctionnent les assurances sociales' (CC 3, 160), and, more importantly, 'la médecine bourgeoise est morte et bien morte' (CC 3, 160). If bourgeois medicine is bankrupt, then the bourgeois state, the Republic, fares no better: 'une porcherie tenue comme une république aurait fait faillite depuis longtemps' (CC 3, 189). The medical writings indicate the same deep anti-republican-ism as that which informs *Voyage au bout de la nuit*, where French society is dominated by a 'cochon aux ailes en or' (V, 9), and which is at the basis of all Céline's writing of the inter-war period. Hence, the limits of Republican legislation as far as health service is con-cerned, and the recognition in the memorandum of 1932, despite the relative optimism of the *Monde* article, that 'les assurances sociales n'ont apporté aucun changement aux statuts anciens' (CC 3, 212).

Seen in this light, the problems which all medical writings are attempting to confront necessitate a rejection of the old humanism and its replacement by a pessimistic and disabused realism. If the necessary transformations in the field of social medicine are frus-trated by the power of capital, the revolution which will definitively solve the problem is by no means imminent. At the same time, any attempt towards progress is checked by one insurmountable ob-stacle: human nature itself. For Céline, in 1932, 'l'homme pratique toute fraternité avec ennui et le pillage et l'assassinat seulement avec passion et frénésie' (CC 3, 188). Only a radical transformation of society and the establishment of a socialist regime will permit the creation of genuine fraternity amongst mankind: a weak and distant hope, definitively crushed in the course of Céline's journey to the Soviet Union in 1936, where the Russian espousal of Fordism showed the inability of socialism to deal with the one irreducible truth: 'l'Homme il est humain à peu près autant que la poule vole' (Mea, 25). From this pessimistic vision of the frustration of human progress and the bankrupcy of traditional humanism, Céline draws a position of resigned realism which recognises the need for social thinkers to adapt to the 'conditions morbides et capitalistes irrémé-diables' (CC 3, 194), and to accept that medicine can only be administered in a minimal way under a capitalist society, containing disease in the same way that society contains prostitution (CC 3, 194).

In this context of a resigned appraisal of the chances of social medicine in France, however, how is the reader to reconcile the enthusiasm for Fordism which leaps from the pages of the lecture and the article on 'assurances'? It is important to underline that, when talking to his own profession, either through the pages of *La Presse Médicale* or at the meeting of the Société de Médecine, Céline is addressing a public which he despises. In his memorandum of 1932, he comments: 'étudions d'un peu plus près encore nos auditeurs, malgré qu'ils nous dégoûtent' (CC 3, 186), and the same contempt emerges from his view of the medical establishment in 'La Santé publique en France' (BLFC 2, 47). Similarly, he is careful to distinguish between two concepts of hygiene: one revolutionary and virtually impracticable before the coming to power of socialism, the other reactionary and, like that of Targowla's traditionalist insurance doctors, designed to repress and control the work-force. Céline's lecture of 1928 and his article of the same year are therefore directed at an audience divided between powerless liberals and dangerous reactionaries. These problematical writings have the effect of denouncing the medical system of the period, 'en froissant les sentiments' (CC 3, 148) of the first category by deploying an exaggerated form of the arguments of the latter. The 'realism' of the insurance-company doctors of the nineteenth century, quoted by Targowla, and the vision of an extended Taylorism are raised to the status of a system which allows Céline to demonstrate the poverty of medical thought in France in the inter-war years and the bankruptcy of bourgeois society in general. Yet Céline is not alone in using an exaggerated form of contemporary ideas to polemical effect: in so doing, he is drawing upon an entire tradition of polemical literature, embodied notably in the English writers of the eighteenth century, Swift and Defoe. Swift's famous pamphlet *A Modest Proposal*, which denounces the indifference of the British to the Irish famine, begins: 'I know a very intelligent American in London who has assured me that a healthy and well-fed young child is, at the age of one, a delicious food'.[43] The message of this American realist, exactly two hundred years before Céline's Ford, is that, in order to resolve the problem of the famine in Ireland, the Irish have only to adopt the course of raising their children, like veal, as fatstock. An even more interesting parallel with Céline's work is provided by Daniel Defoe's essay, *The Shortest Way with the*

43. Jonathan Swift, 'A Modest Proposal' in *Irish Tracts 1728–1733*, Oxford, Blackwell, 1964, p. 111.

Dissenters, which pushed its polemical irony to such an extreme point that the work was not universally recognised as a satirical pamphlet at all, but was taken at face value. In this essay, Defoe, the author of *Robinson Crusoe*, denounces the weakness of the monarchy and the intolerance of the Anglican clergy by ferociously recommending the execution of all dissident Protestants, following the example of the St Bartholomew's Day Massacre in France.[44] This polemical tradition, which is so clearly crucial for a reading of Céline's later anti-Semitic tracts, is helpful in unifying the diverse elements in his medical writings. In the context of this tradition, the broad basis of all the medical writings is Céline's opposition to the bourgeois society in which he finds himself and his pessimistic view of the chimerical nature of any immediate project for change. In this way, the example of Ford, which Céline adopts with enthusiasm and in contradiction to the views expressed in the *Monde* article and the two unpublished memoranda, to say nothing of Bardamu's experiences in Detroit in *Voyage au bout de la nuit*, has the same status as the proposals of the American citizen in Swift's pamphlet: a demonstration of the bankruptcy of humanism in the face of irremediable social injustice.

What makes Céline's choice of Ford as the linchpin of his polemic on industrial and social medicine so important is that it is not merely a symptom of the debate on the introduction of a national health insurance scheme in France in the 1920s, but an essential component of a more general reflection in France on the possibilities offered by the importation, voluntary or imposed, of the American way of life and American industrial and social organisation. Writers on Céline have been too prone somewhat glibly to invoke comparisons with Georges Duhamel's *Scènes de la vie future*, or Paul Morand's *New York*, yet neither work gets to the heart of the central anxiety which exercises Céline. Morand is excited by the often sexual exoticism offered by the American city, an exoticism which, by its very nature, divorces it from any immediate concrete implication for France, whilst Duhamel, although coming closer to Céline's preoccupation with the American system as a symbol for modern life, isolates and defuses his implicit criticism by the adoption for what Henri Troyat, writing on the same subject in the 1940s, calls 'un ton amusé'.[45] Yet, in Europe as a whole, and particularly in France, even before the First World War,

---

44. Daniel Defoe, *The Shortest Way with the Dissenters, and Other Pamphlets*, Oxford, Blackwell, 1927, pp. 113–33.
45. Henri Troyat, *Un si long chemin*, Paris, Stock, 1976, p. 169.

[33]

Americanism constituted, and was perceived as, a serious challenge to the existing social order. A survey of French geography text-books used in schools[46] shows an almost wilful attempt to exclude the United States from discussion, but also indicates that when the North American continent was allowed to appear on syllabuses, it assumed a consistently menacing aspect, embodying an outrageous and inhuman life style which it threatened to export to the countries of Europe. This distrust of Americanism is explained in the case of France to a large extent by that country's industrial primitiveness, its reliance, until the Second World War, on artisanally produced luxury goods, of which the lace and furniture trades in *Mort à crédit* are typical, rather than on an extensively developed heavy industry. Thus, although there was some early interest in Taylor, notably by Rimailho, Hyacinthe Dubreuil and André Citroën, French industry as a whole was slow to show any enthusiasm for America: the assembly-line innovations adopted by Citroën from 1919 onwards and the rare examples of conversion of other large plants to a similar model were more than outweighed by producers such as Renault, who steadfastly refused to adopt an assembly line, and thousands of smaller artisanal enterprises.[47] Similarly, as Charles S. Maier points out, there was little intellectual interest in France in the possibilities offered by the examples of Taylor and Ford, except in the case of rare visionaries such as Le Corbusier.[48] What interest there was largely confined to the Right: the Left's interest in Taylorism being largely restricted to a dwindling rump of Saint-Simonians, with their increasingly obscure review, *Le Producteur*, which is a poss-ible source for Courtial des Pereires's *Le Génitron* and his Saint-Simonian colony at Blême-le-Petit.[49] Orthodox left-wing distrust of Americanisation was more accurately expressed in André Philip's *Le Problème ouvrier aux Etats-Unis*, of 1927, which Céline cites approvingly in his lecture on Ford (CC 3, 141). Nevertheless, Taylor and Ford found their admirers in the late 1920s in a group of technocratic thinkers who, whilst professing political neutrality in the name of national efficiency, gravitated to the Right and the defence of bourgeois interests.[50] As Charles Maier comments: 'The

46. See: Jacques Portes, 'Les Etats-Unis dans les manuels d'Histoire et de Géographie de la IIIe République (1871–1914)', *Revue d'Histoire Moderne et Con-temporaine*, 1981.
47. See: Claude Fohlen, *La France de l'entre-deux-guerres (1917–1939)*, Paris, Castermann, 1966, pp. 73–88.
48. Charles S. Maier, 'Between Taylorism and Technocracy', *Journal of Contem-porary History*, V, 2, 1970, p. 36.
49. See: ibid., p. 38.
50. See: ibid., p. 59.

most typical product of the growing vogue for Americanism was probably Ernest Mercier's *Redressement Français*. This association, founded during the last protracted agonies of the Cartel des Gauches, represented an effort to form a directing elite of economic experts supposedly above party politics, a cadre for institutional and industrial modernisation'.[51] Yet:

> In general, Mercier's managerial elitism emerged as a new defence of that very traditional French bulwark, the bourgeoisie; and his own parliamentary dream was the venerable Union Nationale of the centre groupings. The social policy of the Redressement faded off into the traditional justifications of capitalism by many prominent business politicians of the late twenties, including André François-Poncet and Pierre-Etienne Flandin, some of whom ended up with Vichy.[52]

Nevertheless, although the cult of the engineer as the new Messiah assumed markedly right-wing connotations in France, internationally it cut across ideological lines, embraced by Lenin and Mussolini alike as the architect of the overthrow of bourgeois society, and exploited by exponents of wildly differing political creeds. As Maier writes of the end of the 1920s: 'In different ways, Tardieu and Hoover (and, it might be argued, even Stalin) took over the most easily manipulated aspects of Americanism, but each came to subordinate its claims as an autonomous social vision to his own ideology'.[53] The problem for a writer such as Céline, however, was the sense that Tardieu in France, who finally enacted the social insurance legislation, and Hoover, Mussolini and Stalin, had embraced an internationally prevalent industrial faith which not only threatened the old order in France but made escape almost impossible anywhere in the world: hence the quite specific pessimism of the conclusion in *Mea culpa*: 'Tous les Ford se ressemblent, soviétiques ou non'.

In this context, Antonio Gramsci's essay in the *Prison Notebooks*, 'Americanism and Fordism', provides important confirmation of a potential cultural upheaval. Whilst analysing elements as diverse as industrial production, 'the question of sex',[54] the possibility of an

---

51. Ibid., p. 57.
52. Ibid., p. 59.
53. Ibid., p. 60.
54. In his analysis of sexuality within the context of the Ford system, Gramsci anticipates Marcuse's concept, in *Eros and Civilisation*, of 'surplus repression', the result of the rationalisation of sexual urges in conformity with the demands of the assembly line. That Bardamu, in *Voyage au bout de la nuit*, should be introduced to America by the Eve-like Lola is ironic in view of his subsequent career in Detroit, as

'American epoch', demographic rationalisation, high wages, psycho-analysis, and the role of rotary clubs and the Freemasons, Gramsci insists upon the anti-humanism inherent in Fordism:

> it is from this point of view that one should study the 'puritanical' initiative of American industrialists like Ford. It is certain that they are not concerned with the 'humanity' or 'spirituality' of the worker, which are immediately smashed. This 'humanity and spirituality' cannot be realised except in the world of production and work and in productive 'creation'. They exist most in the artisan, in the 'demiurge', when the worker's personality was reflected whole in the object created and when the link between art and labour was still very strong. But it is precisely against this 'humanism' that the new industrialism is fighting.[55]

Once again, the positive pole to the negative one embodied in Fordism is an idealised vision of artisanal production: a polarisation of clear importance for *Mort à crédit*, in which, however, the life of the artisan in the 1900s is rigorously refused idealisation and is already under threat. Gramsci sees, however, that it is the very repression and dehumanisation of the industrial worker which may provoke change and which therefore needs to be mitigated by social concessions: the industrial worker rejects the role of 'trained gorilla' which the mechanised system maps out for him: 'not only does the worker think, but the fact that he gets no immediate satisfaction from his work and realises that they are trying to reduce him to a trained gorilla, can lead him into a train of thought that is far from conformist'.[56] Once again, it is Bardamu who will emerge, in Céline's work, as spokesman of this non-conformism.

It is now possible to see the way in which Céline's writings on social medicine and Americanism provide a precise historical framework in which to view his literary production of the inter-war years. Tempting as it is to view him as a classic example of a well-defined tradition of right-wing thought, embodied in the social medical thinkers of the nineteenth century, the reactionary radical-ism and anti-Semitism of Ford, and the prevalent use of social hygiene as a metaphor for political and racial purification which will lead directly to the pamphlets of 1937 and onwards, his position is

---

is the fact that he leaves the Ford plant in order to live in a brothel with Molly, the symbol of unrepressed sexuality. In this way, Bardamu's life with Molly has a distinctly subversive connotation.

55. Antonio Gramsci, 'Americanism and Fordism', in *Selections from the Prison Notebooks*, ed. Quintin Hoare and Geoffrey Nowell Smith, London, Lawrence and Wishart, p. 302.

56. Ibid., p. 310.

more complex and any interpretation is forced to accomodate
Bardamu's experiences in Detroit, as well as the two unpublished
memoranda to the League of Nations and the *Monde* article. In fact,
by the time he comes to write *Voyage au bout de la nuit*, Céline has
realised that he is living and writing in a kind of limbo. The existing
bourgeois society, dominated by an all-powerful operation of
money, is incapable of resolving the major social and political
problems which beset the largest and least privileged sector of
society: there remains only one fleeting hope, that of a radical
socialist transformation of structures, and that is snuffed out by the
visit to the Soviet Union in 1936. If the old society offers no reason
for commitment and is, to all intents and purposes, dying on its feet,
the vision of the new is uniformly horrifying. The modern world,
that of the post-war era, will be the world of Taylor and Ford
because the old world is incapable of resisting it, and socialism and
Communism will merely adopt the language and practice of social
engineering. Céline thus finds himself in a world which he cannot
accept and in a profession with a bankrupt philosophy, an outworn
rhetoric and a discredited hierarchy. With polemical detachment,
Céline recognises that all that is left of the heroic adventure of
nineteenth-century medicine in a world which has gone over to
Ford is what he calls 'le fantôme burlesque de la médecine bourgeoise' (CC 3, 160), and it is here that the career of Bardamu begins.

At the same time, if a reading of Céline's medical writings
provides a quite concrete definition of his literary pessimism — that
of a man for whom the world, in which he did not greatly believe
anyway, passed with the First World War — it gives also a privileged insight the workings of his polemic and contains precious
lessons for a study of his anti-Semitic texts. What appears at first
sight as an unproblematic, if bellicose, statement of a position is
rapidly subverted by the procedures of exageration, misquotation
and flagrent self-contradiction, overlaid by a chameleon-like desire
for self-protection whilst adopting the most outrageous of stances.
It is only through an examination of all the works on medicine, with
all their inconsistencies, that the individual prescriptions take on
less importance than the underlying world-view which informs
them all. Even so, this procedure seems unnecessarily perverse and
complicated if it is not born in mind that Céline had already studied,
through Semmelweis, the fate of a nineteenth-century polemicist
whose failure was due precisely to an exaggerated faith in the unambiguous efficacy of straight polemical writing. Moreover, whereas
the medical writings provide a precise historical context for Céline's
work in the inter-war years — the threat of the modern industrial

world — *Semmelweis*, in itself another polemical shot in the battle for social hygiene, situates the struggle in the broader framework of history itself and the ultimate futility of any historical action.

Semmelweis and the Tragedy of Polemic

Two preliminary observations are essential before a detailed study of *Semmelweis* can be undertaken, and they both concern the curious status of the work as a thesis for the award of the degree of Doctor of Medicine and the question of the relationship between Céline himself and his subject. By any academic standards, *La Vie et l'oeuvre de Philippe-Ignance Semmelweis (1818–1865)* is a bizarre thesis for a medical degree: written in a self-consciously belletristic style, in which there is even an element of self-parody, it takes pains to exclude from its subject-matter any material which might be incomprehensible to the layman. In other words, it translates Céline's literary ambition by operating as a popularisation of Semmelweis's career open to as broad a readership as possible and contains no technical analysis of the medical problems involved nor even a professional evaluation of Semmelweis's great work, *The Aetiology of Puerpereal Fever*. In fact, and here perhaps Céline indicates subtly the work's true significance, it stands in exactly the same relationship to Céline's professional medical career as does Semmelweis's own doctoral thesis, not on medicine at all, but on *La Vie des plantes*, and written in another *different* language, Latin. Nor can Céline's doctoral dissertation be termed a work of research: it is, rather, a distillation and compilation of those works on his subject cited in his bibliography (CC 3, 79). Yet, in this first piece of extended writing by Céline, the same relationship between author and the material he is exploiting may be observed as that which characterises the later works and which takes the form of an almost playful deformation of that material. Following Céline's popularisation of his own popularisation, 'Les Derniers jours de Semmelweis', in *La Presse Médicale*, a Hungarian Professor, Tiberius de Gryöry, wrote to the review, generally praising Céline's article, but drawing the reader's attention to a number of factual errors. In the first place, Céline's dating is seriously defective: he gets the wrong date for the onset of Semmelweis's madness; he is nearly six weeks out (22 June instead of 31 July 1865) in situating his subject's last departure from Budapest for Vienna; and, most inexplicable of all, he puts the date of Semmelweis's death at 16 August 1865 and not at its true date three days before, a fact which could be found in any encyclopaedia, let alone the secondary material covered by Céline (CC 3, 95). Secondly, his account contains serious errors of fact in the narrative: Professor de Gryöry dismisses Céline's account of Semmelweis covering the walls of Budapest with posters, points out that the entire episode of Semmelweis's self-inflicted wound 'est de pure invention' (CC 3, 95), and refutes the contention that it was Semmelweis's old professor, Skoda, who travelled to Budapest to bring the mad and dying doctor back to Vienna. Finally, he challenges Céline's statistics: the 96 per cent mortality-rate in Klin's clinic hovered in reality between 16 and 31 per cent (CC 3, 95). If this were an isolated occurrence in Céline's work, it would present little interest and would merely show him up as a slovenly writer. Yet this deformation of existing data is a constant feature in his work and one which invites a deeper interpretation. The errors in dates of *Semmelweis* look forward to the apparently gratuitous mistake of setting the 'Chanson des Gardes Suisses', which introduces *Voyage au bout de la nuit*, in 1793, one year after the Battle of the Tuileries in which the regiment was massacred. The deliberate transformation of the secondary material in the case, say, of Semmelweis's self-inflicted wound or his final journey back to Vienna, is not isolated either; it is the same procedure as that contained in Céline's totally inaccurate rewriting of Macaulay's Monmouth episode in *Voyage au bout de la nuit*. Finally, wild and improbable exaggeration of statistics for polemical purposes, but also to disorientate the reader, becomes a central and perlexing feature of the anti-Semitic pamphlets. It is surprising in this context that critics have not seen the parallel between Professor de Gryöry's courteous questioning of Céline's facts and Emmanuel Mounier's outraged attack on the apparent plagiarism and shameless exaggeration of existing and verifiable statistics in *Bagetelles pour un massacre*:[57] in both cases, the neutral reader is drawn into the polemic by the bait of demonstrably false figures. Of central importance for *Semmelweis*, however, is the fact that all three of these categories of error have the effect of prising the subject away from the realm of history and bringing it nearer to autonomous world of fiction. Hence the most glaring transposition of the factual data: the historical figure, *Ignace-Philippe* Semmelweis, is inverted into the fictional creation, Philippe-Ignace, in the same way that his historical adversary *Klein* becomes the more sinister Klin.[58] Through these

---

57. Emmanuel Mounier, '*Bagatelles pour un massacre*', *Esprit*, 66, March 1938, quoted in HER 2, 341–2.

58. On the inversion of the name, see: Charles Krance, '*Semmelweis ou l'accouch-*

procedures of falsification, therefore, what should begin as an academic doctoral thesis becomes a work of fiction and a polemical fable, in which the polemicist-protagonist fights his struggle with history. Attempts by Charles Krance and, especially, Denise Aebersold,[59] to tie *Semmelweis* too tightly to a notion of covert autobiography do not necessarily facilitate a reading of the work. In the first place, the facts of Céline's own career do not fit easily into the biography of Semmelweis, unless the disturbing notion of predestination is introduced; secondly, to view the work as tending towards a fable of France in the 1920s is to restrict its implications and to obscure its real purpose, which is to tell the story of a medical polemicist of the nineteenth century within the context of the philosophical nature of history itself.

The preface to the 1936 edition and its conclusion accentuate the fairy-story characteristics of the work: 'Voici la terrible histoire de Philippe-Ignace Semmelweis' (CC 3, 96), and: 'Voici la très triste histoire de P.I. Semmelweis' (CC 3, 78). Not only does this stylistic technique situate the work in the context of stories of great men, such as Blaise Cendrars's *L'Or*, which begins with the words: 'Voici la merveilleuse histoire du général Johann Auguste Suter',[60] it reinforces one of the central elements of the tale, its circularity, in the same way that 'Moi j'avais jamais rien dit' and 'Qu'on n'en parle plus' set the parameters for *Voyage au bout de la nuit*. Within this circularity, Céline approaches the two subjects of his work, the one more narrowly concerned with the medical pretext for the thesis, the other leading on to a more general reflection on the nature of truth, the difficulty of its discovery and the almost insurmountable obstacles to its communication.

In its medical preoccupations, the thesis is central to Céline's constant professional concerns: hygiene, infection and fever, expressed in his works on social medicine, the treatise on quinine and malaria and his essay on typhoid.[61] In the case of Semmelweis and puerpereal fever, Céline explores an additional irony: the fact that it is a fever which results from an infection contracted in hospitals and which is caused directly by doctors and medical students, the same

ement de la biographie célinienne', *Revue des Lettres Modernes*, Série: *Louis-Ferdinand Céline*, 2. p. 12.

59. Denise Aebersold, *Céline: un demystificateur mythomane*, Paris, Minard, coll. 'Archives des Lettres Modernes', 1979.

60. Blaise Cendrars, *L'Or*, Paris, Gallimard, coll. 'Folio', p. 21.

61. 'Deux expériences de vaccination en masse et *per os* contre la typhoïde' (1929), CC 3, 167–9. Céline also specifically makes Bébert, in *Voyage au bout de la nuit*, die of typhoid.

carabins of whom Bardamu is a colleague at the beginning of *Voyage au bout de la nuit*. It is precisely the medical profession and, more specifically, medical instruction, which are the guilty parties: the agencies which are the repositories of nineteenth-century humanism in their search for truth and their battle against human suffering become ironically the conveyors of death. Yet, it is a death which threatens specifically women in labour, and here *Semmelweis* begins an extended reflection, continued in *Voyage au bout de la nuit*, on the notion of the abortive childbirth, in which the woman appears as the repository of death. As Yannik Mancel writes:

> Ainsi, de même que tout homme est un 'mort à crédit', une 'pourriture en suspense', toute femme apparaît dans la textualité célinienne non seulement comme sursitaire de la ménopause, mais aussi et peut-être surtout, comme porteuse d'une inflammation/décomposition potentielle des organes génitaux. Mais c'est surtout comme porteur d'une mort virtuelle qu'est généralement présente le sexe féminin dans les textes de notre corpus. Danger de mort pour la mère d'abord, comme en témoigne l'objet même de la thèse de doctorat en médecine de Céline . . . Danger de mort également pour l'enfant, comme le prouvent les séquences d'avortement, de fausse-couche et d'accouchement raté qui jalonnent le récit célinien.[62]

Hence, the inversion of Semmelweis's Christian names automatically mirrors a major thematic inversion of values which dominates the whole work: the act of childbirth, which is traditionally seen as life-giving and ensuring the progression of the species, leads instead to death; the doctor, traditionally an agent of life and the aleviation of pain, becomes the 'auxiliaire de la mort' (CC 3, 36). Similarly, Semmelweis's hard-won discovery, intended to benefit mankind and to guarantee 'les deux grandes joies de l'existence, celle d'être jeune et celle de donner la vie' (CC 3, 52), is stillborn itself and only comes to the notice of history through the later work of Pasteur. Finally, what links *Semmelweis* most closely to the rest of Céline's medical writings and particularly to his work on social medicine is the fact that puerpereal fever in the nineteenth century, as described by Céline, is predominantly, though not exclusively, a disease of the poor,[63] suffered by those who are forced to have recourse to the public hospitals in the same way that they will constitute the

---

62. Yannik Mancel, 'De la Sémiotique textuelle à la théorie du "roman": Céline', *Dialectiques*, 8, 1975, p. 56.
63. The rich by no means totally escaped. Indeed, it is the death of the cousin of Semmelweis's correspondent, Dr Michaelis, which convinces him of the necessity of publishing his discovery.

clientele of the municipal *dispensaires* in France in the inter-war years. Nevertheless, although the later social and economic geography of the novels is hinted at, it would be entirely misleading to see Semmelweis himself as a *médecin des pauvres*: he is, rather, the typical representative of *la médecine bourgeoise* in its purest, least venial form, of which Bardamu will appear as the *fantôme burlesque*. Céline is more interested in using Semmelweis as the example of a man who is accorded a rare and privileged vision of the truth, but who is unequal to the task of expressing it. In this way, in addition to its precise connotations in the context of Céline's work, the discovery of the causes of puerpereal fever is to be seen on the same level as the hypothetical discovery of a cure for cancer (CC 3, 96) or even of the rules of geometry (CC 3, 55). What interests Céline is the process which leads to the recognition of any truth and the difficulties in overcoming resistance to it. Through Semmelweis, Céline portrays the fate of the polemicist who, faced with the hostility and incomprehension of his contemporaries, particularly those in a professional hierarchy, can only react with increasing violence and exageration which lead him to madness and death. In placing the annunciation of the truth about puerpereal fever at the centre of his narrative, Céline therefore accords it prime importance, but is at pains as well to show the long journey which leads Semmelweis to his moment of truth and the dark decline which follows it.

There is nothing in Semmelweis's childhood or upbringing to explain his subsequent fate. It is true that, in the great era of the Austro-Hungarian Empire before the fall of Metternich, as a citizen of Budapest he is an outsider, 'destiné à déplaire' (CC 3, 27) and mocked because of his 'accent hongrois très prononcé' (CC 3, 31). But his Hungarian nationality by no means acts as a barrier to advancement. More important, the picture which Céline gives of Semmelweis's childhood and family is completely positive and could not be more different from the context of *Mort à crédit*. One reason for this is that whilst Ferdinand is an only child, the repository of the aspirations, anxieties and frustrations of his parents, Semmelweis is one of a family of eight,[64] and benefits from a relaxed and happy atmosphere in which parental authority is decidedly mitigated. On two occasions, Céline draws attention to the father's

64. The low birth-rate in France in the second half of the nineteenth century, particularly amongst the bourgeoisie and the petite bourgeoisie, led to a certain cult of the child reflected in the fiction of the period, from Jules Vallès' *L'Enfant*, to which Céline owes much in *Mort à crédit*, to Jules Renard's classic novel of an unhappy childhood, *Poil-de-carotte*.

tolerance of his son's departure from the norm: when the young Semmelweis neglects his studies at the *lycée* of Pest, preferring the spectacle of the streets and jeopardising his father's ambition for him, the grocer still says nothing; more important, he acquiesces, albeit reluctantly, in a crucial decision when Semmelweis reaches Vienna. Semmelweis abandons the study of law, which can still lead him to the coveted position of auditor in the Imperial Army, and transfers to medicine, a discipline which until Claude Bernard and the late nineteenth-century medical thinkers, was theoretical, speculative and with few practical scientific bases. At the same time, if medical science was still in its infancy, a fact which acts as a barrier to any acquisition of a new truth, Semmelweis is determined, like Claude Bernard later, to introduce as much empiricism as possible. It is for this reason that he abandons law and, particularly, is attracted towards the study of surgery, the most practical branch of medicine. This insistence upon the practical, which looks forward to a similar emphasis in Céline's own treatise on quinine, is something he never loses: it marks his entire personality and even dictates his behaviour when, later, he retreats to a kind of temporary exile in Venice. Unlike the Romantic poets, notably Musset, who merely enthuse over the Adriatic City, Semmelweis enters the labyrinth of Venice as he does the maze of scientific knowledge, exploring it in its entirety, even learning how to row a gondola.

Yet, if Semmelweis is led towards his discovery of the causes of puerpereal fever by this innate sense of the practical and the useful, the dominant element in his career is none the less chance. As Céline emphasises at the beginning of the essay: 'L'être qui vient à la conscience a pour grand maître le Hasard' (CC 3, 24). The influence of 'le Hasard' runs through the narrative. Semmelweis is induced to switch from law to medicine by a chance attendance at an autopsy, 'quand la science interroge le cadavre au couteau' (CC 3, 28). With this beginning of Semmelweis's medical career, it is easy to see why Céline should falsify the historical data in order to make him die as the result of an autopsy: the corpse on the dissecting table is the central element in the narrative and establishes its circularity. The corpse initiates Semmelweis into the mysteries of medicine, it is at the origin of puerpereal fever itself, it kills his friend Kolletchka and, in Céline's version, it is the cause of the death of Semmelweis himself. From this initial chance encounter with medicine, Semmelweis is again led on in his career by a series of accidents. By chance, 'il put entendre Skoda' (CC 3, 28) and immediately becomes his student. In the normal course of events, without the intervention of chance, he would have become Skoda's assistant and had a completely different career, but because there is unexpected competition for the post, he is unsuccessful and is directed towards Rokitansky and the study of surgery. Even at this stage chance does not relax: there are no surgeon's posts available when Semmelweis qualifies, so he is obliged to accept the only opening there is: the post of obstetrician under Klin in the Vienna General Hospital. It is in this constant intervention of chance in the career of Semmelweis that the discovery of the causes of puerpereal fever becomes more an accidental revelation of the Truth than the result of long and consciously-directed research. As Semmelweis writes of himself: 'le destin m'a choisi' (CC 3, 41).

Once Semmelweis has been led to his discovery by fate, what clearly interests Céline is the way, not in which a discovery is *reached*, but in which it is *recognised* as such. The truth is there, hidden, at the very beginning of Semmelweis's experience of the Vienna General Hospital, encapsulated in the single conclusion from the mortality rates of the two lying-in clinics: '*On meurt plus chez Klin que chez Bartch*' (CC 3, 42). The essence of the problem which now confronts Semmelweis is contained in the metaphors employed by Céline, one set of which is concerned with circularity and the other with a dichotomy between light and darkness. As Semmelweis approaches the solution to his problem, Céline begins to use images of him turning constantly around the truth without actually recognising it: 'A cet instant, il est si prés de la vérité qu'il est en train de la circonscrire' (CC 3, 46), images which convey both the circularity in which the narrative is imprisoned and the act of writing without progression itself. At the same time, the mystery of puerpereal fever, 'cette tragédie où tout est obscur' (CC 3, 42), is shrouded in darkness. The task of Semmelweis is to shed light. Thus, whilst describing 'cet état présent où tout est obscur' (CC 3, 45), Céline notes Semmelweis's progress: 'Un jour, au loin, il perçait une lueur brève' (CC 3, 44), and defines his ambition as follows: 'il veut voir absolument clair' (CC 3, 44).

This last statement, in the context of a rich image-pattern based upon light and darkness in the context of the search for knowledge, has a quite obvious specific resonance: Semmelweis is applying exactly the same method as Descartes for attaining truth. Both men are motivated by the same ambition: to proceed methodically through the darkness of ignorance and imprecise thought, using only evidence which is proven, to arrive at the light and to benefit mankind in a purely practical sense. Yet, if the adventure of Semmelweis, as narrated by Céline, is calqued upon the mission of Descartes, it reflects yet again that inversion which characterises the entire work. Descartes is pre-eminently the philosopher of tact and prudence who avoids at all costs a head-on confrontation with his detractors: when in difficulties, he retreats. In this way, he is left alone, to proceed through systematic doubt towards the light of incontrovertible truth, a truth instantly transformed into practical utility and which stands at the head of an entire tradition of thought. However, although Semmelweis shares the same ambition and although in his search for truth he starts from the same precepts, his destiny is completely different. He makes the sad discovery that, in order for a truth to exist, it must be *recognised* as such, and it is on this crucial issue that his career falters. The truth about puerpereal fever never becomes of practical value in nineteenth-century science. Rather, Semmelweis's discovery is only recuperated by Pasteur's research into bacteria, to the extent that it occupies in the history of science the tragic and ironic position of glorious precursor, but one deprived of any practical effect. The whole drama of Semmelweis is that, because he cannot convince the medical hierarchy, his discovery is useless and generations of women die because of that failure until they are saved by Lister and the development of antisepsis. Céline is writing about a man who should have been acknowledged as one of the pillars of nineteenth-century medical science but who instead ends up as a footnote in medical histories: 'Here Lister had a predecessor, as he gladly and generously acknowledged'.[65] And, unlike in the case of Descartes, the interest in Semmelweis must necessarily shift away from the nature of the discovery itself to the difficulties encountered in gaining its acceptance. As Bernhard J. Stern writes: 'The devices of social pressure, ridicule, indifference, deliberate misinterpretation and attempts to discredit on the basis of priority, all were used against Semmelweis in an attempt to discourage deviation from the established tradition.'[66] In other words, *Semmelweis* very rapidly becomes the story of the fate of a nonconformist, rather than the history of a scientific discovery. After all, the cause of puerpereal fever as defined by Semmelweis in the *Aetiology* is banal: the transmission of infection to women in labour by doctors and medical students who have just come from the dissecting-room. What interests Céline is the violence and apparent gratuitousness of the reactions to this seemingly inoffensive discovery. Thus, Sem-

65. Charles Singer and E. Ashworth Underwood, *A Short History of Medicine*, Oxford, Clarendon Press, 1962, p. 360.
66. Bernhard J. Stern, *Social Factors in Medical Progress*, New York, AMS Press, 1968, p. 70.

melweis is the victim at Vienna of a brutal persecution, orchestrated by Klin, who is motivated by petty jealousy and appears as 'le grand auxiliaire de la mort' (CC 3, 36). What is interesting in Céline's narrative is that he is careful to emphasise the gratuitousness and pettiness of Klin's opposition, whilst omitting what most biographies of Semmelweis give as a more concrete explanation for his antipathy: Semmelweis's enrolment in the Academic Legion, a revolutionary body, 'formed as a result of the rejection of a petition of the Diet of Lower Austria by Emperor Ferdinand',[67] an act which could not fail to antagonise Klin, who was physician to the Imperial Court. Céline has transformed the conservative court doctor Klein into the irrational Klin, the representative of human stupidity which greets the most beneficial of scientific discoveries with blind hostility. In other words, once the emphasis is removed from Semmelweis himself, the essay is easily integrated into the general anti-humanism and more particular distrust of hierarchies which emerge from the medical pamphlets.

In this context, the reactions of foreign scientists, who are either hostile or indifferent, are of equal importance, but, precisely *because* they are foreign, far from Vienna, they introduce a theme which will be taken up in the fiction, particularly in the English episode of *Mort à crédit*, that of barriers to communication in the form of letters which receive no reply. Attempts by Semmelweis to circumvent the hostility in Vienna by publicising his discovery in an orthodox written style meet the same failure as his application of orthodox Cartesian principles to the problem of puerpereal fever: his letters which are sent off all over Europe announcing the discovery meet with a total silence, and conventional analysis of the disease and its cause in the *Aetiology*, a work which compensates for the relative brevity of the letters by its inordinate length, attempting to impose truth by quantitative means, has no more success. The relative innocence of Semmelweis has led him to announce his discovery in a conventional manner and through conventional channels. The failure of this orthodox publicity will dictate the extreme measures to which Semmelweis resorts as a publicist in Budapest.

Céline is careful, however, in this central section of the narrative, to apportion blame equally and to insist on Semmelweis's own inadequacies. The tragedy of the discovery of the causes of puerpereal fever is twofold: the brutal stupidity of the medical hierarchy, but also the fact that the scientist himself is 'maladroit' (CC

67. Ibid., p. 68.

3, 37) and by his own lack of tact contributes to the failure of his discovery to gain acceptance. As Céline concludes his thesis: 'il semble que sa découverte dépassa les forces de son génie. Ce fut, peut-être, la cause profonde de tous ses malheurs' (CC 3, 78). He is as much the victim of his own inordinate enthusiasm for his discovery as is the hero of Céline's cautionary tale in *La Quinine en thérapeutique*, Doctor Bazire, who kills himself and narrowly avoids killing his wife by believing that if his beloved quinine has not cured their influenza rapidly enough, it is because the dose was too small.[68] Céline's enthusiasts compensate for lack of immediate results by increasing the pressure until disaster strikes.

Undermined by his fatal enthusiasm, beset by his colleagues et home and ignored by his colleagues abroad, Semmelweis embarks on the final, tragic phase of his career. It is at this point that the essentially circular character of the work appears, which sets Semmelweis's problems in a broader, more pessimistic context. Semmelweis has already been dismissed once from Vienna, and has found peace and tranquility in Venice; on his second exile from the Austrian capital, he finds the same relaxation in returning to Budapest, to the extent that the Hungarian capital becomes the repetition and reflection of Venice. Hence, until the very final moments of his career, when Semmelweis succeeds Birley as the Director of the Clinic of Saint-Roch, and when his troubles begin again, Vienna consistently represents conflict and turmoil and any escape from Vienna brings peace. This is certainly true of the first months of Semmelweis's return to his home city in 1848: worn out by the struggles in Vienna, he enters into a period of lethargy and indifference, emerging from it to become for the first and only time in his life a socially acceptable doctor, the darling of the Budapest grande bourgeoisie. This privileged period of acceptance, however, is only transitory and is threatened by two forces which are constant in the story: the march of history and Semmelweis's own uncalculating personality. The repression which follows the Revolution of 1848 and Semmelweis's bizarre behaviour in his treatment of Countess Grandinish (CC 3, 61), rapidly terminate his career as a safe society doctor.

Significantly, this return of Semmelweis to Budapest is marked, in Céline's narrative, by a regression towards childhood and, especially, passivity. Before the Revolution, he has sunk into a state of listlessness, from which he is only awakened by the Revolution itself, in which he rediscovers the music of the streets of his native

68. *La Quinine en thérapeutique*, pp. 631–2.

city which had constituted such a joy and such a distraction during his childhood. Especially, with an almost Nietzschean significance, he rediscovers the world of dance. Yet this period of frenetic play is followed, with the failure of the Revolution, with the return of the 'ténèbres' (CC 3, 63) to Hungary, by a return to passivity. Having lost his rich clientele, he takes, like Oblomov, to his bed, and only survives at all through the help of his friends. Here, Céline sketches out the image of minimal existence which will come to constitute for him the only means of survival: a mixture of inaction, passivity, silence and protection, which recalls childhood, if not the womb itself, and which emerges clearly in the dénouement of *Mort à crédit*.

Yet the constant lesson in Céline's writings is that, save in death, such a minimal existence cannot be anything other than temporary. Semmelweis is dragged out of his inertia and back into the battle, but in such a way that a complex structure of the entire narrative becomes apparent. With the two capitals of the Austro-Hungarian Empire, *Semmelweis* is dominated, not by one centre of gravity, but by two. Budapest (in itself a further duality, Buda and Pest, separated by the Danube, over which the young Semmelweis goes every day to school) and Vienna act in the narrative as its two magnetic poles, attracting and repelling each other throughout. On the one hand, there is the story of the child Semmelweis, leaving the idyllic world of Budapest for the turbulence of Vienna, and who finds peace both in a temporary departure from Vienna to Venice and in a return to his origins which resembles death. At the same time, Vienna asserts itself: it is there that Semmelweis, abandonning law for medicine, meets his destiny, and it is Vienna which, in spite of his escapes to Venice and Budapest, brings him back deeper into the experience of death, to the extent that it comes to poison his life in his native city through the rumours which it spreads. It is entirely fitting, therefore, that Semmelweis should return to Vienna in order to die. The narrative thus has two superimposed and contradictory structures, in which the malefic influence of Vienna remains the strongest. The first runs from childhood in Budapest to escape in Venice and rediscovery of the childhood idyll in Budapest in 1848, with Vienna adopting a merely episodic status. The second structure, however, which dominates, restores primacy to the Austrian capital: it is in Vienna that Semmelweis has his initiation into death, that he learns the hard task of the polemicist and that he dies, and Budapest and Venice now appear as simple illusory escapes. In other words, Vienna is the death-force in the story and, as such, is inescapable, even when there is the illusion of respite in Venice and

Budapest.

The very structure of the narrative, therefore, will not permit Semmelweis eternally to opt out of the Dance of Death, and he is drawn back by an episode which exactly mirrors a previous one. It was on his return from Venice to Vienna that Semmelweis learned of the death of his friend Kolletchka, which provided the essential missing link in his researches on puerpereal fever; in exactly the same way, it is another death, the suicide of Dr Michaelis, who ignored Semmelweis's teaching only to see his cousin die of puer-pereal fever, which drags him out of his torpor in Budapest and sets him on the final stage of his journey. It is at this point that the story becomes unambigously that of a polemicist. When Semmelweis receives the news of the death of Michaelis (which in Céline's version announces exactly the death of Semmelweis himself), he has no more research to carry out into puerpereal fever: he is concerned uniquely with the *transmission* of his discovery. The death of Michaelis, therefore, brings him from the safe world of silence back to the dangerous realm of language. Céline insists upon the link between Semmelweis's period of rest in Budapest and his obstinate silence: 'Rien ne l'intéresse, il n'écrit plus' (CC 3, 64); 'Son passé ne lui parle plus' (CC 3, 64); 'De ses travaux de Vienne, il continue à se taire' (CC 3, 64); 'bientôt sept années de silence' (CC 3, 64). By leaving the safe and comfortable world of silence, Semmelweis re-enters the world of language which will, effectively, kill him, as it will kill Robinson in *Voyage au bout de la nuit*.

Semmelweis's early attempts to publicise his discovery testify to a naive confidence in conventional forms of communication. Yet, as he realises that these forms of writing merely produce a series of failures, he gradually attempts to give to his writing an increased value, just as Ferdinand's father in *Mort à crédit* tries to persuade his son to reply to his unanswered letters by introducing a telegraphic style and by enclosing money and rail tickets. Since Semmelweis's own letters to foreign scientists remain unacknowledged, he at-tempts to remedy this by a sheer mass of writing, the long *Aetiology of Puerpereal Fever* which takes him four years to complete. When this, with its increased value in terms of mass and time, fails to escape the fate of the letters (the Académie de Médecine de Paris does not reply to the abstract which he sends), the stakes are increased still further and Dr Arneth is dispatched to Paris in person to present the manuscript of the *Aetiology* to the session of the Academie dealing with puerpereal fever. Even this fails, however, and at last Semmelweis realises, crucially, that his message can only be conveyed, not merely through an increased value of the written word, but by a dislocation and subversion of written language and medical convention: he abandons academic discourse for polemic. The 'Lettre ouverte à tous les professeurs d'obstétrique' begins: 'Assassins! Je les appelle tous ceux qui s'élèvent contre les règles que j'ai prescrites pour éviter la fièvre puerpérale' (CC 3, 67), and, on the brink of madness, in an episode invented by Céline, he sticks posters on the walls of Budapest, reading: 'Père de famille, sais-tu ce que cela veut dire d'appeler au chevet de ta femme en couches un médecin ou une sage-femme? Cela signifie que tu lui fais courir des risques mortels . . . ' (CC 3, 72). Semmelweis has moved a long way from the balance and modesty of the *Aetiology*: he has abandoned his professional style and his professional readership in order to take up the violent stance of the popular pamphleteer.

Logically enough, this increased violence on the part of the polemicist is matched by a heightened hostility from his audience and engenders a conflict which can only end in death: that of Semmelweis's patients, first, perversely infected by his own staff at the Clinic of Saint-Roch, and, ultimately, that of the doctor-polemicist himself, who goes mad and deliberately inflicts upon himself the infection of a corpse. In this way, the circularity of the narrative is concluded: Semmelweis consciously contracts the illness which killed his friend Kolletchka and which brought him to his discovery, and he dies of the same infection as that which causes puerpereal fever. Similarly, his death in Vienna is the product of a further circularity: he is brought back from Budapest to the Austrian capital, following the same route as that which began his career, and is interned in the same mental hospital as that in which his master Skoda worked when he, in his turn, had been persecuted by Klin. Finally, Céline's long description of the successive stages of Semmelweis's terminal illness constitute an ironic catalogue of the symptoms of puerpereal fever itself: Semmelweis becomes his own *Aetiology*.

Yet this repetition and circularity in Semmelweis's own career is merely part of a broader cyclical view of history which informs the narrative and constitutes the background to all of Céline's inter-war writing. At the same time, a problem is raised which will become increasingly familiar as his writing progresses through the 1930s: the apparently playful gratuitousness of the references. Why, after all, should he begin a thesis on a Hungarian doctor of the mid-nineteenth century with a rather cumbersome evocation of the French Revolution, the Napoleonic Wars and the Restoration? It is not sufficient to attempt to establish a somewhat tenuous connection between the *mal du siècle* of the Romantics following the downfall of Napoleon and the *nouveau mal du siècle* defined by Marcel Arland in the early 1920s,[69] if only because the 'feminine' sensibility of the Romantics is not reflected in the tougher cult of adventurism of the exponents of *inquiétude* in the 1920s. Rather, Céline is attempting to situate the story of Semmelweis in an historical context which is both broad but also highly specific and in which the repetitive and circular elements in the Hungarian's career reflect a certain concept of history.

It is highly significant that the story of Semmelweis should begin, in a line which demonstrates its literary credentials by being almost an Alexandrine, with Mirabeau, the great orator of the early phase of the Revolution: the narrative itself, which is concerned so much with the alternation of speech and silence, begins with speech, indeed with *a* speech, the formal public polemic. For Céline, polemic becomes the spark which unleashes the disorder of the Revolution, the 'tempête' (CC 3, 19), the 'passions' (CC 3, 19) and, the major enemy, 'l'enthousiasme' (CC 3, 19). It is this uncontrollable enthusiasm which leads to the execution of Louis XVI: 'Au tranchant de son cou, jaillit une sensation nouvelle: l'Egalité' (CC 3, 20). Yet, for Céline, equality is not merely a political principle, it is a specifically *feminine* concept, and hence infused with all the pessimistic symbolism with which he invests women, the repositories of death. It is vital to recognise that, in his summary of French history from 1789 to 1820, Céline makes use of a specifically sexual metaphor: 'Comme l'amoureux caresse d'abord la chair qu'il convoite et pense à demeurer longtemps à ses aveux, puis malgré lui se hâte . . . ainsi l'Europe voulait noyer dans une horrible débauche les siècles qui l'avaient élevée' (CC 3, 20). It is as if the masculine principle of 'le Verbe' awakens the uncontrollable and death-directed feminine principle which, henceforth unchecked, drags the world towards disaster, an argument not dissimilar to Freud's reflections on the death-wish of civilisations during the First World War, expressed in essays such as *Civilisation and its Discontents* and *Beyond the Pleasure-Principle*, which re-emerge in Céline's work in the 'Hommage à Zola'. Yet Céline's view of history, like that of Freud, is by no means static and evolves in a metaphorical dialectic of which the two poles are the feminine and masculine principles. For, after the era of the feminine, comes the rule of the male:

69. Marcel Arland, 'Sur un nouveau mal du siècle', *Nouvelle Revue Française*, 125, 1924.

[51]

Aux cours des années monstrueuses où le sang flue, où la vie gicle et se dissout dans mille poitrines à la fois, où les reins sont moissonnés et broyés sous la guerre, comme les raisins au pressoir, il faut un mâle.

Aux premiers éclats de cet immense orage, Napoléon prit l'Europe et, bon gré mal gré, la garda quinze ans (CC 3, 21).

Yet even this period of male domination can last for only fifteen years. Napoleon is overthrown and exiled 'dans une île avec un cancer' (CC 3, 21), and Europe reverts to a system characterised yet again by the feminine principle, and a peculiarly literary one at that. In this context, Céline sees the Romantic *mal du siècle* exclusively in its effete aspects and insists upon it as a pale, literary reflection of the feminine motive force of the Revolution:

Lentement, on se reprit à croire au beau temps, à la paix. Puis on la désira, on l'aima, on finit par l'adorer, comme on avait adoré la mort, quinze ans plus tôt. Assez vite on se mit à pleurer sur le malheur des tourterelles avec des larmes aussi réelles, aussi sincères que les injures dont on criblait, la veille, la charette des condamnés. On ne voulut plus savoir que douceurs et tendresses. On proclama sacrés les epoux attendris et les mères attentives avec autant de déclamations qu'il en avait fallu pour décapiter la Reine (CC 3, 21).

What emerges from Céline's preliminary historical account is a dialectical alternation between masculine and feminine principles following four stages: firstly, Mirabeau, the representative of 'le Verbe', the masculine principle, frightens Versailles, the feminine principle, and unleashes the Revolution; secondly, the feminine principle dominates throughout the Terror and takes two forms: 'la Bête' (CC 3, 20), symbol of death and chaos, and a feminisation of the masculine principle by which the Will is eliminated; thirdly, there comes the rape of Europe by Napoleon, the masculine principle *par excellence*, who restores the reign of will and order; and, finally, with the fall of Napoleon, the Restoration marks a return to the feminine principle, but in a singularly debased fashion: it lacks the bestial energy of the Terror and has exchanged authenticity for bad faith, action for rhetoric. Crucially, it is a period which marks a return to language, but a remarkably feminised version of the 'Verbe' of Mirabeau: 'Cent mignardises furent dites en un jour de printemps pour la volupté des âmes sensibles' (CC 3, 21). Céline's historical vision is based, therefore, upon a dialectical process which leads, not to the elevation of the human species, but to its inevitable decline, a process by which periods of history reflect and repeat each other, but in an increasingly debased manner.

It now becomes clear how these seemingly gratuitous historical references define the context of the career of Semmelweis himself. In the first place, in Céline's narration, the history of the Revolution of 1789 is essentially the story of an infection: France, infected by polemic, is dominated by fever and finally gives birth to a stillborn Revolution from which the nation dies. More important, the four successive phases of French history from 1789 to 1820 in no way constitute a progression: it is as if the passage of time has been dislocated, so that the four historical moments become four mirrors which reflect *ad infinitum* the failure of history itself. This destruction, in Céline's preamble, of any notion of historical progression looks forward to the fate of Semmelweis himself, condemned to repetition and exaggeration in attempts to break through the impregnable circle of history. In particular, the collapse of the 1789 Revolution into the Consulate and the Empire looks forward to a similar process in Hungary in 1848, in which the overthrow of Metternich, after a short period of respite, introduces merely a greater and more all-embracing repression. In this view of historical repetition which leads steadily downwards, it is as if Céline is drawing upon Marx's famous dictum that history repeats itself, the first time as tragedy, the second time as farce. Clearly, 1848 is the ironic reflection of 1789: the entire narrative is imprisoned in an eternal hall of mirrors, and Semmelweis himself, caught between two abortive revolutions, is condemned to the same fate as his patients by producing a stillborn piece of research which will have no concrete effect and will lead to the death of its originator.

The circularity of the narrative, therefore, which will constitute one of the major features of Céline's fiction, is tied to a global vision of the cyclical nature of history which appears to owe much, not merely to the concept of dialectic, but also to the doctrine of eternal reccurrance of Nietzsche. In this context, it is useful to recall one of the major pieces of pure invention in Céline's account: the episode in which Skoda, Semmelweis's old professor and mentor, rushes to Budapest to rescue the mad doctor and bring him back by train to Vienna. As Professor de Gryöry complains, Skoda did no such thing, and Semmelweis was brought to Vienna by his Hungarian colleagues. What Céline appears to have done is to have transposed a well-known episode from the biography of Nietzsche, in which the philosopher, who had gone mad on a visit to Genoa, was brought back to Basle by train by his colleague Frantz Overbeck. This small detail serves to underline a constant underlying consciousness of Nietzsche's work, and especially his emphasis on dance, in Céline's work of the inter-war years, and to draw atten-

tion to one of his most characteristic literary ploys: the transposition and deformation of his sources.

However, all is not unrelieved gloom in *Semmelweis*: there is the
example of a doctor and writer who does succeed: Corvisart, the
great doctor of the Grand Army who, whilst the Battle of Austerlitz
was raging, removed himself from history to work on his translation of Auenbrugger's *Auscultation*. The reference is, like the rest of
the narrative of *Semmelweis*, a complicated one, designed to reflect
both Semmelweis and Céline. Clearly, what Corvisart is doing for
Auenbrugger, this 'acte très pur et très beau' (CC 3, 23), in resusci-
tating a work which has been ignored for fifty years, is precisely
what Céline is doing for Semmelweis: a disinterested act of rehabilitation. Yet the example of the success of Corvisart, in contrast
to the failure of Semmelweis, is not unambiguous: in the first place,
the fifty years' oblivion suffered by Auenbrugger is a confirmation
rather than a refutation of human stupidity in its dealings with great
men and great discoveries; secondly, even though not actually
involved in the battle at Austerlitz, Corvisart can hardly be seen to
be removed from history. Rather, his position as head of the Grand
Army's medical services constitutes the necessary weight to impose
his translation of Auenbrugger, whereas Semmelweis, a man with
no position in the hierarchy, has no means but his own. It is a lesson
which Céline appears to have particularly taken to heart: there are
things which can be said from a position of power or patronage
which cannot be said unpunished by a man alone, unless he dis-
sembles. Semmelweis has no patronage and refuses to dissemble,
and is crushed.

Finally, the examples of Corvisart and Napoleon are not arbitrary
cases of historical greatness, nor is the reference to Bonaparte
isolated in Céline's work. The starting point of *La Vie et l'oeuvre de
Philippe-Ignace Semmelweis*, the Revolution of 1789, is the same
as that of *Voyage au bout de la nuit*, the 'Chanson des Gardes
Suisses 1793'. Similarly, the allusions to Napoleon in the 1924 thesis
are followed up by the considerable presence of Napoleon in
Voyage au bout de la nuit and, through the Passage des Bérésinas, in
Mort à crédit. Indeed, the Napoleonic presence is so definite in
Céline's inter-war writing that it is worth asking the question of
whether his historical and political perspective is ultimately Bonapartist. Be that as it may, it is through the evocation of Napoleon
and Austerlitz that Céline joins the mainstream of French intellectual preoccupations of the 1920s: the *nouveau mal du siècle* was
predicated on the fact that '[nous] avons tous senti la fraîcheur et la
brume du matin d'Austerlitz',[70] and although its main exponents,

especially Malraux, sought to recreate that Napoleonic epic through the cult of adventure in literature, Céline can see the attractiveness of that attempt but is unable to imitate it. Thus, Malraux goes on to produce *La Voie royale*, whilst Céline creates the Bikombimbo of *Voyage au bout de la nuit*.

Céline's medical writings, produced under the name of Louis-Ferdinand Destouches and written, for the most part, prior to the publication of *Voyage au bout de la nuit*, constitute an essential preliminary to a study of his work of the inter-war years, both in terms of their subject-matter and their attempts to manipulate their audience. Thematically, the question of hygiene, in many senses the least exclusively scientific of medical domains, is central to Céline's preoccupations. It is the branch of medicine concerned with combating and preventing infection which leads to fever and delirium and, as such, it constitutes a major metaphor in Céline's fictional and non-fictional writing alike. At the same time, this infection, in the world of hygiene, is the direct result of socio-economic factors of which Céline, more than most twentieth-century French novelists, is fully conscious. Finally, as the basis of a political and racist mythology, by which the body politic, like the human body, must be preserved from alien infection, hygiene looks forward directly to the anti-Semitic writing of the late 1930s.

Nevertheless, the story of Semmelweis is already a potent warning against the overly direct expression of the truth about hygiene, or any other truth which is likely to arouse contention. The direct implication is that prudence is all and that the unambiguous involvement in polemic spells death. For that reason, therefore, Céline's own polemical writing, be it in the form of *Semmelweis* itself or the article and lecture on Ford and social insurance, is careful to use contradiction, self-contradiction, exaggeration, falsification and sheer elusiveness in an attempt to avoid being tied down and punished.

Such complexity in the polemical writing, however, is not due solely to camouflage: it reflects equally a genuine ambivalence towards history itself. In its abstract preoccupations, *Semmelweis* conveys a cyclical view of history in which each cycle represents a debased reflection of a previous one. It is for this reason that the writings on social medicine of the 1920s show such a deep fear of

---

70. André Malraux, *La Tentation de l'Occident*, Paris, Grasset, 1926, p. 95.

the world which has come into being since the First World War and
which threatens to change even more dramatically under the impact
of Americanism on Europe. Yet it is here that the true historical
position emerges which will dominate his writing of the 1930s:
Fordism and the social medicine of the 1920s constitute the brutal
and unacceptable reflection of industrial medicine of the pre-war era
and Céline, whilst noting the historical change, is unable to subscribe to either element, past or future. Where better to situate the
narrator of *Mort à crédit*? Nineteenth-century bourgeois medicine
destroyed its most noble exponent in Semmelweis: what chance
would Semmelweis have in the 1920s? His ghost, the ghost of *la
médecine bourgeoise*, is paraded by Céline to show up the insuf-
ficiencies of modern medical and social thought, but also to demonstrate how outdated that bourgeois medical model is. Aware of this
historical limbo in which he finds himself, caught in a brutally
modern world for which he can feel only fear and loathing, Céline
enters the realm of fiction as a ghost himself, using the name of a
grandmother who was totally a citizen of the *belle époque* and was
never condemned, like her grandson, to witness its overthrow at the
hands of the modern.

[2]

Voyage au bout de la nuit
and the Ghost of the Swiss Guard

In a famous interview in 1957 with Madeleine Chapsal of *L'Express*, Céline commented on his first novel in a way which has not been entirely beneficial for subsequent criticism. He stated: 'Dans *Voyage* . . . je fais encore certains sacrifices à la littérature, la "bonne littérature". On trouve encore de la phrase bien filée . . . A mon sens, au point de vue technique, c'est un peu attardé' (CC 2, 25). With the expansion of critical interest in Céline from the mid-1970s onwards, judgements like this have tended to justify a shift of attention away from the works of the inter-war years to the stylistically richer production of the 1940s and 1950s, from *Guignol's Band* to the trilogy. Quite clearly, on a technical level, as Céline indicates, *Voyage au bout de la nuit* is a tame work in the use of its language, compared even with *Mort à crédit*, and certainly with *Bagatelles pour un massacre*. Nevertheless, this comparative stylistic primitiveness should not justify an implicit relegation of the novel to the status of apprenticeship before the serious production begins. For, if the style is more orthodox than in the subsequent novels, the structure of the work itself and the manipulation of its point of view are as complex as anything which Céline wrote, the only difference being that that complexity is of a kind to which he rarely subsequently returns and is anchored firmly to the ambivalent visions of past, present and future which inform the medical writings of the 1920s. If the medical pamphlets on Fordism are Céline's first non-fictional attempts to grasp the significance of his Golden Age, *Voyage au bout de la nuit* places it at the centre of his fiction.

That complexity is announced in the four or so pages which begin the novel and which stand in the same relation to the rest of the work as the opening section of 'Combray' to *A la Recherche du temps perdu* as a whole. These pages, therefore, are not merely the musical introduction to the entire novel, they contain also the material from which that novel will be generated. Similarly, they have the same chronological status as the 'Combray' section in that they focus fleetingly on the France of the *belle époque* before the First World War, symbolised by the desultory conversation between Bardamu and Arthur Ganate on the warm café terrace of the Place Clichy. It is important to emphasise a fact that is almost buried in the narrative itself, that the opening of *Voyage au bout de la nuit* is not technically about the beginning of the First World War: it is about that Autumn of the *belle époque*, when 'la guerre approchait de nous deux sans qu'on s'en soye rendu compte' (V, 9) and when 'le President Poincaré . . . s'en allait inaugurer, justement ce matin-là, une exposition de petits chiens' (V, 7–8). The novel opens, therefore, in the period before Poincaré's visit to Russia and before the international tension had become so acute that war was a clearly definable threat. Similarly, Bardamu's almost gratuitous act of joining the army is *not* a transposition of the historical events of August 1914; rather, it looks back to the endings of so many of Zola's *Rougon-Macquart* novels, with the unconscious Parisian populace screaming their enthusiasm for war in the cry: 'A Berlin! A Berlin!' In fact, in August 1914, Bardamu's act would have been impossible, since, with the declaration of war, mobilisation had made conscription and not volunteering the rule. Indeed, Roland Dorgelès recalls that, in August 1914, it was virtually impossible to join the army voluntarily.[1] The significance of this subtle emphasis in the chronology of *Voyage au bout de la nuit* is threefold: firstly, from the very beginning of the novel, the work's centre of gravity is placed firmly in the pre-war era; secondly, without the immediate threat of war, Bardamu's act takes on a strongly unreal aspect, an unreality reinforced by the third element, the lack of a logical connection between the Place Clichy introduction and the subsequent section on the war itself — a lack of logical transition which will come to characterise the links between episodes throughout the work.

This introductory section, however, does more than establish a chronological and cultural point of departure for the novel as a whole. It establishes at the very beginning professional, literary and political credentials for the protagonist Bardamu. Céline is careful,

---

1. For difficulties in volunteering after the mobilisation, see Roland Dorgelès, *Au Beau temps de la Butte*, Paris, Albin Michel, 1963, pp. 245–50.

in the very first lines of *Voyage au bout de la nuit*, to identify Bardamu as a medical student, a *carabin*, whose studies, interrupted ostensibly by the war and the journey to Africa and America, will be completed rapidly on his return to France. Equally important, however, is Céline's insistence on Bardamu as poet or writer. His 'prière vengeresse et sociale' (V, 8) is not extemporised: it has already been composed; it has a title, *Les Ailes en or*, and it is *recited* to Arthur in exactly the same way that the doctor–writer Ferdinand, of *Mort à crédit*, will recite the Krogold legend to the similarly unresponsive Gustin. Finally, it is with *Les Ailes en or* that Bardamu emerges at the very beginning of the novel as a subversive and an anarchist, who possesses a deep insight into the complexities of the workings of the capitalist system, an insight which informs with ever increasing power all of Céline's writing in the inter-war years: 'Un Dieu qui compte les minutes et les sous, un Dieu désespéré, sensuel et grognon comme un cochon. Un cochon avec des ailes en or qui retombe partout, le ventre en l'air, prêt aux caresses, c'est lui, c'est notre maître. Embrassons-nous!' (V, 9). This God, who is the very embodiment of capitalism, depends on two essential principles which filter throughout Céline's work of the 1930s: the inescapable connection between time and money ('les minutes et les sous') as dominant elements of the system, which provide the title of *Mort à crédit* itself, and the both mystical and concrete power of gold, which appears constantly in Céline's work, either as part of the plots of the novels (the Gorloge episode in *Mort à crédit*), thematically (the Jewish monopoly of gold in the anti-Semitic pamphlets), or, more intimately still, through the onomastics of the works as a whole (as in *Nora* Merrywin, in *Mort à crédit*).[2] In other words, that Zolaesque concern with the most intimate operations of gold and money at all levels of human life appears in Céline's fiction at the very beginning.[3] In the case of Bardamu, this awareness of the central dominating role of gold, for which the entire 'voyage' is a search for confirmation: 'Je vais voir si c'est ainsi!' (V, 10), is accompanied by a profound distrust. At the very beginning of the novel, even before his journey has begun, he stands opposed to all manifestations of the society built upon a reverence for the 'cochon aux ailes en or': its racial myths, its parliamentary democracy and its international politics. On the question of race, it is important to note Bardamu's response to Arthur's complacent praise of *Le*

2. For a detailed analysis of the psychoanalytical implications of money, of which Céline himself is profoundly aware, see Jean-Joseph Goux, *Freud, Marx. Economie et symbolique*, Paris, Le Seuil, 1973.

3. See also 'Hommage à Zola', HER 1, 169–72.

Temps: 'y en a pas deux comme lui pour défendre la race française!' (V, 8), 'Elle en a bien besoin la race française, vu qu'elle n'existe pas!' (V, 8), and:

> La race, ce que t'appelles comme ça, c'est seulement ce grand ramassis de miteux dans mon genre, chassieux, puceux, transis, qui ont échoué ici poursuivis par la faim, la peste, les tumeurs et le froid, venus vaincus des quatre coins du monde. Ils ne pouvaient pas aller plus loin à cause de la mer. C'est ça la France et puis c'est ça les Français (V, 8).

In terms of the generation of the novel, this description of the French looks forward to the American episode, in which Bardamu works as a *compteur de puces* at the immigration centre outside New York harbour. Moreover, the details of the description constitute an ironic echo of the inscription on the Statue of Liberty, itself, of course, a gift of France, written by Emma Lazarus:

> Give me your tired, your poor,
> Your huddled masses yearning to breathe free,
> The wretched refuse of your teeming shore.
> Send these, the homeless, tempest-tost, to me,
> I lift my lamp beside the golden door.

Indeed, America stands as an exact ironic reflection of Bardamu's view of the French: for him, the French are a mixture of poverty-stricken refugees who can go no further because of the barrier of the sea; the American people are the same mixture of refugees who have managed to surmount the obstacle of the ocean, but are now caught on the land-mass of the United States itself. In other words, America is merely the reflection and repetition of France: as in *Semmelweis*, progression is eliminated, and replaced by stasis. At the same time, if Bardamu's definition of race provides an early insight into the workings of the 'voyage' itself, it also introduces a considerable ideological embarassment in the context of Céline's work as a whole. Just as it is necessary to integrate Bardamu's implicit criticism of the Ford system during the Detroit episode with Céline's apparent praise of the same system in his writings of 1928, so it is essential to recall Bardamu's dismissal of the notion of race when reading the anti-Semitic pamphlets of 1937 onwards. *Bagatelles pour un massacre*, *L'Ecole des cadavres* and *Les Beaux draps*, which are not merely anti-Semitic but racist, will present the same difficulties of synthesis as those presented by a reading of the medical pamphlets.

Bardamu's scorn for bourgeois racial myths is accompanied by a similar distrust of the social organisation which emerges from and reinforces the capitalist system. It is a society which, as Frédéric Vitoux shows, is divided between the mass of *les miteux* and the power of 'le Roi misère',[4] between the galley-slaves of life and the masters: 'On est en bas dans les cales à souffler de la gueule, puants, suintants des rouspignolles, et puis voilà! En haut sur le pont, au frais, il y a les maîtres et qui s'en font pas, avec des belles femmes roses et gonflées de parfums sur les genoux' (V, 9). This opposition is translated throughout the novel into a strong anti-democratic stance, by which bourgeois democracy is viewed as a mere fraud, masking the real power and repression of capital. This anti-parliamentarianism runs from the initial derogatory reference to Poincaré to a precise criticism in the African episode: 'Les indigènes eux, ne fonctionnent guère en somme qu'à coups de trique, ils gardent cette dignité, tandis que les Blancs, perfectionnés par l'instruction publique, ils marchent tout seuls' (V, 139); for '[ils] ne savaient pas, ces primitifs, l'appeler "Monsieur" l'esclave, et le faire voter de temps à autre, ni lui payer le journal, ni surtout l'emmener à la guerre, pour lui faire passer ses passions' (V, 139). This critical vision of the workings of bourgeois parliamentary democracy, which is accentuated by the description of La Garenne-Rancy, with its 'boulevard de la Liberté', its 'place Lénine', its 'coin de la Révolte', its 'boulevard Poincaré', which mock the squalor of the industrial suburb with empty political rhetoric, culminates in a precise awareness of that regime's use of war as an instrument of foreign and domestic policy. Periodically, the slaves on the galley, the *Patrie no. 1*, are dragged on deck by their masters in top hats to attack the rival *Patrie no. 2* (V, 9). In other words, it is the *miteux* who pay the price, socially, economically and militarily for the survival of the bourgeois state.

The introduction to the novel, therefore, establishes a carefully constructed economic and political framework in which the rest of the episodes will take their place, as well as providing a subversive vantage-point for the protagonist, the 'anarchiste' Bardamu (V, 8). At the same time as it provides a political perspective for a reading of the novel, however, it furnishes an imaginative one as well. The introduction ends with a regiment marching past the café, led by its colonel and its band, a regiment which exerts an almost magical attraction on Bardamu and his fellow *miteux*, who are led out of the city to the barracks where, too late, they realise that 'on était faits,

4. See: Frédéric Vitoux, *Louis-Ferdinand Céline. Misère et parole*, Paris, Gallimard, 1973.

comme des rats' (V, 10). The essential ingredients of the episode, the colonel, the music and the *miteux* who follow, are clearly related to the German legend of the Pied Piper of Hamelin, an allusion which possesses a double significance. In the first place, it concludes and reinforces the anarchist social perspective contained in the preceeding pages. The Pied Piper was hired by the burghers of Hamelin to rid the town of its undesirable elements, its plague of rats. In the same way, a common anarchist perception of the First World War in particular, and of the role of any war in general, was that it was a device employed by capitalist society to divert opposition to the regime and eliminate subversive elements by forcing them into a common blood-bath. The legend of Hamelin, therefore, helps to establish the subversive political perspective of the novel as a whole and to situate Bardamu as a *miteux* who should have been wiped out in the ensuing war, but who has inexplicably survived.

In addition, however, the allusion to the Pied Piper contains more complex implications. In the first place, it emphasises the importance of music in the novel, which begins with the military band and ends with Gustave Mandamour's 'danse de feu'. Similarly, the military music which opens the novel and leads Bardamu away to his intended death gives rise directly to the presence of Madelon in the novel, from the Toulouse episode onwards. For, as Georges Sadoul comments:

On chanta beaucoup la *Madelon de la Victoire* à Paris en 1919 après le traîté de Versailles:
Nous avons gagnè la guerre
Hein! Hein! Crois-tu qu'on les a eus
Madelon, ah verse à boire!
C'est pour fêter la victoire
Joffre, Foch et Clemenceau.[5]

By a tragic irony, therefore, Robinson, who has worked so hard to survive the war itself, is finally killed by Madelon, whose name encapsulates the blind chauvinism which he has always instinctively recognised as his enemy and which ushers in the post-war world. More important, however, than the construction of the novel on a system of musical references and allusions, is the fact that the Pied Piper announces a dual journey, firstly towards death itself (the rats and the *miteux* are effectively exterminated, according to the Piper's contract; the 'voyage' goes to the 'nuit'), but also, more import-

5. Georges Sadoul, *Histoire Général du cinéma*, 5, *Le Cinéma muet*, Paris, Denoel, 1975, p. 7.

antly, towards the realm of the imagination traditionally explored in the fairy-story and the fantastic tale. This dual invitation to read *Voyage au bout de la nuit* as a journey towards death and as a fairy-story has the important effect of seriously calling into question the supposedly Naturalist credentials of the novel, and offers a different interpretation of the status of the work's characters and episodes.

In an important study of the novel, Stephen Day examines the beginning of Céline's preface: 'Voyager, c'est bien utile, ça fait travailler l'imagination' (V, 5), and raises the question: 'Ou bien, dans l'"histoire fictive" les choses sont-elles renversées: "de l'autre côté de la vie" on ouvrirait les yeux pour *voir l'imaginaire*, devenu réel . . . ?'[6] In other words, to the extent that *Voyage au bout de la nuit* constitutes a reflection on the novel-form itself, the regiment, with its colonel and its band, effects the transition of the reader from the real world to the world of fiction and artifice which is the only possible world which can protect both reader and narrator from the threat and contingency of real life. In the fairy-story become novel, the real becomes imaginary and the imaginary real. By using the regiment in this way, as a transition from the real to the imaginary, Céline employs exactly the same metaphor as that used by Baudelaire to define the artist's vision in an essay on Constantin Guys, in *Le Peintre de la vie moderne*: 'Un régiment passe, qui va peut-être au bout du monde, jetant dans l'air des boulevards ses fanfares entraînantes et légères comme l'espérance; et voilà que l'oeil de M.G. a déjà vu, inspecté, analysé les armes, l'allure et la physionomie de cette troupe'.[7] For both authors, the passing of the regiment serves as a pretext for artistic vision: the rapid, efficient and serene vision of Guys, set against the frenetic enthusiasm of Bardamu's 'Je vais *voir* si c'est ainsi!', and introduces the reader into a self-consciously aesthetic world. Nor is the comparison with Baudelaire at all gratuitous. The conception of *Voyage au bout de la nuit* itself owes much to the poems 'Le Voyage' and, to a lesser degree, 'Un Voyage à Cythère' in *Les Fleurs du mal*, in which death, frustrated journeys and the search for Eldorado dominate. Similarly, the end of *Voyage au bout de la nuit*, with its bleak dawn breaking:

6. Philip S. Day, 'Imagination et parodie dans *Voyage au bout de la nuit*', Australian Journal of French Studies, XIII, 1–2, 1976, p. 57.
7. Charles Baudelaire, 'Le Peintre de la vie moderne', *Oeuvres complètes*, Paris, Gallimard, coll. 'La Pléiade', 1961, p. 1161.

voici que reviennent de plus loin encore les hommes. Ils s'infiltrent dans le jour sale par petits paquets transis. Ils se mettent du jour plein la figure pour commencer en passant devant l'aurore. Ils vont plus loin. On ne voit bien d'eux que leurs figures pâles et simples, le reste est encore à la nuit. Il faudra bien qu'ils crèvent tous un jour aussi. Comment qu'ils feront? (V, 504),

echoes the last lines of *Crepuscule du matin*:

> L'aurore grelottante en robe rose et verte
> S'avançait lentement sur la Seine déserte,
> Et le sombre Paris, en se frottant les yeux,
> Empoignait ses outils, vieillard laborieux.

It is in their evocation of Paris and modern urban life, however, that the preoccupations of the two authors truly coincide. Both are writers of the urban streets, the *flâneurs* in the crowd whom Walter Benjamin sees as so important to an understanding of Baudelaire.[8] Moreover, both are acutely conscious of their role as witnesses of a changing urban civilisation which threatens to leave them disorientated and vulnerable. Baudelaire stands in precisely the same relationship to the Paris of Haussmann as does Céline to the Paris which followed the 1900 Exposition and the First World War. Finally, their responses to this change politically were identical, taking the form of an apparent lurch to extreme conservatism, with both writers resorting to examples of outrageous polemic, Baudelaire in the *Amoenitates Belgicae* and Céline with *Bagatelles pour un massacre*.

Yet, in *Voyage au bout de la nuit*, Céline goes further than Baudelaire in his exploitation of the regiment metaphor. Bardamu is conveyed by the passing regiment, not merely into the self-conscious realm of art, but also into an imaginary, fantastic world, in which values are inverted. In this sense, the regiment has the same function as that of the White Rabbit in Lewis Caroll's *Alice in Wonderland*: it crystallises the unconscious traces of the conversation between Bardamu and Arthur Ganate and creates an imaginary world from them, in the same way that the Wonderland is created from the traces of the book which Alice's sister is reading out loud.[9]

8. Walter Benjamin, *Charles Baudelaire. A Lyric Poet in an Age of High Capitalism*, London, New Left Books, 1973.

9. The analogy could be developed further: the endless games of chess which Bardamu is forced to play with Baryton, and Parapine's obsession with both mathematics and young girls, bring the novel close to the personality of Charles Dodgson/Lewis Carroll. Similarly, the complex relationship between Bardamu and

More specifically, it helps to situate the novel in a particular literary genre, which is little-known but well-defined: the *voyage imaginaire* itself, of which the most popular and most celebrated form is the *Robinsonade*, the seemingly endless reworkings of the tale of Robinson Crusoe. In one of the rare studies of this sub-genre, Philip Babock Gove, quoting Arthur J. Tieje, gives this definition: 'Of five minor forces in fiction . . . one was the *voyage imaginaire*, consisting in an unrelated series of adventures, determined by a 'purpose' either satirical . . . diverting . . . or reformatory'.[10] Yet the *voyage imaginaire* can take one of two forms. For Geoffrey Atkinson, again quoted by Gove:

> The term *Extraordinary Voyage* is used to designate a novel of the following type: A fictitious narrative, purporting to be the veritable account of a real voyage made by one or more Europeans to an existant but little-known country — or to several such countries — together with a description of the happy condition of society there found, and a supplementary account of the author's return to Europe.[11]

Or, it could take the form of a philosophical journey within the confines of the author's imagination, as defined by Charles Garnier: 'le philosophe a une autre manière de voyager; sans autre guide que son imagination, il se transporte dans des mondes nouveaux, ou il recueille des observations qui ne sont ni moins intéressantes ni moins précieuses'.[12] In other words, the *voyage imaginaire* establishes either the tradition of the adventure-novel or that of the novel of pure imagination. Defoe and *Robinson Crusoe*, with its hundreds of imitations in the *Robinsonades* — of which the most interesting in the context of Céline is Offenbach's *Robinson Crusoë* of 1868, if only because his Théâtre des Bouffes Parisiennes had its

---

Robinson, by which the novel must end after Robinson's death, is not at all unconnected with the problems posed at the end of *Through the Looking Glass* as to who, in a dream-story, is the dreamer and who the dreamed character: 'Lets consider who it was that dreamed it all. This is a serious question . . . it *must* have been either me or the Red King. He was part of my dream, of course — but then I was part of his dream, too!' (*Through the Looking-Glass*, New York, The New American Library, coll. 'Signet Classics', 1960, pp. 236–7).

10. Arthur J. Tieje, 'The Critical Heritage of Fiction in 1579', *Englische Studien*, XLVII, 1913 14, p. 417, quoted by Philip Babock Gove, *The Imaginary Voyage in Prose Fiction*, London, The Holland Press, 1961, p. 7.

11. Geoffrey Atkinson, *The Extraordinary Voyage in French Literature from 1700 to 1720*, Paris, 1922, pp. 7–8; quoted in Gove, *The Imaginary Voyage*, p. 96.

12. Charles Georges Thomas Garnier, *Voyages imaginaires, songes, visions et romans cabalistiques*, Paris, 1787–9, preface; quoted in Gove, *The Imaginary Voyage*, p. 30.

stage-door opening on to the Passage Choiseul in which Céline grew up — stand at the head of a tradition of what will become the adventure-novel, culminating in the work of Conrad and his emulators in France in the 1920s. As Albert Thibaudet wrote in a famous article of 1919: 'L'aventure s'identifie en quelque sorte avec la mer . . . . De sorte que réellement tout roman d'aventures tend à cristalliser sous la forme de Robinson et de l'Ile de Robinson'.[13] At the head of the other tradition, that of the expedition through the imagination, stands Xavier de Maistre and his *Voyage autour de ma chambre*, an important precursor of Proust's *A la Recherche du temps perdu* and a work which throws considerable light on Céline's own novel in the way in which it constructs an entire fictional fabric from an initial rudimentary concrete base.

The establishment of this sub-genre is of immense help in situating Céline's first novel, in that it provides a much more specific meaning than has hitherto been suggested for his comment in the 'Préface': 'Notre voyage à nous est entièrement imaginaire. Voila sa force' (V, 5). This does not mean, or at least does not only mean 'Our journey through life is illusory', or, even 'this work is a work of fiction: hence its strength'. Rather, quite specifically, the comment invites the reader to situate *Voyage au bout de la nuit* in the category of the *voyage imaginaire*, the novel of pure imagination and the adventure-novel, as distinct from the proto-Naturalist or populist category to which the novel is so often consigned. In the 'Préface' itself, therefore, Céline is already distancing himself from Zola and marking out his domain as that of the 'symboles et les rêves' which he identifies in his speech at Médan. Of equal importance for a study of Céline's work as a whole, however, is the fact that, for Gove, the *voyage imaginaire* is closely related to two other fictional sub-genres, the 'Utopia'[14] and the *féerie*.[15] Following this pattern, Céline's production becomes tightly unified, from the *voyage imaginaire* which is *Voyage au bout de la nuit*, through the well-known Utopian vision of *Les Beaux draps* to the two volumes of *Féerie pour une autre fois*. It is also important that, in *Voyage au bout de la nuit*, Céline has chosen to exploit the two possibilities offered by the genre of the *voyage imaginaire* and to fuse them together. Thus, the entire novel becomes one more *Robinsonade*, allowing the author to manipulate an entire range of themes based on notions of exploration, threat, isolation and survival, a complex

---

13. Albert Thibaudet, 'Le Roman de l'aventure', *Nouvelle Revue Française*, 1919, p. 610.
14. Gove, *The Imaginary Voyage*, p. 116.
15. Ibid., p. 24.

interaction between the characters of Bardamu–Crusoe and Robin-son–Friday, by which they constantly change roles, each one be-coming the shadow, reflection and dream of the other, and a profound reflection on the nature and origins of capitalism: it is one of the careful ironies of the novel that, whereas Defoe's novel helped to create the myth of modern capitalism in the eighteenth century, Céline's exploitation of the *Robinsonade* contrives to demolish it. At the same time, by using the tendency of the imagin-ary journey which is concerned with a voyage through the imagina-tion and which runs from Xavier de Maistre to Proust, and which starts from the present in order to reinvent the past or construct a fictitious future,[16] Céline legitimises a further reading of his 'Préface', by which 'Notre voyage à nous est entièrement imagi-naire' means, simply: 'Bardamu's own journey does not actually take place, at least not by any Naturalist criteria'.

It is the presence of *Voyage au bout de la nuit* in the category of the genre of the *voyage imaginaire* which explains elements in the novel hitherto almost impossible to integrate into any global inter-pretation of the work. If Bardamu's journey takes place in the context of the *voyage imaginaire*, however, then the successive implausible, but half-expected encounters with Robinson, the often arbitrary and unexplained transitions from episode to episode, which are more the property of dreams, become simply the stock-in-trade of the genre itself. In particular, the entire episode of the *Infanta Combitta*, which defies interpretation on Naturalist grounds, becomes fully integrated. The problem with this episode is that, whilst the *galère*, the *Infanta Combitta*, is generated by Bardamu's initial reference to the two *galères*, the *Patrie no. 1* and the *Patrie no. 2*, it nevertheless constitutes a blatant incursion of the fantastic into what is ostensibly a Naturalist novel, an incursion which cannot even be explained by Bardamu's fever, because the *galère* continues to exist in the bay outside New York even when the fever has abated: indeed, it is still there when the totally lucid Bardamu jumps ship and seeks asylum in the immigration depot. In the context of the *voyage imaginaire*, however, the episode is merely an extreme example of the imaginary voyage as a whole; indeed, it indicates how to read the rest of the novel and it reinforces the conventions of the genre.

Furthermore, it is only according to the conventions of the

16. For a detailed study of Céline and Proust, see: P.E. Robert, 'Marcel Proust et Louis-Ferdinand Céline: un contrepoint', *Bulletin des Amis de Marcel Proust*, 29, 1979, pp. 34–46.

voyage imaginaire that Céline is able to put into operation a procedure to which he will return lovingly in *Mort à crédit* and *Guignol's Band*, the creation of an invented and hopelessly dislocated topography. Thus, the Paris of *Voyage au bout de la nuit* becomes a city invented according to the conventions of the imaginary voyage and by no means constitutes a realistic transposition of the French capital into fiction. The ambiguous location of La Garenne-Rancy has already been the subject of some critical interest, notably by Henri Godard:[17] initially, Bardamu describes it as being 'tout de suite après la Porte Brancion' (V, 237), in the south of Paris, but thereafter it is systematically located in Clichy, to the north of the city centre, the exact opposite of the original location: in other words, part of the *monde à l'envers* to which the novel introduces the reader. If the sleight of hand in the location of the suburb is significant, so too is the choice of its name: 'La Garenne', as rabbit-warren, introduces the notion of a labyrinth so essential to the concept of the *voyage*; more specifically, it is built upon an earlier reference, in the African episode, to the similarity between Fort-Gono and La Garenne-Bezons (V, 127), to which Céline returns in his writings during the Occupation, both in *Les Beaux draps* and in his preface to Albert Serouille's book, *Bezons à travers les âges*.[18] Similarly, Rancy is derived from the 'eau . . . rance' (V, 162) of the river which leads to Robinson's trading-settlement, but it comes also from the *Cirque Rancy*, one of France's most famous circuses, founded in 1866, a derivation which reinforces the significance of the strangely ubiquitous fair, with its *Stand des Nations*, and which highlights the 'Guignolesque' features of the novel as a whole. La Garenne-Rancy, therefore, provides precious information, not only on Céline's dislocation of the topography in order to create an imaginary setting for his journey, but on the way in which the novel generates itself from previous allusions and on the significance of names in Céline's work in general.

In this context, the falsification of the location of La Garenne-Rancy within the *banlieue rouge* is by no means an isolated example. The positioning of the Institut Bioduret Joseph suffers the same bewildering change in situation. Initially, it is 'derrière La Villette' (V, 279), only to reappear a few pages later, after Bardamu's visit to Parapine, in the rue de Vaugirard (V, 286). Here again, the transposition is deliberate and significant. La Villette is next to Mont-

17. See *Romans* I, ed. Henri Godard, Paris, Gallimard, coll. 'La Pléiade', 1981, p. 1209.
18. Albert Serouille, *Bezons à travers les âges*, Paris, Denoël, 1944.

martre, the real topographical centre of gravity of the novel; more important, it was the great stockyard and slaughterhouse of Paris, and Céline's reference to it constitutes an immediate link with the early episode during the war, when Bardamu comes across the 'prairie d'août' where 'on distribuait toute la viande du régiment' (V, 20), and where his reaction is the famous attack of nausea. In addition to the metaphor of butchery, connected in this precise instance to the practise of medicine and medical research, the reference to La Villette reminds the reader of the unusually frequent presence in the novel of meat and, particularly, preserved meat, the recurrent 'boîtes de conserves'. In his evocation of Paris during the war, the role of the *argentins* figures large: thanks to the meat they import into France, and to their skill as dancers, they are assured of financial and sexual supremacy. Similarly, the 'conserves' of the First World War look forward to the 'boîtes de conserve' which constitute Bardamu's staple diet in Africa and the tins of 'cassoulet à la bordelaise' (V, 167), that non-existent dish, which are his sole legacy from Robinson. Although 'cassoulet à la bordelaise' helps maintain the novel in the sphere of the *imaginaire*, it also has an important function as a junction in the novel between Alcide, who comes from Bordeaux, and Grappa, who comes from Toulouse, the true home of *cassoulet* and the location of an important episode later in the novel. At the same time, Bardamu's own relationship in the novel to the *conserves* is complex. In the first place, they do not act as symbols of preservation: on the contrary, they cause diarrhoea in Robinson, just as the meat on the *prairie d'août* induces sickness in Bardamu. More important, they are objects of theft, both by Bardamu, prior to the death of the colonel, and by Princhard, whom he meets later in Bicêtre. This theft of the *boîtes de conserve* has a specific subversive significance. According to George Orwell, in *The Road to Wigan Pier*: 'The Great War . . . could never have happened if tinned food had not been invented'.[19] The *boîtes de conserve* become, therefore, the very symbol of the ability of a modern industrial society to wage war, and of a specific threat to a potential conscript. Bardamu's theft of the cans, therefore, takes on a symbolic pacifist and subversive connotation.

If the siting of the Institut Bioduret Joseph in La Villette enables Céline to tie together an entire system of imagery throughout the novel connected with butchery, self-preservation and war, the sudden shift of that location from the 20th to the 15th *arrondisse-*

19. George Orwell, *The Road to Wigan Pier*, Harmondsworth, Penguin, 1962, p. 82.

ment has its purpose as well, in that it forces Bardamu to take the rue Bonaparte to the Seine before crossing this urban Rubicon in order to return to the new location of Rancy. Céline has rewritten the geography of Paris in order to give his novel a very broad mythological framework, of which a major component is provided by a number of Napoleonic references, already present in *Semmelweis*, and which will take on a renewed significance with an elucidation of the true meaning of the *Chanson des gardes suisses*.

This procedure of the significant dislocation of Parisian topography culminates, however, in the privileged role occupied by the Place Clichy in *Voyage au bout de la nuit*. It is essential to stress that it is from the Place Clichy that Bardamu, following the regiment and its band, begins his visionary journey, and that it is to the Place Clichy that he returns at every important moment of the novel. Thus, all that is left to him after Robinson's sudden departure from Africa is his 'cassoulet á la bordelaise' and 'une carte postale en couleurs: "la Place Clichy"' (V, 167). When he opens the medicine-chest in search of an antidote to his fever, all he finds is 'un plan du Nord-Sud' (V, 172), the Metro line which connected Montmartre with Montparnasse. On his return from Detroit, Bardamu recalls: 'J'ai tourné encore pendant des semaines et des mois autour de la Place Clichy, d'où j'étais parti' (V, 237), thus expressing the centrality of the square for the narrative and the circularity of the 'voyage' around it. When he flees from Toulouse after the murder of old Madame Henrouille, he gravitates again naturally to the Place Clichy, where he takes on the role of 'Pacha' in the cinema, 'Le Tarapout', presumably modelled on one of the most famous Parisian cinemas, the Gaumont-Palace. Finally, it is from the Place Clichy that Bardamu, Sophie, Robinson and Madelon leave on what is to become Robinson's last journey. In addition, this unusual emphasis on the Place Clichy throughout the novel is reinforced by the extended reflection on the square's presiding spirit, Maréchal Moncey, who defended it against the Russians during the Allied invasion of 1814,[20] and whose statue is now at the square's centre. This reference is, in its turn, reinforced by the fact that the offices of the Compagnie Pordurière are to be found in the rue Moncey, just off the Place Clichy itself (V, 133). Incidentally,

---

20. See: V, 350. Henri Godard (*Romans* 1, 1304) is quite correct in pointing out that, yet again, Céline has got his dates wrong. Céline sets the invasion in 1816, whereas the battle for the Place Clichy was on the night of 29–30 March 1814. This is merely a further example, however, of Céline's dislocation of chronology, as well as topography, to create his *voyage imaginaire* as is exactly the same procedure employed in the dating of the 'Chanson des Gardes Suisses 1793'.

this further important contribution to the Napoleonic system of references in *Voyage au bout de la nuit* also looks forward to, and generates, what are often seen as paranoid fears of foreign invasion of Paris in the pamphlets and the later fiction.

Céline's insistence on the centrality of the Place Clichy in the novel is highly significant. It has the effect of defining *Voyage au bout de la nuit* as a novel of Montmartre, profoundly anchored in the artistic, intellectual, political and social life of the 18th *arrondissement*. It is important to recall, in this context, the fascination exerted on Céline by Montmartre, his very early contact with the *quartier*, and the fact that, as soon as he had a chance, after his departure from the League of Nations in 1927, he set up a medical practice in the rue des Saules, and moved into an apartment at 98 rue Lepic in August 1929.[21] Here he remained for thirteen years, until forced into exile, and Pascal Fouché records how, even when he was in Meudon in the last years of his life, Céline would stare nostalgically across Paris to his real home on the Butte de Montmartre. It is unfortunate that Patrick Macarthy, whilst quite correctly emphasising the importance of Montmartre for Céline,[22] should obscure the issue by playing down the quarter's role as a pleasure centre and try to portray it as a small industrial suburb, inhabited by the working class and the petite bourgeoisie. In fact, the importance of Montmartre for the writers and artists who lived there in the inter-war years had little to do with the social composition of the *quartier*, but a great deal to do with its role as the home of a certain type of artistic community. As Armand Lanoux writes: 'On peut être surpris que l'appellation "école de Montmartre" n'ait pas été utilisée pour qualifier un mouvement littéraire né avec le siècle et éteint en 1973 par la mort de son principal protagoniste, Roland Dorgelès'.[23] This 'école de Montmartre', which comprised novelists like Dorgelès, Pierre Mac Orlan, Francis Carco, Céline and Marcel Aymé, painters like Steinlen, Jules Pascin and Gen Paul, and illustrators and caricaturists like Daragnès, Chas-Laborde, and Ralph Soupault, the cartoonist of *Je suis partout*,[24] together with actors like Robert Le Vigan, clearly drew upon a Bohemian tradition of which, as Marie-Christine Bellosta shows in her analysis of *Nor-*

21. For a detailed account of Céline and Montmartre, see Pascal Fouché, 'Féerie pour un autre Montmartre', *Quinzaine Littéraire*, June 1982, pp. 32–6.

22. Patrick Macarthy, *Céline*, London, Allen Lane, 1975, p. 39.

23. Armand Lanoux, 'Trois personnages en quête d'une bohème', *Quinzaine Littéraire*, June 1982, p. 16.

24. Most of these characters are united in Gen Paul's studio in Marcel Aymé's short story, 'Avenue Junot', which appeared in *Je suis partout* on 14 August 1943.

mance, Céline was plainly aware, but also upon the specific position of Montmartre as capital of the avant-garde in the thirty years before the First World War. The writers and painters of the inter-war years, however, were by no means avant-gardists and tended to concentrate their efforts in certain areas: a harsh social criticism, directed often at the hierarchy of the Third Republic, and which veered to caricature and satire; an exploration of fantasy, both through Francis Carco's and Max Jacob's *école fantaisiste* and through Mac Orlan's concept of *le fantastique social*; an often exoticised interest in the social outcasts and criminals, particularly of Lower Montmartre, the Place Pigalle, in the novels of Mac Orlan, Carco and Dorgelès; an extended exploration of the genre of the adventure-novel, crystallised in Mac Orlan's classic study of Con-rad, '*La Folie-Almayer, et les aventuriers dans la littérature*';[25] and experimentation with the transposition of spoken French and *argot* into prose fiction. Plainly, Céline, by no means an avant-garde writer himself, in spite of his role as an innovator, is at home in these categories of artistic production. In particular, for *Voyage au bout de la nuit*, it is important to underline the elements of carica-tural anti-republican social criticism, development of fantasy, in-version of the classic pattern of the adventure-novel and exper-imentation with the literary language. On this last point, critics have perhaps been too willing to connect Céline's use of *le français parlé* with a Naturalist or populist tradition, or with a similar attempt on the part of Queneau, and to ignore the fact that the use of popular speech is a traditional subversive device in the literature and enter-tainment of Montmartre, from the poet Jehan-Rictus to Richepin, through the entire cabaret tradition, exemplified by Aristide Bruant, in which the insulting of the bourgeois audience by the manipula-tion of popular speech elements was a central feature.

There is one further crucial factor in Céline's association with the 'école de Montmartre' and that concerns its resolutely anti-avant-gardist status. As Francis Carco recalls in *De Montmartre au Quartier Latin*, the significant period of Montmartre in artistic and literary history was from 1900 to 1910. It was in this period, building on the achievements of the Impressionists in Montmartre, that Apollinaire acted as impressario to a whole galaxy of artistic talent, particularly the 'bande à Picasso', who was himself to cross a kind of artistic Rubicon with *Les Demoiselles d'Avignon* of 1907.

---

25. Pierre Mac Orlan, '*La Folie-Almayer* et les aventuriers dans la littérature', *Nouvelle Revue Française*, 81, 1920; see also Pierre Mac Orlan, *Le Petit manuel du parfait aventurier*, Paris, Editions de la Sirène, 1920.

By 1910, however, the avant-garde was moving out of Montmartre, and the artistic centre of gravity of Paris shifted, first to Montparnasse and later to the Latin Quarter. *Le Lapin Agile*, which was the artistic centre of Montmartre in its great period, was supplanted by the *Closerie des Lilas*, the *Coupole* and the *Dôme*, and, later, by the *Flore* and the *Deux Magots*. In other words, those writers and painters who chose to work and live in Montmartre in the inter-war years were quite consciously operating outside and in opposition to literary and artistic fashion: they refused the modishness of the avant-garde, now installed in Montparnasse, and the intellectuality of the Latin Quarter — Céline's reiterated 'je ne suis pas un homme à idéâs' in his interviews of the 1950s has its origins here. Politically, the Montmartre writers and artists of the inter-war years are conservative and reactionary, though in a variety of ways. The important thing about Montmartre in the inter-war years was that it retained its traditional opposition to the government, but that opposition had become inverted, from the Left to the Right. In the 1920s and 1930s, Montmartre accentuated its independance from the rest of Paris and played up its increasingly spurious role as a village surrounded by an urban agglomeration. Nevertheless, to choose to live in Montmartre in that period was to distance onself from Republican politics, to reject the industrial, post-First World War society by retreating into the 'village', to go against literary fashion and intellectuality as the qualities of the Parisian world and, finally, to take on the existence of ghosts of a bygone artistic era.

In this context, *Voyage au bout de la nuit* is more of a Montmartre novel than it may appear initially, and whilst Pascal Fouché is right to draw the reader's attention to the 'repère symbolique' that is the Place Clichy,[26] he is perhaps over-hasty in concluding that 'dans *Voyage au bout de la nuit*, il décrira en fait assez peu Montmartre; l'action est ailleurs'.[27] Description of Montmartre may be limited, though by no means absent, but it is questionable whether the action really is elsewhere. The very beginning of the novel, with its rambling intellectual conversation between Bardamu and Arthur Ganate, is, in itself, a reflection of the predominance of Montmartre in the intellectual life of France just before the First World War, a predominance which, by the end of the conflict, had moved to the Left Bank. In *De Montmartre au Quartier Latin*, Carco describes in detail the importance of the literary cafés on the boulevard de

26. Fouché, 'Féerie pour un autre Montmartre', p. 33.
27. Ibid.

Clichy before the war[28] and their abrupt decline with the onset of the conflict. In an episode which resembles closely Bardamu's own departure for the Army, Carco describes the patriotic delirium which grips Paris on the outbreak of war through its effect on the writer André de Fresnois: from a languid, disinterested intellectual, he is transformed into a fervent patriot by the passing parade: 'Jean Pellerin me saisit dans ses bras, me serra et très bas, désignant notre ami: — Regarde-le, dit-il . . . Regarde . . . Il ne reviendra pas'.[29]

In addition to this awareness of the changing role of Montmartre in the intellectual history of Paris, Céline is equally conscious of the precise social role played by Montmartre in the life of the rest of the capital, to which it was linked by the Nord–Sud Métro line.[30] Thus, the historian Louis Chevalier considers *Voyage au bout de la nuit*, along with Henry Miller's *Black Spring*, as the best chronicle of Lower Montmartre, as opposed to the Butte: what he terms 'le Montmartre du plaisir et du crime',[31] with its fairs, its prostitutes, its great cinema, the Gaumont-Palace, its worrying proximity to the criminal *quartiers* of La Chapelle and La Villette, to say nothing of the 'quartier de la Goutte d'or' of Zola's *L'Assommoir*, its Argentine dancers, its deserters during the First World War and its pre-war anarchists. It is useful to recall that before 1914, Montmartre was the centre of anarchist activity in Paris, with the *Bande à Bonnot*, to which Céline alludes appreciatively in *Guignol's Band*, the young Victor Serge, and the legendary anarchist preacher Libertad, who looks forward to the war-cry of Lola's black servant in *Voyage au bout de la nuit*: 'Liberta!' (V, 217). Finally, it is important to note that, within the life of Paris, Montmartre acted as a code-word, signifying death. As Chevalier reminds us, the popular phrase: 'Je vais voir mon vieux à Montmartre' meant a visit to the husband's grave in the cemetery: 'Bicêtre c'est la maison des fous, Montmartre c'est le cimetière'.[32] Thus, in the course of the novel, Céline makes use of both poles: Bardamu moves from madness in Bicêtre (V, 85) to, and within, the realm of death which is Montmartre itself: the entire *quartier* is one large cemetery, of which the 'petit cimetière' (V, 367) is only a metonymic image. In very precise terms, Céline

28. Francis Carco, *De Montmartre au Quartier Latin*, Paris, Albin Michel, 1927, p. 157.

29. Ibid., p. 223.

30. A line which takes on its full stylistic significance for Céline in the 'métro émotif' of the *Entretiens avec le Professeur Y*.

31. Louis Chevalier, *Montmartre du plaisir et du crime*, Paris, Robert Laffont, coll. 'L'Homme et l'Histoire', 1980, pp. 446–52.

32. Ibid., p. 162.

chooses to situate his first novel between madness and death, between Bicêtre and Montmartre.

Yet Montmartre is not exclusively the realm of death, it is also essentially the domain of play, of pleasure: of imagination and *féerie*. As Jacques Laurent recalls in his novel of 1977, *Les Bêtises*: 'Enfant, pour retarder mon retour à l'A(ppartement), je montais du petit lycée Condorcet jusqu'à la Place Clichy où une triste fête populaire avait lieu presque toute l'année; l'une des baraques avait pour titre: "illusion réelle d'un voyage en mer"'.[33] This concept of the 'illusion réelle d'un voyage' brings us back from the historical aspect of *Voyage au bout de la nuit* to the central question of the operation of the *voyage imaginaire* in the novel: is the obsessive reverting to the Place Clichy so constant and so systematic that the reader must begin to consider whether, in effect, the novel never leaves it? In other words, is the novel less a straightforward chronicle of the First World War and the inter-war years up to the Depression than a projection from the initial scene in the Place Clichy towards a world irremediably cut off from Céline's Golden Age, the society of the *belle époque*, by the war, a world in which characters such as Bardamu would have no place and would exist only as ghosts?

Under this interpretation, *Voyage au bout de la nuit* would convey the same distrust of the post-war world as that conveyed by the medical writings which just preceed it. It is perhaps for this reason that Céline, in a series of contradictory statements after the novel's publication, insists in one interview that: 'C'est un roman, mais ce n'est pas une histoire de vrais "personnages". C'est plutot des fantômes' (CC 1, 38). However literally such a comment was intended, it has the merit of drawing the reader's attention to an aspect of the novel which has received little attention, but which goes hand in hand with the recurrence of the Place Clichy: the considerable presence of ghosts. Thus, Céline is careful to define Bardamu as a man who moves in a world of ghosts, who lives surrounded by them. When describing his last discussions with Molly before leaving Detroit, Bardamu recalls: 'Elle ne comprenait pas très bien où je voulais en venir avec mes divagations, mais elle me donnait raison quand même contre les fantômes ou avec les fantômes, à mon choix' (V, 230), and when he leaves the city, he comments: 'La vie vous force à rester trop souvent avec les fantômes' (V, 235). Gradually, in the course of the novel, its characters are transformed into ghosts, a process culminating in the wilfully

---

33. Jacques Laurent, *Les Bêtises*, Paris, Grasset, 1971, p. 540.

strange scene in the Cimetière Saint-Pierre (V, 366–9). After the death of Tania's lover, she and Bardamu climb to the top of the Butte de Montmartre, in the company of 'des gens qui viennent chercher de la gaîté en haut de la ville' (V, 366). There, by the Sacré Coeur, '[nous] venions d'arriver au bout du monde, c'était de plus en plus net. On ne pouvait aller plus loin, parce qu'après ça il n'y avait plus que les morts' (V, 366). At this point in the novel, Bardamu and Tania are blocked by the dead in the same way that, at the beginning, the *miteux* have been prevented from going further by the sea. Then emerge all the characters of the novel, transformed into ghosts, heading east through the sky, over Rancy towards the fogs of England: the ghosts of Bébert, a Negro from Topo, Grappa and the *curé* who sold Bardamu into slavery on the *Infanta Combitta*. Only Molly is absent from this 'clique de fantômes' (V, 367): 'elle devait avoir un petit ciel rien que pour elle, près du Bon Dieu' (V, 367). In particular, the ghosts of the novel's characters merge with the ghosts from the 'cimetière d'à côté' (V, 367): the ghosts of the Communards, the Cossacks who invaded Paris in 1814 at the end of the Napoleonic adventure, all waiting for their leader, La Pérouse, the doomed navigator. As Henri Godard points out,[34] it was not La Pérouse but Bougainville who was buried in the Cimetière Saint-Pierre, and Céline was well aware of this fact. Yet again, he makes use of a deliberate falsification of his data in order to create his *voyage imaginaire*, and what better patron saint can there be for a 'Voyage au bout de la nuit' than an obsessive navigator who got lost, failed to complete his journey and finally simply disappeared?

This use of the *fantômes* in the novel is the result of a procedure which is highly complex. On one level, the *fantômes* are the ghosts of characters who, like Molly, are irremediably lost in time. On the other hand, 'tous ces salauds-là, ils étaient devenus des anges sans que je m'en soye apperçu!' (V, 367): the ghosts of past characters have become eternal and, like the characters of *Mort à crédit*, threaten to return 'des quatre coins du monde' (MC, 512) in order to destroy the narrator. It is for this reason that Bardamu and Robinson are so apprehensive at the return of Madelon, a metaphor of the war itself: 'Trop de fantômes, par-ci, par-là' (V, 459): the *fantôme*, lost in the past, can only too easily become a *revenant*, full of concrete menace, and it is no coincidence that Madelon's reappearance which leads directly on to the death of Robinson takes place at Toussaint (V, 460).

Yet, faced with this dual threat — the loss of loved ones and the

---

34. *Romans* I, ed. Godard, p. 1305.

possible return of past enemies — Bardamu exhibits a strange complicity: 'j'avais ce sale penchant aussi pour les fantômes. Peut-être pas tout à fait par ma faute' (V, 235), a complicity which leads him to become a ghost or *revenant* in his turn when, one evening, he decides to leave Baryton's *asile* at Vigny-sur-Seine in order to revisit the Henrouilles's villa at Rancy. For, like all the other characters of the novel, Bardamu himself has little choice: there is an increasing sense in *Voyage au bout de la nuit* that, for some, the world is already finished, the march of history already arrested. In invoking the Brittania figure who presides over the one remaining spark of life in a dying West and who looks forward to the London of *Guignol's Band*, the narrator concludes that even that faint ray of hope will soon be extinguished:

> son thé il ne bouillera plus jamais.
> Il n'y a plus de vie pour les flammes.
> Plus de vie au monde pour personne qu'un petit peu pour elle encore et tout est presque fini (V, 369).

It is in this context that must be seen the immense importance of Proust for *Voyage au bout de la nuit*. Not only does the introduction of the novel have the same function as the initial pages of *A la Recherche du temps perdu*, but Céline is careful to introduce a specific reference to Proust in his evocation of Paris during the war: 'Proust, mi-revenant lui-même, s'est perdu avec un extraordinaire ténacité dans l'infinie, la diluante futilité des rites et démarches qui s'entortillent autour des gens du monde, gens du vide, fantômes de désirs, partouzards indécis attendant leur Watteau toujours, chercheurs sans entrain d'improbables Cythères' (V, 74). This reference is vital, not merely because it introduces an extended meditation on *A la Recherche du temps perdu* which will be considerably amplified in *Mort à crédit*, but also because it helps to establish a relationship between Céline and his novel and between Bardamu and the world in which he finds himself after the passing of the regiment. Céline's social context is obviously radically different from that which exercises Proust: in *Voyage au bout de la nuit*, the tortuousness and refinement of Proust's world are set against the 'solidité' and the 'rudes appétits' of Madame Hérote in the significantly-named Passage des Bérésinas (V, 74). Yet, the *gens du vide*, the *fantômes de désirs*, en route to a Cythère which will always horrify them, are an exact grande-bourgeoise reflection of the petite-bourgeois concerns, and language, of Céline's own characters. With a shift in style from the high-literary to the demotic, the concerns remain the same, but extended ironically into a broader social sphere. At the same time, the tantalising phrase: 'Proust, mi-revenant *lui-même* . . .' introduces a parallel, not merely between Proust and his own characters, but also between his own narrator and that of Céline, Bardamu. The evocation of Paris during and after the First World War in *Le Temps retrouvé* is built upon a set of characters, including the narrator himself, recently released from a sanatorium after a breakdown, who had life and vigour in the preceeding volumes but who are now, literally, ghosts, the flotsam of the shipwreck of pre-war Europe who have no right to exist in the post-war era.[35] In exactly the same way, Céline's own characters in *Voyage au bout de la nuit* have ceased to have meaning in real terms in that post-war era, and the pre-war medical student Bardamu, who emerges from several *asiles* to observe the present day, is condemned to the fate of becoming the 'fantôme burlesque de la médecine bourgeoise' (CC 3, 160) whom Céline evokes in his medical writings.

This would already be sufficient to modify significantly our reading of the novel from a Naturalistic perspective to one based upon the *voyage imaginaire*, but it is happily reinforced by the presence, at the very beginning, of the 'Chanson des Gardes Suisses 1793', which Céline uses as an *exergue*. Both François Gibault[36] and Henri Godard[37] have asserted that this poem is a pure fiction, analagous to the Thomas Parke d'Inviliers poem which introduces Scott Fitzgerald's *The Great Gatsby*: a literary joke, purporting to be real, but in reality invented by the author. There are plenty of elements in *Voyage au bout de la nuit*, however, to indicate that the joke is more serious and more complicated, and that Céline does not so much invent as, characteristically, distort existing data. The case of the Monmouth episode towards the end of the novel, when Bardamu is teaching Baryton's daughter English, is a case in point. Contrary to Henri Godard's assertion[38] that Céline has merely compressed Macaulay's original account, his use of the Monmouth story

---

35. It is essential to remember that the publication of the later volumes of *A la Recherche du temps perdu*, from *A l'ombre des jeunes filles en fleurs* of 1919 to *Le Temps retrouvé* of 1928, was a continuing literary event of the 1920s, which impinged considerably on the consciousness of writers like Céline who began their literary careers at that time. *Le Temps retrouvé*, particularly, is contemporaneous with the early period of the composition of *Voyage au bout de la nuit*.
36. Francois Gibault, *Céline 1894–1932, Le Temps des espérences*, Paris, Mercure de France, 1977, p. 306.
37. *Romans* I, ed. Godard, p. 1291.
38. Ibid., p. 1307.

Lorsque nous parvînmes à ce passage, implacable entre tous, où Monmouth le Prétendant vient de débarquer sur les rivages imprécis du Kent . . . Au moment où son aventure se met à tourner dans le vide . . . Où Monmouth le Prétendant ne sait plus très bien ce qu'il prétend . . . ce qu'il veut faire. Ce qu'il est venu faire . . . Où il commence à se dire qu'il voudrait bien s'en aller, mais où il ne sait plus ni où ni comment s'en aller . . . Quand la défaite monte devant lui . . . Dans la pâleur du matin . . . Quand la mer emporte ses derniers navires . . . (V, 437),

is pure fabrication when set against the original.[39] It is difficult even to consider it a condensation, since Monmouth in reality landed at Lyme Regis in Dorset, and not in Kent, a hundred miles to the east, and then proceeded to wage an entire campaign in the south-west before seeing his support dwindle and being finally defeated. In fact, Céline's account of the bewilderment of Monmouth when he lands in Kent has considerable significance for the English episodes in *Mort à crédit*, especially the one in which Ferdinand arrives late in Folkestone, and in the context of the *voyage imaginaire* of *Voyage au bout de la nuit*, in which it stands as yet another example, like that of La Pérouse, of a journey which leads nowhere and where the 'pâleur du matin' is both an ironic reflection of the morning of Austerlitz and an announcement of the end of the novel in the bleak dawn by the Seine.

In fact, the 'Chanson des Gardes Suisses' does exist and is not the product of Céline's imagination. Like Bardamu's account of Monmouth, it is the result of a radical rewriting of the source material: in this case, a transposition of the *Chant de la Bérésina*, dating from the crossing of the Berezina by Napoleon's Grand Army during the retreat from Russia in 1812 and sung, not by the *Gardes Suisses*, but by the *Régiment Suisse* of the Grand Army. In his book *Honneur et fidelité: Histoire des Suisses au service étranger*, P. de Vallière recounts the significance of this song:

Bien avant le jour, le commandant Blattmann et le lieutenant Legler, du 1er, se promenaient de long en large sur la route pour secouer l'engourdissement mortel de la nuit. Legler se mit à fredonner un air qu'il avait chanté, enfant, à Glaris. Blattmann l'encouragea; la voix monta, chaude, dans l'air glacé:

> Notre vie est un voyage
> Dans l'hiver et dans la nuit
> Nous cherchons notre passage
> Sous un ciel où rien ne luit.

39. See: Lord Macaulay, *The History of England from the Accession of James the Second*, vol. II, ed. Charles Harding Firth, London, Macmillan, 1913–15, pp. 563ff.

Des officiers se rapprochèrent, des soldats se levaient pour écouter ce chant qui reveillait en eux la magie des souvenirs. Les hommes arrivaient de tous côtés, attirés par cet écho du pays lointain. Des centaines de voix reprirent en choeur les strophes suivantes. La mélodie s'enflait, toujours plus large, elle passait sur les bivouacs, sur la plaine blanche:

La souffrance est le bagage
Qui meurtrit nos reins courbés;
Dans la plaine aux vents sauvages
Combien sont déjà tombés!

Demain, la fin du voyage,
Le repos après l'effort,
La patrie et le village,
Le printemps, l'espoir — la mort!

Ce fut la diane des Suisses, dans le jour gris, leur adieu à la vie, leur salut au pays.[40]

It is interesting to note that, like the entire novel, the 'Chanson des gardes suisses' 'va de la vie à la mort' (V, 5). More important, however, is the transposition which Céline operates in attributing the song to the '*Gardes* Suisses' and not the '*Régiment* Suisse' of Napoleon: the Swiss Regiment of the Grand Army becomes the Regiment of Swiss Guards of the *ancien régime*; the date of the *Chant de la Bérésina*, 1812, is shifted back to 1793. This fact in itself is highly significant: it is yet a further example of Céline's technique, clearly visible in *Semmelweis*, of playing with dates. In addition, in Céline's version of history, reference is made at the very beginning of the novel to an archaic military unit which saw service under the *ancien régime* but which no longer exists. Even more significant, in this context, is the fact that the *Régiment des Gardes Suisses*, who formed the bodyguard of Louis XVI, were massacred in the Battle of the Tuileries on 10 August 1792, the year *before* the date of their song which opens the novel. This can only mean that Céline's *Gardes Suisses*, still singing in 1793, the year of the Terror and of the execution of the King, are a phantom regiment who no longer exist but who, like Bardamu and his friends, are projected on to an era to which they can never properly belong and are condemned to the same fate as the Flying Dutchman. In other words,

40. P. de Vallière, *Honneur et fidélité. Histoire des Suisses au service étranger*, Lausanne, Les Editions d'Art Suisse Ancien, 1940, p. 697. It is appropriate here to acknowledge here both Stephen Day and Philippe Alméras who, at the Oxford Colloque on Céline in 1975, came close to defining the origins of the *Chanson*, the former by seeing it as a Swiss Protestant canticle and the latter as a version of the German-language *Beresinalied*. See *Australian Journal of French Studies*, XIII, 1–2, 1975, p. 58.

Bardamu's 'voyage' has the same unearthly status as the ghostly 'Chanson des Gardes Suisses' of 1793, and the *régiment-fantôme* of the novel's introduction establishes a *narrateur-fantôme* for the rest of the work.

At the same time, the base from which the transposition departs, the *Chant de la Bérésina* of 1812, picks up the Napoleonic introduction to *Semmelweis* and introduces an entire Bonapartist thread which is present throughout the entire novel. The Berezina itself is present in *Voyage au bout de la nuit* in the passage des Bérésinas, in which Madame Hérote keeps her *maison de passe*, just as it is in the *passage* of the same name in *Mort à crédit*, and it is present by implication in the mock-heroic scene in which Bardamu, having descended the rue Bonaparte, waits at the Seine before deciding to cross to the Right Bank and Rancy beyond: 'Tout le monde n'est pas César' (V, 287). Similarly, imperial traces abound in the novel: the Maréchal Moncey, the hero of the Place Clichy, the ghosts of the Cossacks who finally overcome him, and, in some detail, the extended reflection of Parapine on Napoleon, in which he insists on the Emperor's sexual obsession, an obsession which dominates him even during the retreat from Russia, on Napoleon's contempt for his own play-acting, 'la pièce qu'il joue bien avant les spectateurs' (V, 353), and, finally, on his inevitable decline which contrasts so ironically with the dreams of heroism which he has inculcated into successive generations: 'Ce fut sa torture de ce fou d'être obligé de fournir des envies d'aventures à la moitié de l'Europe assise. Métier impossible. Il en creva' (V, 353).

This reference, which closely ressembles Mac Orlan's distinction between the active and passive adventurer in *Le Petit manuel du parfait aventurier*, the anachronistic man of action and the reader of novels, helps finally to elucidate the role of travel and exoticism in *Voyage au bout de la nuit*. Far from constituting any form of variety or transcendance, the successive episodes of the novel constitute a repetition of sameness, announced at the very beginning by Arthur Ganate's cyncial observation: 'Siècle de vitesse! qu'ils disent. Où ça? Grands changements! qu'ils racontent. Comment ça? Rien n'est changé en vérite' (V, 7). In fact, Albert Chesneau's use of Maurron's concept of the *fantaisie à repetitions* in his study of the pamphlets applies equally well, if not better, to *Voyage au bout de la nuit*.[41] If Céline is unable to subscribe to the post-war world, with its cult, in

---

41. Albert Chesneau, *Essai de psychocritique de Louis-Ferdinand Céline*, Paris, Minard, coll. 'Archives des Lettres Modernes', 1971. For an application of Maurron's theory to the novels, see: Kim Saunders, 'Images of the Foreign in Céline's Early Fiction', MA dissertation, University of Warwick, 1976.

the 1920s, of adventurism as a means of change or, at least, relief, his use of the African episode in the novel appears to derive from, and subvert, the master of adventure literature in England and France, Joseph Conrad.[42] Yet, although Conrad is often glibly associated with stirring sea-stories which appear to reinforce the adventurist cult, his use of travel as a means of displacing his characters from their normal environment allows him to introduce a sombre meditation on the notion of civilisation itself which closely parallels that of Céline. Thus, *Heart of Darkness* shows the decline of the energetic manager Kurtz into primitiveness and, presumably, cannibalism; *An Outpost of Progress* charts the disintegration of a small group of colonists as they plot to kill each other for the most banal and petty of reasons. In *Voyage au bout de la nuit*, like Malraux in *La Voie royale* of 1930, Céline makes use, not only of the cultural pessimism of Conrad's work, but also of the plot-structure of the stories themselves. Thus, Bardamu's journey up the river in search of the mysterious Robinson is exactly calqué on the attempt of Marlow to find Kurtz in *Heart of Darkness*. The result of the journey is the same in both cases: Kurtz has abandonned his role as Western trader and has been lured into primitiveness; Robinson refuses to play the game of trader and neglects to send in even his accounts. In *Voyage au bout de la nuit*, the cultural pessimism is reinforced by the fact that, whereas in Conrad's novella, Marlow, at least, remains unaffected by the 'horror', Bardamu begins to go native: 'En somme, je commençais à me débrouiller dans l'état primitif' (V, 174). It might be added that Bardamu's attempt to make fire in the native method when his matches have been exhausted is not the reflection of a Robinson Crusoe-like struggle for practical survival, which still asserts Western supremacy, but, rather, a subversion of it: Crusoe is well on the way to becoming Friday; *Voyage au bout de la nuit* is a direct and exact parallel of the French title of Conrad's story, *Au coeur des ténèbres*.

In the same way, Conrad's isolated colonists in *An Outpost of Progress* look forward to the equally isolated Grappa and Alcide, although here Céline is not so much concerned with disintegration as with employing the two characters as political symbols. Commenting on Grappa's law-giving and Alcide's highly complicated tobacco deals, Céline notes:

---

42. The extent of Conrad's reputation in France may be gauged by the fact that he was given the rare honour for a non-French writer of a special number of the *Nouvelle Revue Française* on his death in 1924.

Voyage au bout de la nuit *and the Ghost of the Swiss Guard*

A Topo en somme, tout minuscule que fut l'endroit, il y avait quand même place pour deux systèmes de civilisation, celle du lieutenant Grappa, plutôt à la romaine, qui fouettait les soumis pour en extraire simplement le tribut, dont il retenait, d'après l'affirmation d'Alcide, une part honteuse et personnelle, et puis le système Alcide proprement dit, plus compliqué, dans lequel se discernaient déjà les signes du second stade civilisateur, la naissance dans chaque tirailleur d'un client, combinaison commercialo-militaire en somme, beaucoup plus moderne, plus hypocrite, la nôtre (V, 156).

Topo becomes a *topos*, a microcosm of the capitalist world, in which Alcide's exploitation of his soldiers is an exact replica of Ford's major economic discovery, that the factory workers who produced his cars could *also* become consumers and that the market could therefore expand indefinitely. Quite clearly, however, if the colonies are a force for the dehumanisation of Western man and not a field of noble action, and if they constitute merely a mirror held up to the face of Western capitalism, the Napoleonic myth of adventure is redundant and able only to cast an ironic light on those whom it is no longer able to help. The transcendance of the human condition, aimed at, say, by Malraux, who stifles Grabot in order to emphasise Perken, or by Saint-Exupéry, is, for Celine, as unreal as the *Gardes Suisses* of 1793 and as dead as the *Régiment Suisse* after the crossing of the Bérézina.

In his paper at the 1979 Paris Colloquium of the Société des Etudes Céliniennes, Pierre Lainé revealed that, in the creation of Bardamu, Céline had made use, not merely of his own experience, but also of that of other acquaintances, notably Paul F. and Joseph Garcin (BLFC 3, 5–18). This evidence, which serves primarily to lay the ghost of Céline as a thinly disguised autobiographer in his fiction, is, however, by no means isolated: Céline often establishes the episodes of his novels by soliciting information on subjects with which he would normally be expected to be familiar. At the same time, a novel like *Voyage au bout de la nuit* is also woven from a surprisingly wide range of literary references, from Proust and Conrad to Montaigne and Macaulay. What is important, however, is the way in which Céline systematically chooses to subvert his own source material, as he had already begun to do in Semmelweis and the medical pamphlets. Here, however, whilst intimately linked to the same ambivalent social and economic perspective, this procedure allows Céline to create a *voyage imaginaire*, projected on to the future from the Place Clichy in the summer before the First

World War, and which steadily repeats the knowledge that Bardamu does not belong in the post-war world, the world of 'assurances sociales' and Ford, but is caught, like the *Gardes Suisses*, in a ghostly limbo from which he can only escape by retreating once more into silence.

Céline's first novel, therefore, with its protagonist Bardamu as the 'fantôme burlesque de la médecine bourgeoise', demonstrates a profound and sensitive awareness on Céline's part of the historical significance of the First World War, which ushered in a new and increasingly rebarbative society and contrived to invalidate so many of the positive myths by which men live. What makes Céline's fictional pessimism so deep-rooted, however, is that, unlike Proust, he cannot view the pre-war era, Combray and the *belle époque*, with any lasting enthusiasm because the forces which come to triumph in the inter-war years are already at work in the France of 1900: Céline's Golden Age is already seriously tarnished. Having taken the reader on his imaginary journey through the 1920s, he returns, in *Mort à crédit*, to the date and the event which maintain an obsessive presence in all his work: 1900 and the Universal Exposition.

[3]

Mort à crédit *and the Ghost of the Petite Bourgeoisie*

In his survey of the 1930s, Nino Frank draws attention to the upsurge, in the last half of the decade, of a cult of superstition and the irrational. This took the form of the introduction, in newspapers like *Paris-Soir*, of horoscopes, of the popularity of imported mechanical games from the United States, like those miniature cranes which persist in failing to land a prize for the player, and of a vogue for the anomalous and the absurd, enshrined in the comedy of Pierre Dac.[1] As Philippe Muray has indicated, it is precisely in this context of 1930s irrationalism that Céline's second novel, with its oscillation between nineteenth-century positivism and the temptation of the occult, must be situated.[2] Yet, central to this context was a vogue for the *belle époque*, Céline's Golden Age. Nino Frank comments: 'C'est en ce temps-là que s'amorce officiellement une mode 1900'.[3] Thus, Céline's comment towards the beginning of *Mort à crédit*, 'Le siècle dernier je peux en parler, je l'ai vu finir' (MC, 544), and the subsequent narrative set in the period before the First World War can be seen as both reflecting and contributing to the 1930s vogue for 1900. Nevertheless, whereas in most cases this vogue may be seen as taking the form of a superficial *mode rétro*, an easy antidote to the political, military and economic uncertainty of the period, Céline's use of it in *Mort à crédit* is considerably more sophisticated and far-reaching, continuing his meditation on the bankruptcy of the post-war era in the medical writings of the 1920s and in *Voyage au bout de la nuit*. In one sense, as Merlin Thomas

1. Nino Frank, *Les Années 30*, Paris, Horay, 1969, pp. 137–8.
2. Philippe Muray, 'Mort à credo. Céline, le positivisme et l'occultisme', BLFC 8, 95–116.
3. Nino Frank, *Les Années 30*, p. 144.

suggests,[4] Céline accords to his evocation of childhood and ado-lescence in pre-war central Paris the same status as that accorded by Proust to Combray. Yet, for reasons both economic and psycho-logical, Céline is unable to endow this period of the narrator's experience with the same unambiguously optimistic qualities. Rather, the evocation is uniformly pessimistic, precisely because Céline discerns in the events of the period the pressures which will lead, by the arrival of the inter-war years, to the destruction of that bastion of pre-war French society, the artisanal petite bourgeoisie.

In his elegant conclusion to his essay on Proust in *Axel's Castle*, Edmund Wilson refers to *A la Recherche du temps perdu* as the 'Heartbreak House of capitalist culture', in which the narrator is not long to be master.[5] Céline's narrator Ferdinand stands in exactly the same relationship to the society and culture of which he is both the victim and the exponent. *Mort à crédit*, therefore, is consciously calqued upon *A la Recherche du temps perdu* and, continuing the Proustian meditation begun in *Voyage au bout de la nuit*, turns its attention to the period when its characters were not yet the gro-tesque *fantômes* of the inter-war years, but discerns that they are already beginning to lose substance. Thus, the novel constitutes clearly an exploration and exposition of the reasons for the decline and exclusion of the urban petite bourgeoisie but also, and this is its originality, raises the question of the profound psychological symptoms of such exclusion and reflects its cultural implications. If Proust's novel, with its grand-bourgeois narrator washed up on the shores of the inter-war years, is the elegy to the Heartbreak House of capitalist culture, then *Mort à crédit*, narrated by the excluded petit-bourgeois Ferdinand, who has been denied from the outset the elegance and poise of Proust's protagonist, mirrors the same bank-ruptcy, but from a different social and economic perspective.

Voyage au bout de la nuit opens in the summer of 1914 and projects itself forward to the inter-war years; *Mort à crédit* begins in the 1930s and looks back to the *belle époque*, the period when decline became inevitable. In other words, Céline is careful to establish two historical poles to his novel: 1900, when the disaster set in; the 1930s, when that disaster was perceived as irreversible and plainly visible. Thus, the novel opens with the death of Madame Bérenge who, as concierge, is not merely an intermediary, through

4. Merlin Thomas, *Louis-Ferdinand Céline*, London, Faber and Faber, 1979, pp. 65–6. See also N. Hewitt, '*Mort à crédit* et la crise de la petite bourgeoisie', *Australian Journal of French Studies*, XIII, 1–2, 1975, pp. 110–17.
5. Edmund Wilson, *Axel's Castle*, London, Fontana, p. 154.

the circulation of letters, between Ferdinand and the outside world, and the figure who protects Ferdinand from the outside world, but is also the very symbol of a fast-declining Parisian way of life. Similarly, Ferdinand's role as doctor, reinforced by that of his cousin Gustin, is again that of the 'fantôme burlesque de la médecine bourgeoise', first alluded to in the essay on the 'assurances' and sketched out in detail in the career of Bardamu in Rancy. 'Je n'ai pas toujours pratiqué la médecine, cette merde' (MC, 511): not for Ferdinand and Gustin the life of consultations and visits which ensures financial well-being and a comfortable faith in the role of the doctor as the repository of humanism. Instead, the municipal *dispensaire*, designed as an ineffectual holding operation against the two plagues of urban French society, tuberculosis and syphilis. Finally, Céline provides a clue as to the political consequences in the inter-war years of the erosion of the petite bourgeoisie which began before the war. Ferdinand's delerious pursuit of Mireille through Paris ends with the comment: '25 000 agents ont déblayé la Concorde. On y tenait plus les uns sur les autres. C'était trop brûlant. Ça fumait. C'était l'enfer' (MC, 535). For the French reader in 1936 such an allusion would be quite unambiguous: it would be seen as referring directly to the riots of 6 February 1934, the culmination of the attempt by the fascist *ligues*, staffed by *anciens combattants* and disaffected petits bourgeois, to overthrow the Republic which they believed had tricked them out of their inheritance. Yet even this attempt was doomed to failure and, ironically, began the train of events which led to the victory of the Front Populaire in June 1936. It is important to stress that the social and political climate in which Ferdinand narrates his pre-war history is also that of *Bagatelles pour un massacre*: the decline of the petit-bourgeois world, the erosion of central Paris, the redundancy of nineteenth-century humanism and the irreversible encroachment of the modern world. All that occurs in the transition from one work to the other is that Auguste's imprecations against the Jews and the Freemasons, which appear peripheral in *Mort à crédit*, are at the centre of the stage in *Bagatelles pour un massacre*: the worldview remains the same. Yet the groundwork for such a diatribe has already been laid in the novel, where Céline combines a number of complex and crucial issues: historical decline, social change, economic strength and psychological weakness, all centered on the set piece of the novel and the period which it evokes: the 1900 Universal Exposition which took place around the Place de la Concorde from which, in a sense, Ferdinand's journey back to the past begins and to which he returns throughout the novel.

The Exposition

The Exposition of 1900 occupies the same privileged status in *Mort à crédit* as that held by the Place Clichy in *Voyage au bout de la nuit*, both in the way in which it is announced and narrated early on in the novel and in its reverberations right to the work's conclusion. The Exposition defines the kind of world in which the narrator's family now find themselves and in which they feel increasingly vulnerable and isolated; more specifically, as the consecration of the rise of the 'petit inventeur',[6] it is ever-present in the novel, first in the career of the ever-benevolent *oncle* Edouard and then, in burlesque form, in the person of Courtial des Pereires. Finally, for broad social and economic reasons, it is rapidly assimilated into the Pantheon of Auguste's pet hatreds, against whom he rails whenever his vulnerability is made too clear. The importance of the Exposition for the novel, however, is accentuated, not merely by the way in which it appears early on in the narrative, but by the fact that it appears twice, in rapid succession, once as pure reminiscence and secondly as hallucination or delirium.

In his recalling of the family's visit to the Exposition, Ferdinand is at pains to emphasise the intense heat and the vast crowds, and in this he is doing no more than recording historical fact. Pascal Ory, in *Les Expositions Universelles de Paris*, notes that in July 1900, at the height of the Exposition, the temperature rose to 38.5°C[7] and one witness, Jean Lorrain, records in his diary: 'Dimanche, à l'Exposition, une foule, un peuple, plus de six cent mille êtres entassés dans si peu d'espace, la population de trois grandes villes piétinant et tournant en ronde entre le pont d'Iéna et celui de la Concorde et ces troupeaux humains admirant surtout les canons, le formidable attirail du Palais de la Guerre . . .'.[8] Yet, whereas Lorrain's crowds are responding to the aims of the Exposition, by being instructed and diverted, the experience of Ferdinand's family is quite different:

A la place de la Concorde, on a été vraiment pompés à l'intérieur par la bousculade. On s'est retrouvés ahuris dans la Galérie des Machines, une vraie catastrophe en suspens dans une cathédrale transparente, en petites verriéres jusqu'au ciel. Tellement le boucan était immense que mon père on ne l'entendait plus, et pourtant il s'égosillait. La vapeur giclait, bondissait par tous les bords. Y avait des marmites prodigieuses, hautes comme trois maisons, des bielles éclatantes qui fonçaient sur nous à la charge du fond

6. Pascal Ory, *Les Expositions Universelles de Paris*, Paris, Ramsay, 1982, p. 38.
7. Ibid., p. 128. Ory records the total number of visitors as 48 million (p. 26).
8. Jean Lorrain, *Poussières de Paris*, Paris, Ollendorf, 1902, pp. 364–5.

de l'enfer . . . A la fin on y tenait plus, on a pris peur, on est sortis . . . On est passés devant la Grande Roue . . . Mais on a préféré encore les bords de la Seine (MC, 579).

This description of the centrepiece of the Exposition, the *Galérie des Machines*, which constitutes a nightmarish distortion of the passage des Bérésinas, is significant for the way in which the experience of Ferdinand's family is atypical but prophetic. They are not one with the crowd; rather, it is the crowd which is the means of their exclusion from most of the exhibits. Ferdinand's family in fact learn nothing from their visit: Auguste's commentary is drowned by the very machines he is attempting to explain; most of the exhibits are too crowded to allow them access; like the *Grande Roue*, which stands as a symbol of all of Céline's narration, they revolve, getting nowhere, chased on by the leitmotifs of flight: 'On a pris peur, on est sortis'; 'On s'est encore une fois barrés'; 'On s'est enfuis par une autre porte'; 'On s'est faufilés au plus court' (MC, 580). What Céline is at pains to create in *Mort à crédit* is the impression of that 'énorme brutalité' to which he refers in his 'Hommage à Zola': thus, the central elements of Ferdinand's reminiscences of the Exposition are vulnerability, rejection, fear and flight, and it is these elements which will come to dominate the novel as it progresses, as they have already dominated the prologue, ending with the mature narrator's breakdown in delirium on the old site of the Exposition on the Place de la Concorde.

Yet Céline is careful to link this initial delirium, which opens the door of the childhood and past of the narrator, and the reminiscence of the Exposition of 1900 with a further episode of delirium which takes us closer to the real meaning of the Exposition, as well as providing an interesting demonstration of Flaubert's definition, in his *Dictionnaire des idées reçues*: 'Exposition: sujet de délire au XIXe siècle'.[9] Ferdinand, under the guidance of his *grand'mère* Caroline, has learned to read and write so well that he is sent to school. On the ninth day, he falls ill and is sent home. There, he begins to hallucinate: 'D'abord j'ai vu tout en rouge . . . Comme un nuage tout gonflé de sang . . . Et c'est venu au milieu du ciel . . . Et puis il s'est decomposé . . . Il a pris la forme d'une cliente . . .' (MC, 586). It is this gigantic client who operates in much the same way as the military band-Pied Piper in *Voyage au bout de la nuit*: she leads all the small shopkeepers of the passage out into the street, off over the Place Vendôme, over the rue de Rivoli, towards the Exposition,

9. Quoted in Ory, *Les Expositions Universelles de Paris*, p. 6.

the entrance-fee to which she will pay because: 'C'est la Dame, la cliente qu'avait tout l'argent sur elle, tout le pognon des boutiques planqué dans ses trousses . . .' (MC, 590). Yet, when they all arrive at the turnstiles, the 'cliente' suddenly vanishes:

> Elle a retroussé d'un seul coup tous les volants de ses jupes . . . son pantalon . . . plus haut que la tête . . . jusque dans les nuages . . . Une vraie tempête, un vent si glacial s'est engouffré par-dessous qu'on en a hurlé de douleur . . . On restait figés sur le quai, abandonnés, grelottants, à la détresse. Entre le remblai et les trois péniches la cliente s'était envolée! . . . Tous les voisins du Passage ils sont devenus tellement blafards que j'en reconnaissais plus aucun . . . Elle avait trompé tout son monde! La géante, avec ses larcins magnifiques . . . L'Exposition y en avait plus! . . . Elle etait finie depuis longtemps! . . . On entendait déjà les loups hurler sur le Cours-la-Reine (MC, 591).

The entire episode is a particularly rich one, but the essential ingredient is the fact that it establishes explicitly what was only hinted at in Ferdinand's conscious reminiscence: namely, that the Exposition of 1900 was a diversion for the petite bourgeoisie, a trick to blind them to the fact that their relationship with their clientele, the grande bourgeoisie, was essentially one of duplicity of which they were the victims. Thus, Céline is able to introduce the entire notion of social change at the expense of the petite bourgeoisie which constitutes one of the main lines of the novel. At the same time, this childhood hallucination on the part of the narrator, by concentrating on a gigantic female client, combines a specific reference to the 1900 Exposition — Moreau-Vautier's huge statue, *La Parisienne*, which dominated the main entrance — with a transposed phantasm of the encounter with the *cliente* of the Place des Ternes (MC, 554–6), thus linking the notions of economic and sexual aggressivity and domination. Similarly, the episode stands midway between the unhappy present in which the doctor Ferdinand composes his reminiscences and the ambiguous past in which Gwendor battles with Krogold: the wolves on the Cours-la-Reine suddenly transpose the scene into the vaguely medieval past of the comic-book legend; the disappearing confidence-trickster reinforces the echoes of Stavisky and 6 February, an echo reinforced in its turn by the fact that the childhood hallucination, like that of the adult Ferdinand, ends with rioting, destruction and chaos at the end of the Tuileries: 'Il ne reste rien au monde, que le feu de nous . . . Un rouge terrible qui vient me gronder à travers les tempes avec une barre qui remue tout . . . déchire l'angoisse . . . Elle me bouffe le fond de la tétère comme une panade tout en feu . . .

avec la barre comme cuiller . . . Elle me quittera plus jamais . . . '
(MC, 593). Finally, the gigantic *cliente* who floats up into the air
from the Tuileries looks forward to the presence in the novel of
Courtial and his balloon, the *Zélé*, for, as a plaque still indicates, it
was from the Tuileries that Charles and Robert made the first flight
of a gas-filled balloon, in 1798.

The fact this attack of delirium, of crucial importance for the
psychological meaning of the novel, should occur after the child
Ferdinand's first experience of school, the jewel in the crown of the
early Third Republic, serves to underline the extent to which
Céline's novel parts company with the optimistic positivist philosophy underlying the Universal Expositions. The 1900 Exposition
was the fifth in a series which began in 1855 and recurred at regular
intervals in 1867, 1878, and 1889, with a belated postscript in the
form of the International Exposition of 1937, one of the ostensible
causes of the anti-Semitism of *Bagatelles pour un massacre*. Whilst
all of these exhibitions espoused of necessity an enthusiastic belief in
the possibilities of science and technology, derived from the same
Saint-Simonian utopianism which produced 'la médecine du travail'
and which is reflected in Courtial's *colonie* in Blême-le-Petit, the
1900 Universal Exposition was particularly conscious of its additional role as the messenger of a new century. The *décret* of 1892,
setting out the Exposition's aims, emphasised its Janus-like position,
astride two centuries: 'Ce sera la fin d'un siècle de prodigieux efforts
scientifiques et économiques; ce sera aussi le seuil d'une ère dont les
savants et les philosophes prophétisent la grandeur et dont les
réalités dépasseront sans doute les rêves de nos imaginations. L'exposition de 1900 constituera la synthèse, déterminera la philosophie
du XXe siècle'.[10] It was entirely fitting, therefore, that the one
major innovation to be celebrated by the Exposition should be the
new energy source, electricity, personnified by 'La Fée Electricite'.
It is no less fitting, however, that that innovation and all it stands for
should be implicitly rejected by a narrator whose reminiscences
include the gas-infected *Passage des Bérésinas* and whose previous
work is the novel, *Voyage au bout de la nuit*.

Not for nothing, therefore, do Ferdinand's family have an initial
distrust of the Exposition. The narrator records that '[d'abord,]
mon père il a boudé' (MC, 578), and, more interestingly, that
'[grand'mère,] elle s'est bien méfiée de l'Exposition qu'on annonçait.
L'autre, celle de 82, elle avait servi qu'à contrarier le petit commerce
. . . ' (MC, 576). Not only does this translate a popular, albeit

10. Quoted in ibid., p. 30.

unfounded, belief amongst the petite bourgeoisie that Expositions caused inflation, but it also constitutes a continuing example of one of Céline's favourite fictional and polemical devices, the blatant and wilful distortion and invention of objective data: there was no Exposition in 1882. As Philippe Julian points out, this initial distrust of the Exposition was widespread amongst the Parisian population as a whole: 'At first the Parisians, bored with the whole affair even before it had begun, and deriding it for political reasons, shunned the exhibition; then they came, attracted chiefly by Lorrain's articles in *L'Echo de Paris*, and many of them spent all their Summer evenings there'.[11] He then goes on to offer a more plausible reason than Jean Lorrain's articles for the belated conversion of the Parisian population to the Exposition: complimentary tickets. He notes: 'nearly half the total number of visitors were entitled to at least one free admission. Only those far from the corridors of power failed to receive anything'.[12] Ferdinand's family's attendance at the Exposition, therefore, is representative both of their time and of their class: Julian notes that 'the majority of visitors . . . belonged to the lower bourgeoisie'.[13] Initially, and rightly, distrustful of the event, they are lured to it by Rodolphe's free tickets, thus inverting the process by which Bardamu is persecuted on board the *Amiral Bragueton* for being the 'seul payant du voyage' (V, 113). Ironically, however, the family's complimentary tickets come, not from a source of Republican patronage, but from the marginal *oncle* Rodolphe, who participates in the Exposition dressed as a minstrel, a constant cause of shame for Ferdinand's parents. A further departure from the norm is the fact that, unlike the majority of visitors to the Exposition who, once they overcame their initial distrust, were captivated, Ferdinand's family, prophetically, are driven away and return definitively to their home as if to a refuge. Significantly, the orthodox response is provided by Auguste who, by narration and the power of language, turns defeat into victory, until his precarious and fragile spell is shattered by Madame Méhon's notice: 'MENTEUR', posted against the window (MC, 581): 'tous les chagrins viennent dans les lettres' (MC, 511).

With the breaking of the father's spellbinding power as a storyteller, the Exposition comes to join his traditional list of enemies, along with the Jews and the Freemasons: 'Le Destin . . . Les Juifs . . . La Poisse . . . L'Exposition . . . La Providence . . . Les Francs-Maçons'

11. Philippe Julian, *The Triumph of Art Nouveau. Paris Exhibition 1900*, London, Phaidon, 1974, pp. 197–8.
12. Ibid., p. 205.
13. Ibid., p. 199.

(MC, 688–9). Irrational as this inclusion of the Exposition may appear, it is by no means inconsistent with a certain body of right-wing thought which saw in the event a coalition of all the forces which threatened to undermine traditional French values. Thus, Pascal Ory notes conservative opposition to the moral depravity supposedly unleashed by the Exposition, encapsulated in Barrès' dismissive phrase: 'limonade et prostitution', [14] that same prostitution which, encouraged by the 1900 Exposition, moved to Lower Montmartre and established that area of Paris as a 'lieu du plaisir et du crime'. At the same time that the Exposition was seen to present a moral danger to French society, it was also recognised as being a major culprit in the destruction of the old Paris: as Jean Lorrain commented: 'Paris s'en va'.[15] And that destruction was hastened by the construction of the first Métro line in time for the opening of the Exposition, from Porte de Vincennes to Pont de Neuilly, which, together with the Nord-Sud of *Voyage au bout de la nuit*, provides in its turn the basis for Céline's own 'métro émotif' of the *Entretiens avec le professeur Y*. In the place of traditional French values and the recognisable structure of traditional Paris was substituted a creeping Americanism, perceived by hostile critics to have been endemic to all of the preceeding exhibitions. Thus, Baudelaire, commenting on the average Frenchman's reactions to the 1855 Exposition, writes: 'Le pauvre homme est tellement américanisé par ses philosophes zoocrates et industriels qu'il a perdu la notion des différences qui caractérisent les phénomènes du monde physique et du monde rural',[16] and the Goncourts follow a similar line in their description of the 1867 Exposition: 'L'Exposition Universelle, le dernier coup à ce qui est, l'américanisation de la France, l'Industrie primant l'Art, la batteuse à vapeur régnant à la place du tableau'.[17] Céline's description of the 1900 Exposition, therefore, falls into the same category of distrust of Americanisation as his ambiguous medical polemics and the Detroit episode of *Voyage au bout de la nuit*. The Exposition has merely completed the work begun by Haussmann. Finally, if, for right-wing critics, the Exposition was the cause of moral dissolution, the physical destruction of the old Paris and a process of Americanisation which would irreversibly transform France at the expense of the French, a unifying factor could be found in the traditional scapegoat figure of the Jew. Ultimately, conservative criticism of the Exposition was

14. Ory, *Les Expositions Universelles de Paris*, p. 31.
15. Lorrain, *Poussières de Paris*, p. 228.
16. Quoted in Ory, *Les Expositions Universelles de Paris*, p. 50.
17. Quoted in ibid.

allied to anti-Semitism, which combined distrust of cosmopolitanism with charges of profiteering. Thus, Jean Lorrain, whilst noting
the defeat of the Dreyfusards in the 1900 municipal elections, lashes
out at the way in which Jews have enriched themselves at the
expense of the French through the Exposition.[18] Similarly, Paul
Morand, in his retrospective evocation of the Exposition,[19] whilst
asserting that the causes of the state of France in 1931 are to be
found in 1900, flavours his account with constant doses of anti-
Semitism. There is a certain logic, therefore, in Auguste's perception
of the Exposition as an enemy on the same level as the Jews and the
Freemasons, just as there is in his son's choice of the event as a
privileged indicator of the decline of his family and his class.

For, whilst opposition to the Exposition was, even at the time, a
narrowly conservative, anti-Semitic political issue, which shows
through clearly in *Mort à crédit*, and is reflected in *Bagatelles pour
un massacre*, the novel recognised that the questions were broader
and concerned the erosion of an entire class and way of life. The
Universal Expositions were not merely the celebrations of scientific
and industrial achievement: their main purpose was that of legitimisation — legitimisation of regimes, of classes, of economic
philosophies, of fashion and, by the same token, the consecration
of a number of defeats and exclusions. The 1855 Exposition, for
example, was in part designed to legitimise the illegitimate regime of
Louis-Napoleon, a process repeated and extended in 1867, of which
Zola has left a crucial depiction in *Nana*. Here, the Second Empire
is shown as striving to win respectability by acting as host to
European monarchs, an attempt reflected exactly, and ironically, by
Nana's own efforts to enter legitimate society by inviting well-
known figures to her dinner-table. In the latter case, however, the
dining-room is overcrowded, there is not enough food to go round
and, necessarily, some of the would-be guests find themselves
excluded. With a Universal Exposition there are always victims: in
1900, those victims were the petit-bourgeois shopkeepers and artisans of central Paris, and legitimacy was granted to the bourgeoisie
who had achieved hegemony by the end of the nineteenth century
and to their regime, the Third Republic.[20]

Yet, if Ferdinand and his family fall victims to the historical process
which consecrates the bourgeoisie at the expense of the petite
bourgeoisie, their predicament is connected also to a further, pro-

18. Lorrain, *Poussières de Paris*, p. 276.
19. Paul Morand, *1900*, Paris, Éditions de France, 1931.
20. See: Roger Magraw, *France 1815–1914: The Bourgeois Century*, London,
Fontana, 1983.

found aspect of the Universal Expositions. 'World exhibitions were places of pilgrimage to the fetish Commodity', writes Walter Benjamin, who goes on to quote from Renan in 1855: 'L'Europe s'est déplacée pour voir des marchandises'.[21] This aspect of the Expositions entailed a process by which: 'The world exhibitions glorified the exchange-value of commodities. They created a framework in which their use-value receded into the background'.[22] In the luxury-goods trade, at least, the result of this process, through the invention of modern advertising, was the transitory *spécialite*[23] — in other words, the domination of production by fashion: 'Fashion prescribed the ritual by which the fetish Commodity could be worshipped'.[24] This analysis is important because it sheds light on an important aspect of Ferdinand's downfall. His family are sellers of antique furniture, but, more particularly, lace, *articles de Paris*, those luxury goods which constitute for Benjamin the commodity fetish ruled by fashion. Yet fashion is the translation into commerce of time, one of the interlocking components of the title *Mort à crédit*, and it is from time and the march of time that the family are excluded: their wares, resolutely *old-fashioned*, are no longer appreciated by the clientele; on the one occasion when the family do attempt to compromise with fashion, by ordering a vast quantity of *boléros d'Irlande*, they discover that they are no longer in vogue and Clémence is then forced to work for one of the new departmental stores. A further sly reference to fashion, centered firmly on the Exposition of 1900, is to be found in Ferdinand's recurrent recollections of his staple diet at home, *nouilles*. The explanation given is that, since lace can only too easily be impregnated with any smell, the family are obliged to cook and eat only those things which are odourless: in this case, noodles. Yet these recollections contain also a reference to fashion. Philippe Julian, in his evocation of the 1900 Exposition, notes 'the stands displaying leather and lace goods, wildly Modern Style and showing little evidence of Art Nouveau, represented what soon came to be known as the "nouille" (noodle) style'.[25] The family's diet is precisely an element of fashion which will kill them.

The prominence given at the beginning of *Mort à crédit* to the 1900 Universal Exposition shows a considerable awareness on

---

21. Walter Benjamin, *Charles Baudelaire. A Lyric Poet in an Age of High Capitalism*, London, New Left Books, 1973, p. 165.
22. Ibid.
23. Ibid.
24. Ibid., p. 166.
25. Julian, *The Triumph of Art Nouveau*, p. 111.

Céline's part of economic and historical forces. As the consolidation of the scientific and social processes of the nineteenth century and as the archway to the twentieth, it embodies a world in which Ferdinand, his family and his class can no longer belong, and crystallises all those forces which have led to their exclusion. In this respect, it forms part of the same pessimism concerning the modern world to be found in the medical writings of the 1920s or in *Voyage au bout de la nuit*. Significantly, Céline does not refer to one of the most popular exhibits of 1900, the *Pavillon du Tour du Monde*, even though it is echoed in the *Chanson de prison* which begins the novel: 'Habillez-vous! Un pantalon!/Souvent trop court, parfois trop long./Puis veste ronde!/Gilet, chemise et lourd béret/Chaussures qui sur mer feraient/Le tour du Monde!' (MC, 509).[26] There is to be no travelling to escape, and the family remain locked in the prison of their decline. What is remarkable about *Mort à crédit*, however, is the extent to which Céline is able to chart that decline: the two Exposition scenes, the first as reminiscence, the second as delirium, lead in two directions: to a detailed analysis of the social, economic and historical processes behind that decline, and also to an explanation of the psychology which accompanies it.

The Decline of the Petite Bourgeoisie

In confronting the social and historical aspects of *Mort à crédit*, however, some caution is necessary, for the novel combines and interconnects two chronicles, one of which is general and relates to the passing of the pre-war world and the other of which is more specific and concerns the erosion of a particular class and social group, the Parisian petite bourgeoisie. Into the first category come episodes in the novel which, although part of the same process as

26. As with the 'Chanson des Gardes Suisses' which begins *Voyage au bout de la nuit*, the 'Chanson de Prison' is by no means Céline's own composition. I am indebted to M. Philippe Lejeune who gave me the song's full text, which appears in: Abbé Moreau, *Souvenirs de la Petite et Grande Roquette*, Paris, J. Rouff, 1884, vol. I, p. 54. The passage of the book quoting the song described the process of entry into the prison of the Grande-Roquette, by which the prisoner goes first to the *parloir*, for the last private conversation with a loved one, then to the prison archives, the *greffe*, and finally to the *avant-greffe*, where 'les détenus nouvellement arrivés changent de vêtements et prennent le costume de la prison' (Moreau, p. 53): 'Que chacun de vous à l'instant/Se déshabille./On ne nous laisse en attendant/Qu'un costume très peu gênant/Et fort commode;/C'est le léger accoutrement/Qu'Adam dès le commencement/Mit à la mode./Puis on fouille le detenu/C'est très facile il est tout nu/Entends-je dire,/Et, d'ailleurs n'est-ce pas la loi?/Ce souvenir évoque en moi/Un

the decline of the petite bourgeoisie, are not directly connected to it. The inevitable defeat of the traditionalist Meanwell College at the hands of the brash and technological Hopeful Academy, a defeat contained in the contrast between the names, in which good intentions pale into insignificance beside confidence in the future, is a sign of the transition to the modern world. This transition is reinforced by a similar process which takes place in the career of Courtial des Pereires, whose constantly leaking lighter-than-air machine, the *Zélé*, is driven from the fairgrounds of France by its heavier-than-air rival, the aeroplane. Indeed, there could be no more fitting shroud for Courtial than the remnants of an earlier balloon, the *Archimède* (MC, 1058). Neither of these episodes, however, is specifically symptomatic of the fate awaiting the petite bourgeoisie: rather, they signal the passing of an era and the vulnerability of certain manifestations of that era to the twin factors of time and money, combined in the complex operation of credit. In this way, the narrator of *Mort à crédit*, who has already evoked Proust in such a significant manner in *Voyage au bout de la nuit*, plays upon the Proustian model to such an extent that *Mort à crédit* becomes in many respects a calque of *A la Recherche du temps perdu*: the 'déclic' from present to past which introduces both novels; the presence throughout of a sick, neurasthenic narrator, both as adult and child; the role of a legend — Golo and Geneviève de Brabant for Proust, Krogold and Gwendor for Céline; the composition of the family — mother, father and initiatory grandmother whose name in *Mort à crédit*, Caroline, retains links with Charlemagne and looks forward to the Holy Roman Empire invoked in the pamphlets. Similarly, whereas Proust's novel is on one level a specific social chronicle of the decline of the pre-war nobility and grande bourgeoisie and their replacement, through the catalyst of the war itself, by the rising mercantile bourgeoisie symbolised by Madame Verdurin, its general implications concern the passage of

---

gai sourire./Habillez-vous! Un pantalon/Parfois trop court, souvent trop long/Puis veste ronde./Gilet, chemise et lourd béret,/Chaussure qui sur mer ferait/Le tour du monde'. Similarly, whilst the context of the 'Chanson des Gardes Suisses' is as important for *Voyage au bout de la nuit* as the quoted text itself, the 'Chanson de prison' takes on added significance from the fact that it details the final point of a. process which passes through the *parloir* and the *greffe*. The rare moments of intimate conversation allowed the new prisoner in the *parloir* announce the first words of the novel: 'Nous voici encore seuls', and the *greffe*, which, as Moreau notes, at the Grande-Roquette also contained the Bicêtre archives, introduces a favourite image of Céline's, i.e. the official scribe as a reflection of the novelist-chronicler.

time and the loss of the past, in the same way that Céline is not solely concerned with the destruction of his past, the petite bourgeoisie, but concentrates on the complicated operation of time and value in the twin poles of *mort* and *crédit*. Ultimately, however, the effectiveness of the calque depends upon the fact that it is debased and that even the fragile optimism open to Proust is denied to Céline: Ferdinand is viewing the passing of the *belle époque*, not from the vantage-point of the financially-cushioned Proustian narrator, but from that of the ever-impoverished petite bourgeoisie. For the grand bourgeois who is Proust, the elegant aesthetic solution to the historical process is still possible; for the narrator whose childhood has been spent in the gas-filled Passage des Bérésinas and whose adult life is confined to the municipal *dispensaire*, that solution seems more removed and less plausible. Similarly, the Célinian narrator must necessarily exhibit less refined and more savage psychological symptoms: the world of Combray is opened up by a gentle *rêverie* in a luxury bedroom; the prison of the Passage des Bérésinas is rediscovered through a violent attack of delirium.

At the same time, that integral pessimism which ultimately separates Céline from his Proustian model has its origins in a precise awareness of the trials of the Parisian petite bourgeoisie in the period surrounding the 1900 Exposition, dramatised through the evocation of the destinies of Ferdinand's parents, Auguste and Clémence. Although the father and mother represent different facets of the petite bourgeoisie, they are maintained as a composite symbol of the entire class, both by virtue of their being married and through a sly literary joke by Céline which nevertheless has considerable implications. On one level, Céline has simply borrowed the names from Zola's *L'Assommoir*, in order to signal the fact that his novel is a new attempt to describe the life of the Parisian *petites gens*. On another level entirely, however, the choice of names is connected to the fact that the subtitle of Corneille's *Cinna* is, precisely, 'La Clémence d'Auguste'. This not only constitutes yet another cultural referent in a writer whose work has, until relatively recently, been held to be remarkably free of a cultural background, but it also introduces into the novel a number of elements which are burlesque, yet which must be taken seriously. On the face of it, the problems facing Ferdinand's parents and their responses to them are far removed from the world of Cornelian tragedy: Auguste is merely the powerless and petty tyrant of his own family and Clémence is in such a position of vulnerability that clemency is all she can hope for. Yet, what adds tension and pathos to the novel is that the elements of tragedy and heroism are not entirely lacking in *Mort à crédit*: there is a modest, daily heroism in Clémence's journeys to sell her wares and in Auguste's constant battle to ward off humiliation at his office. Indeed, much of *Mort à crédit*, like Joyce's *Ulysses*, seems to operate upon a mock-heroic register which is not totally devoid of seriousness. Above all, Corneille is the poet of stoicism, and in their tenacious resistance to the historical forces which threaten to overwhelm them, Auguste and Clémence are not so far removed from the heroic model as they may at times appear.

In one sense, it is Clémence who is the more interesting of the two parents, in that she stands at an important crossroads of artisanal activity. Her work entails the buying and selling of lace, antique furniture and expensive new furniture. As such, she is both an entrepreneur, commissioning work from artisans, and a *commerçante*, emmeshed in the problems of the retail trade. She therefore combines two vital aspects of the Parisian petite bourgeoisie: the artisan and the small shopkeeper, and she is vulnerable in both areas. As a shopkeeper, she is constantly menaced by the proliferation of big stores, on the lines of Zola's *Au bonheur des dames*, those able to respond to fashion in a way in which she cannot, and whom she is ultimately forced to join. As an entrepreneur dealing with artisans, she meets two categories: the makers of lace, luxury goods, *articles de Paris*, but also the broader category of *fils et tissus*, represented by Madame Héronde, and the furniture-makers, the *ébénistes*, represented by the Alsatian family, the Wurzems. It is to be noted that, as a shopkeeper-entrepreneur who commissions work from the artisans, Clémence, in the carefully maintained hierarchy of the petite bourgeoisie, is superior to those she employs. She nevertheless suffers personally the results of their own difficulties: Madame Héronde gets further and further behind with her work and can never deliver on time: 'C'est triste qu'elle aye pas de parole' (MC, 548), comments Clémence, neatly encapsulating at least two meanings of credit; the Wurzems are unable to pay their rent and 'se réfugient dans un maquis, rue Caulaincourt' (MC, 548), in that Montmartre which remains Céline's heartland. It is again important to stress that Céline, in an attempt to avoid transparent didacticism, introduces personal reasons for his artisans' failures: Madame Héronde is honest as regards money, but dishonest in her promises, and she dies in childbirth, like Semmelweis's patients; the Wurzems' problems are due as much to the father's passion for fishing, which he inherits from the fishermen on the Seine in the 'Rubicon' episode of *Voyage au bout de la nuit*, as to general economic forces. Nevertheless, the Wurzems, having to move from their workshop near the *Cirque d'Hiver* on the Boulevard du Temple (MC, 548) to Montmartre, and Madame Héronde in her *bicoque* in Ivry, which does not even have gas lighting, even though it is the era of 'la Fée electricité', are, in their decline, representative of a certain historical process.

In an early work, *Histoire des populations françaises et de leurs attitudes devant la vie depuis le XVIIIe siècle*, Philippe Ariès charts the shifts in population in Paris from the Second Empire to the inter-war years. He notes in general that, in the period from 1845 to 1931, the working-class population of the city declined rapidly, with a corresponding growth in non-industrial professions,[27] to the extent that, by the end of the First World War, the bourgeoisie appeared to have taken over the city.[28] More precisely, with the process of urban renewal begun under Haussmann, prices began to rise both in terms of commodities and rents, and the workers were forced to leave, to be replaced by an influx of office-workers needed to staff an increasingly bureaucratic society.[29] At this point, for Ariès, Paris ceases to be 'red' and becomes moderate, if not downright conservative, and, after 1893, is composed of two antagonistic blocks, the dwindling population of industrial workers and the growing population of the bourgeoisie, with the increasingly vulnerable petite bourgeoisie squeezed in between.[30] Whilst the modernisation of Paris had as its first effect the virtual exile of the industrial proletariat to the *banlieue rouge* beyond the city limits, a second wave of change took place in the mid-1900s which radically affected the standing of the petite bourgeoisie. Ariès records that the artisanal industry of *fils et tissus*, with which Clémence is so intimately involved through Madame Héronde, was established in the capital around 1850[31] and had maintained its strength, with a workforce of 160,000, right up until 1906.[32] Indeed, in that year, the order of Parisian industries was unchanged from 1845, with the artisanal trades still in a prominant position. In the period from 1906 to 1931, however, which is roughly the time-scale of *Mort à crédit*, the situation had changed drastically, with all artisanal trades in decline and *fils et tissus* down by 80 per cent,[33] possibly as the

27. Philippe Ariès, *Histoire des populations françaises et de leurs attitudes devant la vie depuis le XVIIIe siècle*, Paris, Self, 1948, pp. 293–4.
28. Ibid., pp. 294–5.
29. Ibid., p. 300.
30. Ibid., p. 303.
31. Ibid., p. 292.
32. Ibid., p. 308.
33. Ibid., p. 309.

result of the introduction of artificial fibres from 1891 onwards.[34] Céline's novel, therefore, through the activities of Clémence, constitutes an accurate and well-informed reflection of the decline of the Parisian petite bourgeoisie immediately following the 1900 Exposition, a process accelerated by the First World War itself. Yet, as the novel's title suggests, that decline was a slow agony, a death in small instalments, resisted tenaciously by the artisans. As Guy Palmade reveals, in spite of the process of erosion, there were still, by 1914, two *patrons* for every five workers;[35] and, after all, the Temple is still the centre of the French jewellery trade, just as the Sentier still dominates the French garment industry.

If Clémence represents a type of artisanal activity and retail trade which rapidly became out of date within the time-scale of the novel, Auguste, at first sight, appears more positive, as an *employé de bureau*, one of those office-workers who, for Philippe Ariès, displaced the Parisian proletariat in the last half of the nineteenth century and changed the political complexion of the capital. The problem, however, is that, in his profession too, events are moving more rapidly than he can control them. The fact that his place of employment is an insurance company provides a further permutation to the title of the novel, in that insurance constitutes a privileged link between money, good faith, time and, ultimately, death. Nor is it coincidental that the name of the company, La Coccinelle, should look forward to the real name of that financial adventurer Courtial des Pereires, which is Léon-Charles Punais. What is crucial in Auguste's employment, however, is the fact that he is a *bachelier-employé*, a member of a sad caste whose constant tragedy is chronicled in French literature from the Second Empire onwards. In this respect, Auguste and his relationship with his son present close analogies with the relationship between Jacques Vingtras and his father, in Vallès's trilogy. Vallès's depiction of Vingtras *père* as an educated *pion* in a rich college, who is caught between the contempt of the teaching-staff and the insolence of the pupils, and who takes out his humiliation and frustration on his son, establishes a clear connection between *L'Enfant*, of 1882, and *Mort à crédit*, a connection reinforced by the style: Vallès makes a tentative and sparing use of exclamation and the three dots which will be fully exploited by Céline. If Jacques Vingtras's father, an educated man but reduced to humiliation because of his lack of qualifications, is a precursor in Auguste's own martyrdom, the experience of his son is

---

34. See Guy P. Palmade, *Capitalisme et capitalistes français au XIXe siècle*, Paris, Armand Colin, 1961, p. 237.
35. Ibid., p. 238.

no less significant. Jacques Vingtras discovers that the possession of the *baccalauréat*, even as early as the Second Empire, is no passport to success at all and that the doors to the professions are maintained firmly locked by the bourgeoisie. His experience in *Le Bachelier* prefigures that of Auguste: the *baccalauréat*, by itself, with no other diplomas, is a sop thrown to the petite bourgeoisie which presents no danger of allowing them access to positions of real power. Auguste's complaint to Ferdinand, therefore, has profound echoes in recent French literary history: 'De mon côté, à la Coccinelle, je dois subir quotidiennement les attaques sournoises, perfides, raffinées dirai-je, d'une coterie de jeunes rédacteurs récemment entrés en fonctions . . . Nantis de hauts diplômes universitaires . . . ces jeunes ambitieux disposent, sur les simples employés de rang, tels que moi-même, d'avantages écrasants' (MC, 762). The *bachelier* can only become a 'simple employé de rang': the future lies with those who are 'nantis de hauts diplômes universitaires'. Auguste is an almost anachronistic nineteenth-century clerk faced with extinction or, at least, eternal subordination in an increasingly professional and technological world.

He does, however, make one attempt to cross the barrier into the twentieth century, by buying a typewriter and learning how to type. That this is a totally deluded enterprise, which will at best render him eligible for employment as a typist rather than as a clerk, is ultimately less important than the fact that the object itself cruelly stands as a symbol for Auguste himself: both are *machines à écrire*, and it is undoubtedly this assimilation which makes Ferdinand's assault on his father with the typewriter so crucial to the psychological structure of the novel.

The Passage des Bérésinas, an anachronism in its own right, with a First Empire name and a Second Empire function,[36] serves as a last refuge in *Mort à crédit* for a whole class which is itself anachronistic and about to disappear. Clémence, Auguste and the petit bourgeois who surround them are made progressively redundant by vast economic and technological changes, consecrated by the 1900 Exposition, which will wipe them off the map of the new Paris and the new France. Squeezed between the triumphant bourgeoisie and the rapidly organising proletariat, the petite bourgeoisie began to lack weight and credibility in the Third Republic. Ironically, the petit bourgeois instinctively sided politically with the architects of their downfall, the bourgeois, rather than with the Left. J.-J. Chevalier, in his *Histoire des Institutions et des Régimes de la France Moderne*

36. See Benjamin, *Charles Baudelaire*.

(1789–1958), shows how the Parti Radical was logically the natural party of the *petites gens*: 'Ce puissant "tiers parti" . . . s'intercale entre "les gens bien" de la droite et le socialisme qui à ce moment-là est trop "peuple" et fait trop "rouge"',[37] but that the petite bourgeoisie tended to move to the Right of that party. Thus, the Parisian petite bourgeoisie moved from Radicalism to Boulangism in the 1890s, which translated in itself a refusal of dynamics, a shift from support of *mouvement* to defence of *ordre etabli*, what Chevalier terms the 'progressive provincialisation of the Parisian petite-bourgeoisie',[38] and which culminated in a massive petit-bourgeois vote for the Right in the legislative elections of 1902.[39] Auguste's progressive conservatism, deepening with every new disaster and constantly searching for scapegoats, is an accurate reflection of the political evolution of his class and its lack of political consciousness in the period before the First World War, to which Clémence's insistence on the moral code of honesty, probity and hard work, the only credit they possess, is an essential pendant. At any rate, it is the conservatism and delusion of those who are about to disappear: at no point in the novel is the family's name ever mentioned, a sure sign that they will have no descendants. When questioned by the police after the death of Courtial, the narrator gives his name simply as: 'Ferdinand, né à Courbevoie' (MC, 1062). Stripped of a surname, the narrator, his family and his class are equally stripped of a future.

Mort à crédit is therefore an extraordinarily accurate and relatively rare evocation of the crisis facing the French petite bourgeoisie in the period leading up to the First World War. Indeed, apart from Vallès's trilogy, written in the 1880s, its closest parallel is to be found, not in French literature at all, but in English Edwardian fiction, in the novels of H.G. Wells, and a discussion of Wells provides a useful conclusion to Céline's own treatment of history. Nor is the parallel too distant: Wells achieved great popularity in France, particularly through his scientific romances, but also as a political thinker, to the extent that he was invited to give a lecture at the Sorbonne in 1927 on 'Democracy under Revision'.

The connection with *Mort à crédit* comes initially through the Meanwell College episode. This is normally seen as exhibiting some Dickensian influence, particularly from the evocations of school life

37. J.-J. Chevalier, *Histoire des institutions et des régimes de la France Moderne 1789–1958,* Paris, Dalloz, 1967, p. 468.
38. Ibid., p. 416.
39. Ibid., p. 471.

in *Nicholas Nickleby* and *Oliver Twist* and in the use of allegorical names for the institutions themselves, such as Dotheboys Hall. Also, the location of the Merrywins' school, between Chatham and Rochester, is the very centre of Dickens country. Nevertheless, Dickens has by no means a monopoly on the locality or the subject of schooling. The south-east coast of England and the southern Home Counties are equally the geography of Wells and his novels abound in the evocation of the area's seedy private schools, from the 'private school among the Kentish Hills'[40] attended by the youthful narrator of *Tono-Bungay*, to the Cavendish Academy attended by Kipps, in his parent's search for upward social mobility, of which the narrator remarks: 'And of course there were boys from France',[41] a comment which seems to indicate that Ferdinand's experience, or that of Céline himself, is by no means isolated. Above all, it is Wells rather than Dickens who is the privileged witness and historian of the vulnerability and limitations of a threatened petite bourgeoisie. As Patrick Parrinder writes:

> Wells' fiction reveals this precarious world of retail trade, at the lower edge of the middle class, as one of the characteristic sources of English social consciousness . . . It is a shabby world, clinging to the illusion of gentility and combining the deference of servant-hood with a jealously-guarded sense of respectability and status; a world where personal identity becomes a bulwark against the threatening anonymous crowd around and below, and where the nearness of the crowd and the fear of catching one's own reflection in it, can lead to a social outlook tinged with hysterical uncharity.[42]

Nowhere are we closer to the paranoia of Ferdinand's family, desperately attempting to maintain credibility as petit bourgeois whilst their economic status pushes them further towards the crowd.

Wells, in his autobiography, makes the same observations about his parents as those recalled by Ferdinand: 'They were both economic innocents made by and for a social order, a scheme of things, that was falling to pieces all about them. And looking for stability in a world that was already breaking away towards adventure, they presently dropped me into that dismal insanitary . . . hole in which I was born'.[43] And, of his mother, he comments: 'My mother's

40. H.G. Wells, *Tono-Bungay*, London, Pan Books, 1964, p. 23.

41. H.G. Wells, *Kipps*, London, Fontana, 1961, p. 11.

42. Patrick Parrinder, *H.G. Wells*, Edinburgh, Oliver and Boyd, coll. 'Writers and Critics', 1970, p. 4.

43. H.G. Wells, *An Experiment in Autobiography*, I, London, Gollancz, 1934, p. 59.

instinct for appearances was very strong. Whatever the realities of our situation, she was resolved that to the very last moment we should keep up the appearance of being comfortable members of that upper-servant tenant class to which her imagination had been moulded',[44] concluding: 'my little mother, you see, becomes a symbol of the blind and groping parental solicitude of that age, a solicitude which enslaved and hampered where it sought to aid and establish'.[45] It is interesting that Wells should give an example of an idealised figure who can no longer stand the imprisonment to which she is subjected and who, like Nora Merrywin in *Mort à crédit*, takes her life by drowning. Writing of his cousin Clara, he concludes: 'All light and hope had gone out of life for her and late one night she flitted in her nightgown down the lawn from a sleepless bed to the river and drowned herself in a deep hole under a pollard willow'.[46]

Critics have tended to see Wells's visionary scientific writing as an antidote to the stifling decaying world of the petite bourgeoisie,[47] much as Courtial des Pereires may be seen as an unhoped-for escape from the same climate to the 'world that was already breaking away towards adventure'. In fact, however, exactly in keeping with *Mort à crédit*, the scientific vision is rarely able permanently to change the situation — at least for the good. Wells's fiction is a succession of chronicles of grandiose scientific experiments which fail. One recurrent experiment is to do with 'intensive culture', which looks forward to Courtial's project of 'agriculture radio-téllurique' (MC, 977), and which, like Céline's version, always ends in failure, often with the same image of decomposition. This pattern culminates in *The Food of the Gods*, in which scientists' attempts to produce giant vegetables succeed also in producing giant rats and mice. In other words, Céline's description of Courtial des Pereires, although it clearly owes much to the author's own experience with Raoul Marquis, fits into a fictional pattern, crystallised in the work of Wells, by which escape from the world of the petite bourgeoisie into science leads instead to a simplistic attempt to transform nature, with disastrous results. Both Céline and Wells ultimately reject the positivist scientific utopia as a means of transcending their class. It is entirely fitting, therefore, that both writers should carefully downgrade their scientific visionaries and inventors to the

44. Ibid., p. 73.
45. Ibid., p. 134.
46. Ibid., p. 131.
47. See Bernard Bergonzi, *The Early H.G. Wells. A Study of the Scientific Romances*, Manchester, Manchester University Press, 1961.

status of charlatans. Courtial is a mischievous mixture of the serious inventor who, like Wells, admires Flammarion, and the confidence-trickster; one of Wells' finest creations, Arthur Ponderevo, the hero of *Tono-Bungay*, is of the same blend: he invents the patent medicine which makes him a millionaire purely to escape from bankruptcy. In both writers, the inventor appears as a disquieting amalgam of the ideal of the petite bourgeoisie, education and the work ethic, and its worst enemy and recurrent nightmare, the confidence-trickster who will spirit away its humble fortune.[48]

Finally, both novelists show a certain ambivalence in their depictions of the petite bourgeoisie. In spite of its self-delusion and its limitations, it possesses a certain modest heroism. Yet both Wells and Céline are aware of how fragile that heroism really is and how it can easily give way to aggression and the search for a scapegoat: *Tono-Bungay* begins with the narrator's embittered reflections on the wealth and cunning of the Jews, and this general anti-Semitism of the petite bourgeoisie is expanded by Wells to a pervasive authoritarianism which begins with his description of the typical petit bourgeois, Kipps. As J. Kagarlitsky points out, no respect is possible for Kipps,[49] either as a character in his own right but also because of the way in which the type which he is takes on increasingly authoritarian characteristics as Wells's fiction progresses. Kipps becomes the fascist Bert Smallways, in *The War in the Air*,[50] and the fascist Tewler, in *You Can't Be Too Careful*.[51] Auguste is clearly moving in the same direction, as is his son, who becomes the narrator of *Bagatelles pour un massacre*.

Wells and Céline both appear, therefore, as chroniclers of the petite bourgeoisie in a time of crisis and decline, which engenders in both authors a perception of political movement to the Right and a deep metaphysical pessimism. Where Céline goes far beyond Wells, however, is in the way in which his portrait is concerned not merely with social decline and tension, but also with the complex workings of that decline through the economic system and with the profound psychological traumatism which that decline subtends.

48. See H.G. Wells, *The New Machiavelli*, London, Odhams, 1911, pp. 28ff; Wells, *Tono-Bungay*, p. 193.

49. J. Kagarlitsky, *The Life of H.G. Wells*, New York, Barnes and Noble, 1966, p. 152.

50. Ibid., p. 153.

51. Ibid., p. 156.

'Crédit est mort'

It is upon the notion of credit that the entire novel turns. Whilst, in some ways, not too much can be made of the title *Mort à crédit* itself, since its choice was an arbitrary one from several other possibilities, it is difficult to avoid the fact that the interaction between the title's two components reflects to an astonishing degree the play of forces within the novel as a whole. For the commonly accepted meaning of the title, conveyed by its English-language translation *Death on the Instalment Plan*, by concentrating purely on the notion of a lingering death, is ultimately inadequate. What the title transmits so clearly is also the profound connection in the context of the 1900 petite bourgeoisie between the twin poles of death and credit, the interplay of which provides the motive force for the whole work.

One of the most characteristic features of Auguste and Clémence as representatives of their class is their belief in the connection between financial independance and credibility. Clémence's criticism of Madame Héronde, '[c'est] dommage qu'elle aye pas de parole', implies an entire structure of belief in which the adherence to time, the keeping of promises and financial solvency are all interlinked. Clearly, Ferdinand's parents, as members of the petite bourgeoisie, strive to maintain their standing, their *crédit*, in a changing society, by being beholden to no man, by owing no money: in other words, by rejecting financial credit. A rigid distinction is made between moral credit and credibility and the financial system of credit instinctively refused on the lines of the old shopkeepers' print: 'Crédit est mort, les mauvais payeurs l'ont tué', massively popular from the early seventeenth century onwards, but particularly in the nineteenth century.[52]

This petit bourgeois morality, however, is in constant danger of being overwhelmed by financial reality and of having nothing else to fall back on but the superficial vestiges of respectability. Even as early as 1839, Michelet records an early example of an ironic contrast between actual poverty and the images designed to combat it. Describing a visit to silk-workers in Lyon, he records his impressions of the house of a poor Republican weaver and contrasts it

---

52. See Jean Adhémar, *Imagerie populaire française*, Milan, Electra, 1968, pp. 15–16; R. Saulnier and H. Van der Zee, 'La Mort de crédit', *Downa Sztuka Lwów*, II, 1939, pp. 217–18; Pierre-Louis Duchartre and René Saulnier, *L'Imagerie populaire. Les Images de tous les provinces français du XVe siècle au Second Empire. Les Complaintes, contes et chansons, légendes qui ont inspiré les images*, Paris, Librairies de France, 1925, pp. 62–3.

with that of a more intelligent inventor:

> Tout à côté de ce pauvre ménage, demeure un chef d'atelier plus aisé et plus intelligent. Celui-ci est un inventeur qui, sans cesse, trouve des perfectionnements, entre autres le *battant*, qui économise dans les soies brochées toute la soie qu'on perdait dans les revers de l'étoffe. Il nous reçut avec une dignité modeste. Secrétaire de noyer. Le principal ornement était un tableau-pendule exécutant des airs, tandis que le pauvre tisseur républicain orne ses murs de Napoléon à deux sous et de vieilles images (*Crédit est mort*, etc.).[53]

In other words, the man of the future, the inventor, has already reaped the financial rewards of his discoveries and his place in history, whereas the Republican weaver must be content with decorations which implicitly mock his redundancy. The very image, *Crédit est mort*, may be seen to symbolise a financial ethic increasingly out of touch with reality but which constitutes the only dignity to which the victims of the historical process can aspire. Thus, in *Mort à crédit*, by 1900 the financial ethic of Ferdinand's parents and their work ethic, encapsulated in Edouard's print of Millet's *Angélus*, again, one of the most popular decorations of petit-bourgeois homes, are increasingly irrelevant and no longer correspond to the workings of the modern economic system. Rather, they serve to maintain the petite bourgeoisie in their role as victims, as powerful myths but without concrete reality. At a period when the powerful forces in French society, consecrated by the 1900 Exposition, were exploiting a sophisticated financial system based on credit, the petite bourgeoisie took refuge behind its traditional anti-credit rhetoric and celebrated savings as the only honest way of manipulating spare capital.[54] For this very reason, their deepest fear was that of theft: 'Sa terreur, maman, c'était les voleuses' (MC, 547), and their recurrent nightmare was the confidence-trickster. It is worth recalling that, for the French petite bourgeoisie, the worst confidence-trick of all was not Panama or Stavisky, but the refusal of the Soviet government in 1920 to honour the 'Emprunts Russes' which had constituted a safe and modest form of saving for all the *petites gens* before the First World War, and it is this which is one of the major causes of French anti-Communism during the inter-war years, reflected in *L'Ecole des cadavres*.

The problem — and it emerges with extraordinary clarity in *Mort*

---

53. E. Michelet, *Journal*, I, 4 April 1839.
54. See Palmade, *Capitalisme et capitalistes français au XIXe siècle*, p. 223.

à crédit — is that, by 1900, France was operating a financial system based on credit and underwritten by the gold standard and that the petite bourgeoisie in some way found itself cut off from both. Thus, Paul Einzig, in *The Destiny of Gold*, comments: 'It was substantially correct to say that the period of the pre-1914 gold standard had been (in more than one sense) the golden age of mankind',[55] and adds: 'In the nineteenth century it was absolutely essential to base the credit structure on money with intrinsic value . . . Gold had played a historical role in creating the degree of confidence necessary for building up an extensive credit structure'.[56] Ferdinand's parents have no gold and they refuse to participate in the credit system; therefore, they lose their credibility and their place in the modern world and cease to have any lever on time. Furthermore, Einzig's reference to a golden age is useful for an understanding of Céline's ambiguous attitude to the modern, post-war world and the era which preceeded it: the world before 1914 was the Golden Age, in that it was not a world dominated by Ford, but it was a Golden Age from which Céline and his class were excluded because they had no gold and no credit. From this intuition stems not merely the highly specific pessimism of Céline's inter-war writings, but also his search for scapegoats: the reiterated lament throughout *L'Ecole des cadavres* that '[les] Juifs ont pris tout l'or!', and the attacks upon England as the centre of the world's gold markets. At the same time, Céline is careful to introduce gold itself into the novel, in the same way that Zola introduces it into *L'Assommoir*, both in the form of the broach, the *Çakya-Mouni*, and also in the form of the reiterated phoneme *or* in *Mort, Nora, Gwendor*, and in the Germanicised *Krogold*.

With Krogold, however, and later with Gorloge, the two poles of the title *Mort à crédit* are brought together. Both Krogold and Gorloge contain within their names the concepts of gold and time, just as one of the well-known variations of the *Image d'Epinal*, *Crédit est mort*, was the *Horloge du crédit*, with its picture of a clock-tower set at eleven o'clock and the legend:

Mauvais payeurs qui entrez céans, remarquez bien ce cadran.
Quand l'aiguille marquera midi, on vous donnera à crédit.[57]

Krogold is composed of *Kronos* and *Gold*, Gorloge of *gorger, or*

55. Paul Einzig, *The Destiny of Gold*, London, Macmillan, 1972, p. 6.
56. Ibid., p. 7.
57. Jean-Marie Dumart, *La Vie et l'oeuvre de Jean-Charles Pellerin*, Epinal, Imagerie Pellerin, 1956, Plate X.

and *horloge*, and, if it is recalled that Kronos, as Saturn, devoured his young, both names constitute a dual threat to Ferdinand and his family: with no gold, with no intrinsic value, they are deprived of credibility, are cut off from time since, literally they have no future, having no name, and, in the course of the novel, are gobbled up. It is bitterly fitting that their defeat should be signified by the fact that, after the theft of the *Çakya-Mouni*, in which Ferdinand's word is totally ignored, the family should, for the first time in its life, enter the world of credit by being forced to repay Gorloge in instalments. It is, furthermore, fitting that Ferdinand's family should fall foul of the combination of money and time, for it is precisely here that there begins a certain strain of anti-Semitism centred on the traditional hatred of usury. As Jacques le Goff points out, in an article on attacks on medieval merchants: 'Au premier rang de ces griefs faits aux marchands, figure le reproche que leur gain suppose une hypothèque sur le temps qui n'appartient qu'à Dieu',[58] and he goes on to quote from Guillaume d'Auxerre: 'L'usurier agit contre la loi naturelle universelle, car il vend le temps, qui est commun à toutes les créatures'.[59] It is from this conflict between a 'Temps du Marchand' and a 'Temps de L'Eglise'[60] that stems, not only an embryonic credit system and attempts to organise work and time along more rational, pre-Taylorian lines, but also apocalyptic, millenarian resistance to such innovations. Thus, like his denunciation of the Exposition, Auguste's anti-Semitism has its profound roots in his victimisation at the hands of a financial exploitation of time.

Céline thus portrays the parents of Ferdinand, and Ferdinand himself, as the victims of a society in a state of change, a society in which they have no concrete role and in which even their rhetoric becomes as embarrasing as their over-grandiose names. Denied financial weight and a future in a rapidly changing French society, their credibility is seriously eroded, to the extent that, even though they speak the truth, no-one believes a word they say. Clémence's criticism of Madame Héronde appears increasingly naive in the course of the novel: to have a *parole*, it is not enough simply to speak the truth and keep one's promises, it is necessary that one's good faith and credibility be recognised as such. Yet Ferdinand's version of events in the episodes concerning 'le petit André' and the theft of the *Çakya-Mouni* are not believed, even though the reader

58. Jacques Le Goff, 'Au Moyen Age, Temps de l'Eglise et Temps du Marchand', *Annales*, 15, 1960, p. 417.
59. Ibid.
60. Ibid., p. 418.

knows them to be true, and Auguste's 'conscience irréprochable' and 'parfaite probité' (MC, 763) are irrelevant when set against the attacks and lies of the *jeunes rédacteurs* in the offices of *La Coccinelle*. Céline depicts a relativist society in which money and position determine credibility, and not absolute truth. It is a recognition which Auguste himself implicitly makes in his correspondence with his son: as letter after letter goes unanswered from Ferdinand in England, Auguste apparently perceives the fragility of mere language: in order to elicit a response, he abandons the formal letter form for the telegram, which not only embodies the telegraphic stylistic subversion so dear to Céline's literary theory, but costs more: if mere words are inadequate, words supported by money constitute a different value.

In a sense, Courtial des Pereires is a victim of the same syndrome as that which destroys Clémence and Auguste. They subscribe to a system of values contained in the formula *Crédit est mort* which, far from helping them maintain their position in society, renders them redundant. Courtial, in spite of his change of name, is a victim of a process which successfully eradicates him by the end of the novel. On one level, this publicist, follower of Flammarion, inventor and charlatan, by his very name encapsulates many of the financial considerations of the novel as a whole: *Courtial* derives from *courtier*, a banker, a money-dealer; *des Pereires* is borrowed from the two brothers, Isaac and Emile Pereire, 'les meilleurs représentants du dynamisme Saint-Simonien au service de l'économie impériale',[61] who founded the Crédit Mobilier under the Second Empire and left their name to the Porte Pereire, near the narrator's clinic at the Fondation Linauty (MC, 516). Courtial, therefore, born himself in 1852 (MC, 1050), at the beginning of the Second Empire, by choosing a name which links, through a pseudo-aristocratic *particule*, a money-dealer with a family of financial adventurers under Napoleon III, seems to embody precisely those forces of high capitalism to which Ferdinand's own family are so vulnerable. Similarly, the two competitions he organises, as editor of the *Génitron*, one for a perpetual-motion machine and the other for a device to lift gold from the sea-bed, reflect yet again the two poles of the novel, *mort* and *crédit*. The problem is, however, that Courtial, like Ferdinand's parents, has too great a faith in words unsupported by financial credit. It is not enough to have chosen the name of a family of financial grandees of the Second Empire (who, incidentally, went bankrupt themselves after the crash of the Crédit

61. Palmade, *Capitalisme et capitalistes français au XIXe siècle*, p. 138.

Mobilier); it is also necessary to have the same positive position at the head of the financial community, and it is this which Courtial so glaringly lacks. Indeed, his major positive quality is his ability with words which keeps him half-way between the populariser and the confidence-trickster, half-way between Flammarion and Stavisky. Words, however, are not enough to keep the creditors at bay, nor to transform a parody of a Saint-Simonian community into a success, nor even to keep the antiquated *Zélé* in the air. When the realities of money and time finally intrude, words are revealed as deceptive allies: Courtial shoots himself in the mouth and falls in the figure of the last letter, Z (MC, 1041).

Faced with the operation of time and money, which in rapid succession wipes out his own parents, the Merrywins' Meanwell College and Courtial des Pereires, Ferdinand opts for a rapid dissociation from the values of Auguste and Clémence which delude them and contribute directly to their decline. This takes the form, on the part of the mature narrator, of a progressive demolition of the values of the 1900 petit-bourgeois world. Education, since the *Loi Ferry* of 1882 the ostensible guarantee of upward mobility for all, is portrayed as a cruel deception: the pupils learn nothing and, at the *Certificat* examination, '[tout] le monde était reçu!' (MC, 633). There is no attempt to make the *Certificat* into a meaningful qualification for the whole of French society. Rather, it acts as a bastion, protecting the real preserve of the bourgeoisie, the *lycée*, by giving to the petite bourgeoisie the illusion of education. In the same way, Ferdinand's parents' devotion to the work ethic is the result of a similar delusion: however hard they work, they nevertheless decline. Ferdinand's own efforts for Berlope and Gorloge are easily destroyed by lies, to the extent that, at the end of the novel, Edouard's print of *L'Angélus* is no more than a bitter caricature of what has preceeded. Small wonder, then, that the child Ferdinand should prefer to the life of work the ludic activities of a Courtial and that the mature narrator should comment: 'J'aime mieux raconter des histoires' (MC, 512). This process is accompanied fittingly, by an increasing scepticism about language itself, in which silence appears as the only way of avoiding the delusions inherent in the rhetoric of Courtial and Ferdinand's parents. This 'autism' achieves a specifically economic significance with the journey to Meanwell College: Ferdinand has been sent there, through the good offices of Edouard, to learn English in order to exchange that knowledge for money. It is, in the eyes of Auguste and Clémence, a straightforward commercial project, and Ferdinand's refusal to speak and learn English is not merely the culmination of his rejection of the entire education process, but also an act of conscious economic sabotage.

This sabotage, this rebellion against the tyranny of gold and credit, reaches its highest point on Ferdinand's return from England, when he is sent out to buy food for the family dinner. Having bought his father's favourite ham, a lettuce and *coeurs à la crème*, instead of going straight home, he wanders into the Tuileries, the scene of two previous episodes of delirium and the setting of the Exposition, and, amongst the crowd, casually divests himself of his purchases in exchange for wine: 'J'échange la tranche de jambon pour un "kil" de rouge tout cru!' (MC, 815). Two things of crucial importance occur in this episode. In the first place, Ferdinand goes consciously against all his family's petit-bourgeois pretentions by fraternising with the *peuple*, that crowd from which the petite bourgeoisie, in France or England, strove to distinguish itself by the maintenance of the narrowest but the most important of lines; Ferdinand even imports a *style peuple* into his languange. Secondly, that social *déclassement* is accompanied by an act of economic regression: by bartering the ham for wine, by sharing the lettuce, Ferdinand returns, for a privileged moment, to a primitive era of *troc* which is implicitly incompatible with the economic world in which his parents are sinking. In this way, the phonetic emphasis of the narrator's name, *Ferdinand*, conveys within itself an objection to the gold-dominated modern economy.

Mort à crédit, therefore, may be read as the chronicle of the decline of a particular social class, centered on the Exposition of 1900, in which the detailed workings of the modern economy are part of the very structure of the novel. The erosion of Ferdinand's parents, the disappearance of his class, are the result of a progressive loss of credibility brought about by their isolation from the operation of the system of credit. The final example, though, the scene of exchange in the Tuileries, is not merely of economic or social significance: it preceeds the violent quarrel between Ferdinand and Auguste which culminates in the attack with the typewriter. This pivotal scene in the narrator's reminiscences, coupled with the repetitive scenes of delirium, is sufficient to remind the reader that the crisis of the petit-bourgeois family depicted in the novel cannot be undergone without deep psychological scars and that, as a historical chronicle, the novel is complete in providing in addition an informed psychological, even psychoanalytical perspective.

'La Clémence d'Auguste'

It is unfortunate that, whilst the presence of psychological components in Céline's fiction and, especially, in *Mort à crédit*, has been noted, the subject has been by no means as well explored as might have been expected. Henri Godard, in his excellent analysis of the cultural background to the novel, documents Céline's interest, in 1933, in Freud and the Vienna school of psychoanalysis,[62] but is reluctant to apply this evidence to a reading of *Mort à crédit*, preferring instead to discuss Céline's debt to Léon Daudet's *Le Rêve éveillé* of 1926.[63] Unfortunately, whilst this work may have confirmed Céline in a certain mysticism, it offers very little in the way of an alternative to a psychoanalytical reading of the novel and is more usefully seen simply as an additional document. At the same time, when the psychological elements of Céline's fiction have been explored, often by practising psychologists, there has been an unhelpful tendency to eliminate the literary status of the texts themselves by eradicating any distinction between narrator and author. This approach, shown at its clearest by Willy Szafran, who argues: 'Le drame de Céline réside précisément dans le fait qu'il y a une abolition presque totale de la distance entre l'homme et son oeuvre',[64] leads to a situation in which not only is the text viewed as transparent autobiography, but even some of the most elemental precautions of Freudian psychoanalysis, such as the recognition of screen-memories, are ignored.

In *Mort à crédit*, however, the psychological problems are surely nothing less than obvious. Through the two scenes of delirium at the end of the Tuileries, Céline is deploying a psychologically disordered mature narrator who, throughout the bulk of the novel, recalls a disordered childhood within a psychologically disturbed family, and, by situating his disordered child protagonist within a family context, Céline is doing no more than pointing the reader in the same direction as that taken later by psychiatrists such as Maud Manoni and R.D. Laing.[65] Indeed, by concentrating upon the forces

62. *Romans* I, ed. Henri Godard, Paris, Gallimard, coll. 'La Pléiade', 1981, pp. 1387–9.

63. Ibid., pp. 1389–90.

64. Willi Szafran, *Louis-Ferdinand Céline. Essai psychologique*, Brussels, Editions de l'Université de Bruxelles, coll. 'Arguments et documents', 1976, p. 196.

65. Maud Manoni writes, 'As analysts, we find ourselves grappling with the history of a family', in *The Child, his 'Illness' and the Others*, Harmondsworth, Penguin, 1973, p. 60, and R.D. Laing makes the same point in *The Divided Self*, Harmondsworth, Penguin, 1965, through the case-histories of James (Chapter 6) and Julie (Chapter 11).

at work within the narrator's family itself, in particular the tension between Ferdinand and Auguste, the reader is able, not only to move closer to the very centre of the novel, but to do so through an understanding of gold and credit. In other words, symbolically as well as socially, the family's economic vulnerability is connected intimately to its neurotic state. Thus, in his study, *Freud, Marx: Economie et symbolique*, Jean-Joseph Goux explores the deep connection between Marx's economic theory and Freud's theory of the Unconscious, and develops this on a symbolic level in a chapter entitled: 'Numismatiques: L'Or, Le Père, Le Phallus, Le Monarque et La Langue. (Essai de numismatique théorique)'. He begins:

> A présent, le monde des marchandises *converge* vers cette forme unique (L'OR historiquement), se rapporte unanimement à cet 'équivalent universel' qui fonctionne, de par ce 'monopole social' comme monnaie; le monde multiforme des marchandises se trouve centré et centralisé vers ce qui, à chacune des marchandises, donne du prix et *fixe* un prix.
> Telles sont les péripéties de la forme de valeur, et l'issue monétaire de la crise. Or qu'en est-il dans le régistre des comptes du rapport à l'autre (du rapport entre sujets), sinon que le PERE est choisi à un certain moment du dévelopement du moi pour résoudre une situation conflictuelle,[66]

and in order to construct an 'axe de la *métaphore paternelle* (monnaie, phallus, langue, monarque)'.[67] In other words, the monopoly of gold as an 'équivalent universel' in the financial world is reflected by that of the monarch in politics, the phallus in sexuality and the father in the family. All the elements of *Mort à crédit* are now present in this metaphor, yet these are positive images from which Ferdinand's family are either excluded or in which they are deformed. On gold, Goux quotes from Marx: 'la société "salue dans l'or l'incarnation éblouissant du principe de la vie"':[68] the family are excluded from gold and hence condemned to a world of living death. At the same time, Auguste, with his imperial name, combines the role of father and monarch, with crippling effects upon his son.

These effects take the form of two major psychological symptoms, that of constant excretion and that of silence. As regards the former, it is recurrent throughout Ferdinand's childhood up to his departure for England and is clearly abnormal, and not to be confused at all with a Rabelasian celebration of excrement as 'la

66. Jean-Joseph Goux, *Freud, Marx. Economie et symbolique*, Paris, Le Seuil, 1973, p. 61.
67. Ibid., p. 65.
68. Ibid., p. 73.

matière joyeuse'.[69] In classic psychoanalytical terms, excrement is assimilated to gold, but, as Jean-Joseph Goux warns, it may be used in both a positive and negative sense. Positively, it may be seen as a present for the father, a means of gaining the father's attention, and therefore part of the absolute system of 'équivalents universels'. At the same time, Freud also sees it as a sympton of regression: 'L'or donné *par le diable* à ses victimes se transforme immanquablement en excrément'.[70] In the case of the child Ferdinand in *Mort à crédit*, the process is clearly negative: if the child's excrement is a symbol of gold in the form of a present to the father, the present is brutally rejected by Auguste who, on each occasion, flies into an uncontrollable rage. If the implicit unconscious aim has been to gain the father's attention, even love, it has manifestly failed, with permanent psychological damage to the narrator.

That damage is translated by an abnormal retreat into silence, a retreat which has clear psychological, if not specifically schizoid, connotations. Thus, Erik H. Erikson, discussing one case of schizophrenia, in which '[meaning] is quickly replaced by parrotlike repetition of stereotyped phrases, accompanied by guttural sounds of despair',[71] notes his child-patient's reaction to constant criticism by his nurse for his bodily smell: 'Ah, baby, you stink!', as 'the child had turned against speech',[72] and he concludes, of schizophrenic children in general: 'They have a defective screening system between the inner and outer world; their sensory contacts fail to master the overpowering impressions as well as the disturbing impulses which intrude themselves upon consciousness. They therefore experience their own organs of contact and communication as enemies, as potential intruders into a self which has withdrawn "under the skin"'.[73] Whilst R.D. Laing comments: 'In a world full of danger, to be a potentially seeable object is to be constantly exposed to danger. Self-consciousness, then, may be the apprehensive awareness of oneself as potentially exposed to danger by the single fact of being visible to others. The obvious defence against such a danger is to make oneself invisible in one way or another",[74] concluding: 'Being visible is therefore a basic biological

69. See Mikhail Bakhtine, quoted in Yannik Mancel, 'De la Sémiotique textuelle à la théorie du "roman": Céline', *Dialectiques*, 8, 1975, pp. 47–8.

70. Goux, *Freud, Marx. Economie et symbolique*, p. 75.

71. Erik H. Erikson, *Childhood and Society*, Harmondsworth, Penguin, 1965, p. 190.

72. Ibid., p. 192.

73. Ibid.

74. Laing, *The Divided Self*, p. 109.

risk; being invisible is a basic biological defence'.[75] In the case of the young Ferdinand, self-defence takes the form of a retreat into an almost autistic silence and of a quest for invisibility, culminating in the final scene of the novel, in which he is literally buried under his uncle's coats:

C'est pas les pardessus qui manquent! . . .
— Non mon oncle (MC, 1304).

The danger against which these procedures are defence mechanisms takes two forms: it is the entire process of decline and vulnerability experienced by Ferdinand's class; more narrowly, it is his own family, particularly his father, who continually goad him into conforming to their suicidal social ethic. Yet, Ferdinand's response is, again, ambiguous. On one level, his retreat into silence is the exact negation of Auguste's hysterical verbiage; at the same time, the search for invisibility unites, rather than divides, father and son: when life becomes too unbearable, Auguste, like Courtial, hides in the *cave*, much as Ferdinand will hide at the end under Edouard's *pardessus*. Finally, if Ferdinand's attempt at self-defence most often takes the firm of a refusal to communicate, it neatly rejoins the numismatic concerns of the novel: 'silence est or'.

In the context of the child Ferdinand's concern with *caca* and silence and invisibility, it is important to consider the novel's repetitive structure, which similarly possesses a psychological significance. It is unfortunate, yet again, that Albert Chesneau did not see the application of Maurron's theory of 'fantaisie à répétions' to *Mort à crédit*, where there is first of all the helpless repetition of the father's imprecations against his enemies, but also, more importantly, the way in which, for the child Ferdinand, each episode repeats and accentuates the same unalterable disaster. Given the role of the mature narrator in his selective recall of these repetitive failures, it becomes clear that they lead the way still further to the psychological core of the novel. Examining the phenomenon of repetition, Freud originally considered it as a positive attempt on the part of the child to master his surroundings: the 'fort da!' syndrome. In his later work, however, with which Céline appears particularly familiar, he was less optimistic. As A. Hesnard writes:

De plus, Freud fait faire à la conception moderne de l'homme — entrevue par Kierkegaard — un pas decisif en ravissant à l'agent humain, identifié à

75. Ibid., p. 110.

la conscience, la nécessité incluse dans la contrainte de répétition (*Wiederholungszwang*). Cette répétition étant symbolique, il s'avére que l'ordre du symbole ne peut plus être conçu comme constitué par l'homme, mais bien par comme le constituant. Freud, qui adopte, en les précisant, les notions opposées de répétition et de rémémoration (revivis- cence fidèle d'événements évoqués) et d'activité inconsciente, est, de plus, contraint d'évoquer dans son expérience un élément qui gouverne l'au-delà de la vie, qu'il appelle l'*instinct de mort*.[76]

Mort à crédit, therefore, may be seen, through repetition, as explor- ing that Freudian notion of the death instinct which interests Céline so much in the 'Hommage à Zola'; like *Voyage au bout de la nuit*, 'il va de la vie à la mort' and it is helped on its way by the very repetitive nature of credit itself in the payment of installments.

Through the repetitive process, in the mature narrator's remi- niscences, of the principles of *caca* and *silence*, both of which are connected to gold, it becomes increasingly clear that, on one level at least, *Mort à crédit* can be read as the account of a childhood neurosis and one, moreover, which is centered on the father Au- guste: if *caca* and *silence* both lead to gold, they lead also, following Goux's schema, to the father and monarch, combined in the name and persona of Auguste himself. And this centrality of the father- monarch is unmistakably underlined by the prominence given in the novel to the almost caricaturally Oedipal scene of the assault on Auguste by Ferdinand with the *machine à écrire*. What is significant about this scene is, firstly, the fact that it is the ultimate rebellion of Ferdinand's quest for silence against his father's speech: the assault is directed against Auguste's mouth, to the extent that the death of Courtial, who shoots himself in the mouth, constitutes a fantasised transposition: 'Je vais lui écraser la trappe! . . . Je veux plus qu'il cause!' (MC, 822), and that, secondly, it is part of a process by which Ferdinand searches throughout the novel for a substitute father: Peter Merrywin, Courtial and the constantly available Edouard. Yet in this respect, Céline's portrayal is complicated. If Ferdinand is searching for a substitute father-figure, the assault on Auguste is not Oedipal, in that it is a protest at neglect and rejection, a cry for concern. At the same time, at Meanwell College and with Courtial, the relationships are more complex: Ferdinand supplants Peter Merrywin to the extent that, when he walks around the grounds of Meanwell with Nora and Jonkind, it is he who is the *père de famille* and Nora his wife, a process which culminates in the real or fantasised scene in which Nora, just before her suicide,

76. A. Hesnard, *De Freud à Lacan*, Paris, Les Editions E.S.F., 1970, p. 89.

comes to his bed; similarly, whilst on one level Courtial is Ferdinand's employer, and forty years his senior, both he and Irène are so innocent that it is the narrator who fulfils a parental role, and discovers a parental language to go with it, by organising them and protecting them as much as he is able. In both cases, however, the Oedipal motivation is just beneath the screen, with Nora as the transposition of Clemence and Merrywin and Courtial as transpositions of Auguste. It is in Courtial that the clearest reflection of the father takes place, with Ferdinand able to show to the inventor the affection he is unable to demonstrate openly to Auguste, yet with Courtial's death constituting the fantasised revenge on his own father.

If the main bulk of *Mort à crédit* is made up of the account of the career of a disturbed child and adolescent, whose disturbance arises principally from an ambigous love–hate relationship with his father, it is essential to recall that the novel is also the product of a disturbed mature narrator — that, indeed, the selected reminiscences form part of the neurosis of the present. Thus, the delirium of the mature Ferdinand following the loss of his manuscript and centred on the Place de la Concorde is in fact the repetition of the original delirium following the hallucination of *la grande cliente*. It is essential to see that the precise causes of this later delirium are to be found in the experiences of Ferdinand's parents recounted as the novel progresses: the loss of the manuscript by Madame Vitruve, Ferdinand's typist, hence his employee, merely repeats the recurrent fear of his mother at being swindled by Madame Héronde: 'Sa terreur, maman, c'était les voleuses'; the lies told about Ferdinand in the *quartier* by Mireille, whilst also introducing at an early stage the notion of credibility, are an exact reflection of those told against Auguste by his young rivals. In other words, the paranoia of the mature narrator is the result of the assumption of the fears and insecurities of his parents. At the same time, this delirium of the mature narrator has two stages: the first, unleashed by Mireille, and a second provoked by Ferdinand's mother when he is convalescing and which leads into the past: 'Le siècle dernier, je peux en parler, je l'ai vu finir . . .'. Significantly, the second wave of delirium is provoked by references to the father:

> Je chie dans mon pyjama! La combinaison trempée . . . Ça va terriblement mal! Je vais débloquer sur la Bastille. 'Ah! si ton père etait là!' . . . J'entends ces mots . . . Je m'embrase! C'est encore elle! Je me retourne! Je traite mon père comme du pourri! . . . Je m'époumone! . . . 'Y avait pas un pire dégueulasse dans tout l'Univers! de Dufayel à Capricorne! . . .' (MC, 543).

The reminiscences which constitute the novel, therefore, like the memories which make up *A la Recherche du temps perdu*, are, in *Mort à crédit*, introduced through a delirium induced by a repetition of the pattern: *caca* — paternal outrage — filial insult. It is the father who constitutes the passage to the past, through a repetition of his son's guilt. Céline's comment to Robert Poulet on *Mort à crédit*, that it is 'le drame de la mauvaise conscience',[77] takes on a more specific meaning when the role of the father is fully explored.

At the same time, the role of excrement which, far from constituting a 'present' for Auguste, was the cause of dissention between father and son, remains an important, if subtle feature for the mature narrator, infecting his professional life. He is careful to establish himself at the beginning of the novel as a writer, not merely of legends, but also of *Voyage au bout de la nuit*. In his discussion of 'la fonction de dévalorisation (sexuel et/ou idéologique) qu'occupe l'excrémentiel dans le texte célinien',[78] Yannik Mancel recalls a comment in *L'Eglise*: 'Faire dans sa culotte, voyez-vous, c'est le commencement du génie' (E, 85). More subtly, the excremential role is present, not merely in Ferdinand's vocation as a writer, but also in his profession of medicine, and in such that a way that it incorporates the element of gold and constitutes a further link between child-protagonist and mature narrator. This concerns Gorloge's golden brooch, the *Çakya Mouni*. The word is deliberately spelt in order to maintain echoes of *caca*: the *Çakya Mouni* is therefore, of itself, a link between gold and excrement. It is much more, however: the *Sakya Muni* was the incarnation of the Buddha in his role as physician, which leads the reader back to Ferdinand's opening statement: 'Je n'ai pas toujours pratiqué la médecine, cette merde' (MC, 511). The excremential symbolism, therefore, is essential to the mature narrator's function as a writer and as a doctor, and poses clearly the relationship between the adolescent and the mature narrator with Auguste: the 'present', which alone confers value upon the giver, be it excrement, medicine or literature, is refused.

It is in this context that the 'Légende du roi Krogold' takes on a new significance. Krogold (Kronos-gold) is the nexus of time and money within the novel; he is the absolute monarch; in his connotations of Kronos–Saturn, he is the devourer of his own children. It is by no means stretching a reading of the novel to see the narrator's Krogold legend as not merely the repetition of the story

---

77. Robert Poulet, *Entretiens familiers avec Louis-Ferdinand Céline*, p. 75.
78. Mancel, 'De la sémiotique textuelle à la théorie du "roman"', p. 52.

he learned and recounted when a child, a petit-bourgeois version of Proust's use of George Sand, but also as the transposition of his own relationship with his father, particularly since he takes care to note that: 'Papa aussi portait une montre, mais en or lui, un chronomètre ... Il a compté dessus toutes les secondes jusqu'à la fin ... La grande aiguille, ça le fascinait, celle qui court vite. Il bougeait plus à le regarder pendant des heures ...' (MC, 635). Yet the legend of Krogold is the story of a betrayal, by Gwendor, and of an ineluctable punishment of death: 'Il n'est pas fainéant Krogold ... Il fait sa justice lui-même ... Gwendor a trahi ... La mort arrive sur Gwendor et va terminer son boulot ...'(MC, 522).

From this identification of Krogold with Auguste, two interlinking responses are possible for the adolescent Ferdinand as for the mature narrator, and they take the form, already observed, of attraction and repulsion. The affectionate description of Auguste in Dieppe and of his painting of the roofs of Paris as if they were seen from a ship goes hand in hand with the hatred which culminates in the assault with the typewriter and in the dream of the death of the father in the transposed form of Courtial. At the same time, in a covert way, the literary devices of the mature Ferdinand may be seen as attempts to placate and threaten the departed father at one and the same time. The obvious similarity of names between Gustin and Auguste, of which the former is a contraction, leads the reader to wonder whether the recitation of the Krogold legend is not more directed at the father than at the cousin, whether it may not constitute a final attempt to capture Auguste's attention and affection: to obtain, finally, the 'clémence d'Auguste'. If it is, it fails, since Gustin goes to sleep. Yet the search for affection veers quickly to the opposite: the search to wound. The child Ferdinand hits his father with a *machine à écrire*: the mature, but equally disturbed narrator will assault his father's memory, first of all in verbal insult to the mother, but then with a massive manuscript of reminiscences.

What makes the alternating relationship so tense, however, is that there is more than a little identification with Auguste on the part of the narrator. It is this which makes the encounter with the 'cliente de la Place des Ternes', immediately transposed into 'la grande cliente', so genuinely traumatic: it is a joint sexual humiliation for father and son which binds them very closely together. It is this also which adds significance to the way in which Ferdinand, as narrator of *Bagatelles pour un massacre*, with Gustin again as interlocutor, employs the same irrational exaggeration as that seen in Auguste's outbursts against the forces by which he feels threatened. It is this, finally, which suggests a further meaning of the very first words of the novel: 'Nous voici encore seuls' (MC, 511). It is not just the reunification of the mature Ferdinand with his adolescent counterpart, nor that between the novelist, his characters, his manuscript and, ultimately, his reader. In a sense, it is a coming together of the narrator and the one reader who can confer meaning on the novel, the absent Auguste.

It is interesting that, according to Henri Godard, the one Freud essay in which Céline showed particular interest in 1933 was 'Mourning and Melancolia', of 1915.[79] Not only does this essay lie at the origins of two roughly contemporaneous works, Louis Guilloux's *Le Sang noir* of 1935 and Sartre's *La Nausée*, of 1938,[80] but it helps to draw together the psychological components of *Mort à crédit*. In his essay, Freud distinguishes between mourning and melancholia on the grounds that, whereas the former is the healthy recognition of the definitive disappearance of a love-object, melancholia is the unhealthy inability to accept that reality, a failure which leads to lassitude, paralysis of the will and, often, suicide. Céline's novel does not record the death of Auguste, that death of the father which, for Jean-Joseph Goux, can alone transform into a fetish along with gold,[81] but it does record the death of Courtial. That death leads to breakdown, vomiting, the total paralysis of will which is translated into a search for ultimate authority in the *Régiment* and the return to the womb in Edouard's *pardessus*. For the mature narrator, this paralysis has not resolved itself and the lassitude still persists: 'Tout cela est si lent, si lourd, si triste' (MC, 511). The *facteur* is the emissary of death for both Courtial and the concierge, but for the mature narrator refuge is to be sought, not in the authority or protection of others, but in the ultimate non-existence to which the child Ferdinand has been tending throughout the novel: 'J'aime mieux raconter des histoires. J'en raconterai de telles qu'ils reviendront, exprès, pour me tuer, des quatre coins du monde. Alors ce sera fini et je serai bien content' (MC, 512). Once again, the narrator of Céline's fiction conjurs up his ghosts, but this time as a specific means of self-destruction. Deprived of the Proustian concept of the transcendence of art, Céline can believe only in its ultimately auto-destructive qualities.

Mort à crédit is arguably Céline's most complex novel. Quite apart

79. Romans I, ed. Godard, p. 1387.
80. See N. Hewitt, 'Looking for Annie. Sartre's *La Nausée* and the Interwar Years', *Journal of European Studies*, XII, 1982, pp. 96–112.
81. Goux, *Freud, Marx. Economie et symbolique*, p. 62.

from its stylistic and literary density, it exposes a complicated historical and psychological case history. Its significance lies primarily, however, in the way in which, after the frightened evocation in *Voyage au bout de la nuit* of the world following the First World War, it records the Golden Age of France at precisely the time when its victims were already beginning to feel their insecurity. Not only does Céline describe this is detail, through the decline of Clémence and Auguste and the real and symbolical operation of credit as the conjuncture of time and money, he also shows the psychological legacy which the child of that declining family can never shake off and which informs even his mature writing. The Exposition of 1900 leads not only to the riots of 6 February 1934, but also to the melancholia of the novel's fictional narrator. The question is, however, whether that melancholia need be definitive, whether the effects of the 1900 Exposition can ever be exorcised, and it is to this that Céline turns his attention in 1936, with his attempt at a third novel, *Casse-pipe*, which will explore Ferdinand's quest for authority in the pre-war cavalry, and with his investigation of the Soviet Union as a possible means of reversing the process begun in 1900.

[4]

Trente-six, le grand tournant

In 1974, the French film-maker Alain de Turenne produced a documentary film on the Front Populaire called *Trente-six, le grand tournant*. In it, the scriptwriter, the journalist Jean-François Revel, emphasised the way in which the Front Populaire translated a massive desire for change on the part of certain sectors of French society, but also how that apparently revolutionary break with the past was more symbolic than real and how the government's progressive policies were so limited by constraints at home and abroad that no lasting change had really taken place: Daladier, the Prime Minister at the time of the 6 February riots, returned to power with the fall of Léon Blum in 1937.

The notion of a *grand tournant* which is more apparent than real, is useful for an understanding of the events of Céline's career in the same year as the Front Populaire election, 1936. In that year, he journeyed to the Soviet Union and wrote the pamphlet which would appear the year after, *Mea culpa*. To many commentators at the time, and since, this publication constituted a political *volte face*: he was still largely considered, on the reputation of *Voyage au bout de la nuit*, a left-wing author, and *Mea culpa* appeared to mark a radical change in course and to send him off on that path which would end in collaboration during the Occupation. At the same time, his professional career as a novelist encountered difficulties when, after the controversy surrounding the publication of *Mort à crédit*, that novel's sequel, *Casse-pipe*, seemed to run out of steam. Even though Henri Godard, in his Pléiade edition of Céline's fiction between *Mort à crédit* and the German trilogy, shows that Céline did indeed, as he claimed, actually produce a bulky manuscript, far longer than the fragments which are now available, Céline undoubtedly ran into trouble with the work and felt unable to complete it. Thus, the novel's composition, begun in the autumn of

1936, was definitively halted in May or June 1937, even though he had the manuscript formally typed up in November of that year.[1] The year 1936 was marked, therefore, for Céline, by an unpopular political decision, which appeared to many a radical change of course, and by difficulties with his new novel. It could be argued that the result of this apparent ideological shift and failure in the genre of fiction is the extended excursion into polemic, which begins with *Mea culpa* and continues through the three anti-Semitic pamphlets, in the same way that the lack of success of the plays of the 1920s, *Progrès* and *L'Eglise*, turn Céline towards the medical polemic and the novel form itself.

Crucial as these events are, however, they should not serve to disguise the profound continuity in Céline's work, which is based upon an ambiguous juxtaposition of the modern world of the inter-war years and the world of the *belle époque*, a juxtaposition which is seen to operate clearly in the two major pieces of Céline's writing of the 1936–7 transition period, the evocation of the enclosed world of the pre-1914 cavalry in *Casse-pipe*, and the acerbic denunciation of Soviet Fordism in *Mea culpa*. From the exploration of these two works, united in their nostalgic distaste for the past and their fear of the present, the reader is in a better position to evaluate and understand the work which follows: the anti-Semitic pamphlets and the final affectionate look back at the world which vanished in 1918, in the two volumes of *Guignol's Band*.

Casse-pipe

At the end of her excellent analysis of the theatrical properties of the first chapter of *Casse-pipe*, Christine Sautermeister comments on the almost insuperable difficulties presented to the critic by the fragmentary nature of the work.[2] Indeed, the reader is faced with the task of coordinating four different fragments of the novel, all that remains of the once considerable manuscript: the major fragment, published in 1949 by Frédéric Chambriaud, dealing with the

1. For all these details on the state of the manuscript I am grateful to Henri Godard.
2. Christine Sautermeister, 'Lecture théâtrale et cinématographique de *Casse-pipe*' (BLFC 3, 221). For other important studies of the novel, see Christine Sautermeister, 'Quelques traits caractéristiques du comique de Céline à partir de *Casse-pipe*' (BLFC 1, 335–52), Aart van Zoest, 'Une Analyse sémiotique de *Casse-pipe* (1)' (BLFC 8, 75–82)) Michèle Out-Breut, 'Une Analyse sémiotique de *Casse-pipe* (II)' (BLFC 8, 83–94); and the remarkable study by Jean-Pierre Richard, 'Casque-pipe', *Littérature*, 29, 1978, pp. 3–17.

first night of the young *engagé* Ferdinand with the *17e Régiment des Cuirassiers Lourds*; the second, published in Robert Poulet's *Entretiens familiers avec Louis-Ferdinand Céline* of 1958, and describing the young volunteer's first days of training as a cavalryman; the third episode, published by Dominique de Roux in the *Cahiers de l'Herne*, and coming much later in the novel, when Ferdinand is no longer an *engagé*, a *bleu*, but has been promoted to the rank of brigadier and is participating in the 1913 *Quatorze juillet* parade in Paris; and the final fragment, published along with the third, which deals very briefly with Ferdinand's behaviour towards his men now that he has been promoted. It is unfortunate, despite its undoubted fascination, that the first and longest fragment should have so monopolised critical attention, to the extent that it alone is associated with the title of the novel as a whole. In the first place, this monopoly has been allowed to overshadow the importance of the later fragments and, secondly, and more crucially, it has disguised the fact that, even in its highly fragmentary form, the work as a whole follows an undoubted progression, which goes far beyond the narrator's first night in the *caserne*.

At the same time, it is important to emphasise the contrived, fictive nature of *Casse-pipe*, which situates the novel firmly amongst the preoccupations of *Voyage au bout de la nuit* and *Mort à crédit* and demarcates it from autobiography. Thus, in *Casse-pipe*, the narrator is using the fictional form to evoke the brutality and charm of the pre-war cavalry, with exactly the same mixture of abhorrence and nostalgia as that which informs the evocation of the artisanal petite bourgeoisie in *Mort à crédit*. It is for this reason that the mannered and adolescent posturing of the *Carnets du cuirassier Destouches* are of little interest for a reading of *Casse-pipe* which, like the preceeding novels, places an inter-war years narrator in an ambiguous relationship with his own present and his own past. Similarly, the fictive credentials of *Casse-pipe* are established by the way in which, again, like the earlier novels, it self-consciously takes its place in a literary tradition: this time it is the nineteenth-century tradition of the anti-militarist novel. Christine Sautermeister[3] and other critics draw attention to Céline's debt to Courteline's *Les Gaîtés de l'escadron*, Jean Drault's *Soldat Chapuzot*, Charles Leroy's *Le Colonel Ramollot*, Lucien Descaves' *Sous-Offs* and, especially, Abel Hermant's *Le Cavalier Miserey*, which so outraged military circles when it was published in 1887 that, according to one com-

---

3. Christine Sautermeister, 'Lecture théâtrale et cinématographique de *Casse-pipe*', p. 214.

mentator, the Colonel of the *12e Chasseurs* the Duc de Chartres, publicly burnt it.[4] To this list could be added not only novels of the turn of the century, such as Georges Darien's *Biribi*, but also earlier works, notably Vigny's *Servitude et grandeur militaires*, Stendhal's *Lucien Leuwen* and Erckmann-Chatrian's *Histoire d'un conscrit de 1812*. Yet, in contrast to the latter work, and unlike a great deal of French military fiction, Céline's novel chooses to deal with an *engagé* and not a *conscrit* and it is in this fact that is to be found its singular ambiguity.

Christine Sautermeister concludes her analysis of the first fragment of *Casse-pipe* with the comment: '*Casse-pipe* dans son premier chapitre représente, grâce à un heureux concours de circonstances, la réussite d'un spectacle total',[5] thus underlining the extraordinary unity and completeness, as well as the theatricality, of the major fragment of the novel. This unity is established by the unwavering concentration of the narrator on the disorientation and isolation of the recruit Ferdinand during his first night as a *bleu*. Thus, the conventional, expected, cry from the gate, a gate which in its grotesqueness acts as a barrier and as the bars of a prison, 'Brigadier! C'est l'engagé!', is met with the unexpected response: 'Qu'il entre ce con-là!' (CP, 9), a response which is unexpected, not because of its aggressivity, but because it seeks to exclude the would-be recruit and even ridicule his pretension to join the army.[6] This alienation is conveyed primarily by the unswerving hostility of which Ferdinand is the object throughout the episode, from the brigadier Meheu, and from the entire platoon. It is signified by the fact that, whereas all the other characters, quite naturally, are in military uniform, of which the *casque* is the salient feature, Ferdinand is clothed throughout in his civilian *raglan* which, as the night progresses, bears up considerably less well than the uniforms to the intense rain and begins to shrink. Similarly, Céline is at pains to emphasise throughout that Ferdinand, along with Arcile, the guardian of the stables, is one of the rare Parisians in a regiment which is predominantly Breton. Finally, and here Céline exploits a paradox which he has already used in the *Amiral Bragueton* sequence of *Voyage au bout de la nuit*, Ferdinand is isolated and suspect precisely because he is an *engagé* and not a *conscrit*: whereas the expected response would be

---

4. See Jean Roman, *Paris 1890s*, London, Prentice Hall International, 1961, p. 59. Some doubt is cast on this story by the fact that the Duc de Chartres retired from command of the *12e Chasseurs* in 1883.

5. Christine Sautermeister, 'Lecture théâtrale et cinématographique de *Casse-pipe*', p. 221.

6. See Aart van Zoest, 'Une analyse sémiotique de *Casse-pipe* (1)', p. 77.

to welcome the volunteer and to distrust the conscript, in the same way that the paying passenger would normally be accorded greater respect than the employee with a free ticket, Céline reverses the values, so that it is conscription which is seen as natural, the only way in which any honest man would come to the Army, and volunteering which is considered a suspicious form of flight from unspoken crimes in civilian life (CP, 17). With this inversion of values which necessarily casts an ironic light on the symbolism of the Army, the novel departs radically from representations of the Army as a political or moral solution, such as that conveyed in Psichari's *L'Appel des armes*, written and set at the same time as the action of *Casse-pipe*.

This generalised hostility of which Ferdinand is the victim during his first night with his new regiment is condensed and centered on the exaggerated and instinctive hatred directed at him by the *maréchal des logis* Rancotte. What is interesting about Rancotte is the way in which he exceeds the bounds of the stereotyped Naturalist or caricatural sergeant-major: as Ferdinand himself feels, there is something uncanny about the way in which Rancotte singles him out for special distrust and persecution. At the same time, this reaction takes on a specific and significant form:

> — Mais il pue, cet ours, ma parole!
> C'etait trouvé! Il exultait!
> — Mais il cogne abominable . . .
> Ça m'étonnait comme réflexion, vu que ça tapait si infernal dans l'endroit où nous nous trouvions que c'était un terrible effort pour ne pas abandonner les choses et tout simplement défaillir. Y avait donc de la prétention.
> — Mais il va me faire dégueuler! qu'il annonce alors à tue-tête.
> Il rappelle Meheu.
> — Emmenez-moi cet ours dehors, brigadier, tout de suite! Je veux plus de ça ici! De l'air! de l'air! nom de Dieu! Il est pas possible ce sagouin! je peux plus respirer! Y a de quoi faire crever tout le poste! En l'air! en l'air! allez ouste! Emmenez-moi tout ça, Meheu! Faites-moi lui voir du quartier! (CP, 16).

By quite uncannily, and illogically, given the all-pervading stench of the cavalry stables, singling out Ferdinand because of his alleged smell, Rancotte is doing no more than continuing Auguste's favourite system of abuse to his son in *Mort à crédit*, to the extent that, if *Casse-pipe* is read as a sequel to Céline's second novel, Rancotte appears as a repetition of the persecuting father-figure from whose clutches Ferdinand is unable to escape, and who will only be exorcised by imitation and emulation, rather than by flight

or by outright rebellion. Hence, the significance, in the later fragments of *Casse-pipe* and in the anti-Semitic pamphlets, of the way in
which the narrator consciously adopts his father's irrational aggressivity. This is a reading reinforced by Jean-Pierre Richard's
theory that the *casque* is ultimately a symbol of castration,[7] and is
related to the sequence when Ferdinand and the platoon hide from
Rancotte in the mountain of horse-droppings in Arcile's stable: an
ironic reflection of the gold–excrement–father nexus observed in
Mort à crédit and a symbol of the return to the womb and the search
for non-being.

In more general terms, Ferdinand's disorientation is not merely
the result of the hostility of which he is the object, but of the
strangeness of the experience of the cavalry regiment at night.
Throughout the first fragment, Céline is at pains to exaggerate the
distortions of size and noise, culminating in the epic description of
Arcile's Augean stables, though it must be questioned whether, in
its existing form, the fragment sustains and exploits the classical
allusion as fruitfully as it might. In any case, by distorting effects of
size and sound, Céline is able to accentuate the disparity between
Ferdinand's isolation and vulnerability and his surroundings, to the
extent that he employs the same techniques as those used by Carrol
in *Alice* to create a strange blend of nightmare and *féerie*.

Once again, in order to create his dream or nightmare, Céline
reverts to procedures already employed in *Voyage au bout de la
nuit*, notably the use of night-time as a setting for the action. It is by
no means for purely formal reasons that this first fragment of
Casse-pipe, theatrical in nature, follows perfectly the classical unity
of time, as well as those of place and action, in taking place in one
single night, beginning in total darkness with Ferdinand's arrival at
the *grille* and ending with dawn breaking and the trumpet sounding
the *diane*. Ferdinand is therefore plunged into the strange, unreal
world of the cavalry barracks at night, in which Meheu's platoon of
Bretons wander aimlessly through the darkness and the rain, from
which occasionally dream-like frantic horses erupt, and which is
dominated by the fear of authority. In his evocation of this unutter-
ably lost platoon, Céline is returning to a subject which is familiar
from a reading of *Voyage au bout de la nuit*: the 'Chanson des
Gardes Suisses' itself, which begins the novel with the evocation of a
military journey through the night, and, more precisely, the episode
in which Bardamu and his cavalry comrades, having spent the day as
escort to General des Entrayes, are sent out at night to roam the

7. Jean-Pierre Richard, 'Casque-pipe'.

hostile countryside until dawn comes to restore them to comparative safety.

This general concept of *errance dans la nuit* is rendered more precise by the way in which night-time is used consistently as a barrier to vision. *Casse-pipe*, in its first and major fragment, is the story of people who can hardly see or hear. Thus, Ferdinand comments on his first meeting with Rancotte: 'Je pouvais pas lui voir bien les yeux à ce Rancotte à cause de la lampe fumeuse, un tison, et puis surtout de son képi, en avant, en éventail, une viscope extravagante' (CP, 14), and establishes a pattern, sustained throughout the fragment, by which the protagonists are almost deaf and blind and are unable to perceive and communicate clearly. Specifically, this limited vision, which affects all the characters, alters their ability to read or to understand language. Hence, on Ferdinand's arrival: 'Le Brigadier il avait du mal à ouvrir ma feuille . . . Elle lui collait entre les doigts . . . puis à lire mon nom' (CP, 11), and, when the patrol erupts into the guard-room, 'Ils ont repondu des choses que j'ai pas comprises' (CP, 12). This goes further than a new recruit's inability to understand a particular jargon: it is an affliction which affects all the characters in the episode and which places them in the confines of a genuine mystery. It is this affliction, above all, which is encapsulated in the strange search for the password, the *mot*, which dominates the entire fragment. On one level, the search for the password which will see the platoon safely through the *ronde* marks a shift in allusion from that to Hercules and the Augean stables to the myth of the labyrinth, the Minotaur and Ariadne's thread, an allusion by which Ferdinand plays the role of reluctant and unlikely Theseus. On another level, the search for the *mot* points simply to the difficulty of reading itself and to the problems inherent in decoding the text. Most important of all, however, is the enormous, tantalising fascination exerted by the lost *mot*, a word which intrigues everyone but which no-one can remember and which is never finally elucidated. What is known about it is that it is a proper name — of a battle, of a flower, or of the delerious *planton*'s mother, Margueritte, the name of Céline's own mother (CP, 93) — which possesses the magical ability to captivate everyone and reflects the inability of Meheu and Rancotte to decipher Ferdinand's name. In other words, out of a conventional piece of military comedy, in which an incompetent platoon blunder through the night in search of a password which is assumed to be the precondition of any military activity, Céline fashions an episode which is both mythologically mysterious and psychologically complex: the forgetting of the name which will take them through the night is a significant act of unconscious abdication connected with the refusal of their own identity. As Céline has already suggested in his two previous novels, the attractiveness of non-assertion and minimal survival, symbolised by acceptance of the night and refusal of the day, is more than equal to the demands of action, responsibility and lucidity.

Where *Casse-pipe* begins to depart from the pattern laid down in *Voyage au bout de la nuit* and *Mort à crédit*, however, is in the ending of the major fragment. *Voyage au bout de la nuit* ends with a bleak dawn which echoes Baudelaire's *Crépuscule du matin* in its inversion of conventional imagery: the dawn does not indicate a change for the better, rather, a continuation of the same inescapable repetition; *Mort à crédit* ends with the protagonist Ferdinand about to seek escape from the world in sleep and in the minimal survival offered by Edouard's 'C'est pas les pardessus qui manquent!'. In *Casse-pipe*, however, after the persecution of which Ferdinand is a victim throughout the night and the aimless wandering without the password, there comes a dawn which is more positive than that which concludes the first novel: Rancotte finally orders the sounding of the *diane*: 'Alors tout autour de nous il a sorti comme des yeux . . . des choses dans la brume . . . des mille fenêtres à nous regarder . . . des reflets, je crois . . . des reflets . . . Il faisait presque jour à present . . . ça pâlissait d'en haut . . . des toits . . . et tout le quartier . . . les murs . . . la chaux . . .' (CP, 101). Not only does this dawn bring light and lucidity in contrast to the night which has dominated thus far, it also brings with it the 'brume' which echoes the 'brume d'Austerlitz' and permits a re-entry into the heroic mould at last. The major fragment of *Casse-pipe*, therefore, can be read as the narration of an initiation or, more appropriately, as a *veillée d'armes*, which, in some mysterious way, guarantees Ferdinand entry into the world of the army and ushers in a more positive, more dynamic pattern of conduct than that evoked in the first two novels.

This increasingly positive depiction of the cavalry before the war is continued in the second fragment of *Casse-pipe*, originally published by Poulet, in his *Entretiens familiers avec Louis-Ferdinand Céline*, which deals with the tortures undergone by Ferdinand in learning to ride: from unlikely Theseus, he becomes incompetent centaur. As in the major fragment, there is considerable emphasis on the 'servitudes' of military life: the alcoholism and brutality of the *sous-offs*, those *anciens* who are supposed to instruct the *bleus* but who keep their knowledge to themselves, and, centrally, the hardships of daily exercise in the *manège*, to which the narrator

attributes his lifelong head-pains which he will later falsely ascribe
to the war:

> S'il arrive que je divague, loin des tempêtes à présent, c'est d'avoir trop
> raclé ma tête dans tous les bastringues des pourtours, d'avoir trop fendu
> la camelote avec mon tarin, à vif, dans toutes les pistes au galop, de tous
> les manèges du 16e, au petit bonheur des biques folles, à la frénésie
> chevaline.
> Je me suis senti battant de cloche pendant des années, le crâne en gong
> pour ainsi dire. Je titube encore de la mémoire. Je peux plus voir un
> cheval en peinture! La vie du Guignol au suicide!... La ronde con-
> tinue!... (CP, 106–7).

Yet, alongside this complaint, which announces closely both the
style and the subject-matter of the later Céline, from *Bagatelles pour
un massacre* onwards, there are more positive images: the skill of
Capitaine Dagomart, 'un véritable Centaure' (CP, 108), with his
mount 'Rubicon' who echoes the anti-heroic 'Tout le monde n'est
pas César' of *Voyage au bout de la nuit*, and, crucially, the importance of the cavalry regiment as the repository of the world of
dreams. At the very beginning of the fragment, evoking Lieutenant
Portat des Oncelles, whose death Ferdinand will witness in the First
World War (CP, 103), the narrator recalls how even the chaos of the
manège is unable to provoke him into speech: 'ça le laissait reveur'
(CP, 103). Yet those who fall totally under the dreamlike sway of
the regiment are, significantly enough, the Bretons. As Ferdinand
comments: 'J'étais le seul de Paris, les autres ils venaient du
Finistère, peut-etre deux, trois des Côtes-du-Nord. Ils n'avaient pas
les yeux très francs, mal ouverts, bleu lavé ...' (CP, 111), and 'ils
venaient faire les militaires, ça les rendait tout rêveurs, d'un rêve un
peu animal' (CP, 112). This is in marked contrast to Céline's later
non-fictional account of his regiment in a letter to Roger Nimier
from exile in Denmark, in which he refers to the '12ème Cuirassiers
— absolument breton — ah pas proustien du tout — même pas de
sensualité élémentaire', and concludes:

> et quels ploucs! Spécialement recrutés pour les grèves parisiennes — qui
> étaient chaudes!... Tristes gens — *mystiques*. Je les ai vus foncer à la
> mort — sans ciller — les 800 — comme un seul homme et chevaux — une
> sorte d'attirance — pas une fois — dix! Comme d'un débarras. Pas de
> sensualité — pas un sur dix parlant français — doux et brutes à la fois —
> des cons en somme.[8]

8. 'Inédit, deux lettres de Céline à Nimier', *Libération*, 4 June 1984.

In the novel, the mystic side of the Breton cavalrymen is never totally absent. Nor is the narrator himself, looking back on his experience, wholly impervious to its fascination. On one level, he is perfectly prepared to indulge in nostalgic pride at the minutiae of the cavalryman's daily work: 'Le plus delicat dans une bride, c'est la gourmette rendue miroir' (CP, 112). More profoundly, amongst the continuing descriptions of the misery of the *bleu* as a scapegoat, again continuing the role of *souffre-douleur* accorded to Ferdinand in *Mort à crédit*, there emerge what will become familiar examples of Céline's post-Occupation language: 'Le garde referme l'enorme lourde . . . La fantasia continue . . .' (CP, 110); and, describing the hectic activity of the nights before reviews, Céline writes: 'C'est pire que la transmutation, c'est de la perversité magique, la féerie d'embrouillamini, la cambrouille sorcière des choses' (CP, 117). Into what began as the uniformly dark world of the barracks, magic and *féerie* make their modest entrance.

This progression towards an at least fleeting optimism is confirmed startlingly in the third fragment of the novel, published in the *Cahiers de l'Herne*, which deals with the regiment's participation in the 14 July parade through Paris in 1913, the last great parade of peacetime. By this time, the narrator is no longer a *bleu* and has even just been promoted to brigadier: 'A force de me faire tabasser je devenais un parfait militaire' (HER 1, 167). Significantly, this success has had the effect of reconciling him with his parents, as well as maintaining the support of Edouard. Indeed, it has so mollified them that they pay for the ritual celebration: 'J'avais annoncé à mon oncle, à mes parents, qu'on pouvait fêter la chose. Ils m'ont payé la cantine' (HER 1, 167). Not that this payment is sufficient: as Ferdinand comments: 'J'ai refait trois fois autant de dettes' (HER 1, 167). What is significant about this comment, however, is that by now the guilt associated with debt, which hangs over the characters of *Mort à crédit*, has plainly been exorcised by the military way of life. Undoubtedly, the fragment is remarkable for an almost unique expression of comradeship and solidarity in Céline's whole fiction, which is concentrated upon a rare and emphatic use of the first person plural. Explaining the use to which the parents' contribution has been put, the narrator describes the journey from the barracks to Versailles, the first stage of their journey to Paris: 'On a bu du curaçao tout le long de la route. L'escouade aimait ça avec les pommes de terre robe de chambre. Une combinaison à nous' (HER 1, 167). The isolated *bleu* of the opening fragment, so characteristic of the protagonists of the first two novels, has now become integrated into a military unit of which he is intensely and unambiguously proud: the *grandeur* has finally come to follow the *servitude*.

Yet that unit into which Ferdinand has become so successfully integrated and to which he looks back with such unalloyed nostalgia is hardly neutral, either politically or ethically. The narrator is pleased to emphasise the elite nature of the military in general and particularly his own cavalry regiment: it is an honour for the civilian population of Paris to be allowed to mingle with the soldiers as they make their triumphal progress to and from the parade. At the same time, the fragment expresses the same anti-Republicanism as that which pervades *Voyage au bout de la nuit*, although now it is rooted, not in vague anarchism, but in the soldier's contempt for civil power. This takes the form of disparaging remarks made by the narrator about President Fallières and his entourage:

> Je vois Fallière [*sic*] en habit. Il est à vingt metres du colon. Il nous domine dessus son balcon fleuri. Sa rombière est là à gauche. Elle est devant les gonzesses. C'est elle la plus laide de toutes. Elle a une robe rose à fleurs grises. Il relève son gibus. Il recommence encore. Jamais j'avais vu tant d'huiles comme il était entouré. Ils étouffaient dans les plumes entre les barrières et les épaulettes en or. Lui j'y suis à qui il ressemble. De face comme ça au Bon Dieu, qui est à Saint-Roch en peinture. Je l'ai vu souvent quand j'étais petit, qu'il pleuvait (HER 1, 168).

This extended description which vibrates with controlled contempt takes up the reference to Poincaré at the beginning of *Voyage au bout de la nuit*, 'qui s'en allait inaugurer, justement ce matin-là, une exposition de petits chiens', and looks forward in a more sinister way to the photograph of Fallières which appears in the edition of *L'Ecole des cadavres* published during the Occupation, with the seemingly irrelevent and anodyne title: 'Le Président Fallières se laisse aimablement photographier par l'Aide de Camp du Prince de Monaco'. Fallières, much more than his predecessor Emile Loubet, was the President of the *belle époque* and is used by Céline as a symbol of that period's kindly charm and ineffectualness against the more profound forces which were even then changing the world. Interestingly, Céline returns to Fallières in another fragment of the novel, which recounts his regiment's role as official escort whenever the President was in residence at Rambouillet:

> Heureusement que le Président ne se promenait jamais la nuit dans les allées de son parc . . . Il faisait tout de suite ralentir si on allongeait le moindrement. Nous l'escortâmes bien des fois au moment des chasses, le peloton entier, ou bien seulement deux escouades. Notre lieutenant des Oncelles, plumet, gants blancs, à la portière, piaffait, contenait son

bourdon. Assujetti dans la banquette, le Président tronait, il étendait encore les cuisses, pour s'étayer, mieux s'adosser, plus carrément. Il voulait pas qu'on aille vite. Doucement. . . . Il étendait encore les cuisses, se passait des coussins sous les jambes pour que son ventre tremble plus du tout. Comme ça il était bien paré, campé adossé convenable, calé . . . Il restait comme ça bouche ouverte à respirer avec un bruit, la tête en arrière cahotante, le nez tout en l'air. Il faisait presque double à cause d'une loupe qu'était dessus. Ses deux ordonnances . . . ils faisaient des mines à des Oncelles, que le Président. . . . Et nous parcourions ainsi tous les abords de la forêt, à très noble allure, au trot somptueux des attelages.[9]

Finally, in his letter to Nimier, Céline hints at homosexual rumours in connection with Fallières: 'Le 1er Cuir à Paris était renommé pour la pédale. A Rambouillet, y avait son Fallières. C'est peut-être ça'.[10]

Set against this well-meaning but slightly comic and slightly unrespectable Republican leadership, is the distant but by now admired figure of the Regiment's colonel, Colonel des Estranges. The name itself, of course, takes the archaic form of *étrange* as its base, but more importantly, it is similar to the Général des Entrayes under whom Bardamu serves in the war episode in *Voyage au bout de la nuit*. The transition, however, has been significant: the general was a figure of fun who, in his serious aspect, looked after himself at the expense of his men. The fleeting reference to the colonel of the regiment in this fragment, however, implies respect for the auto-cratic leader: 'Le colonel des Estranges était paraît-il très content de nous. Il a levé toutes les punitions' (HER 1, 168). Finally, this militarist, anti-Republican narrator is at home in a regiment whose major activity in peacetime is, as Céline emphasises in his letter to Nimier, strike-breaking, and here he is following in the footsteps of *Lucien Leuwen*. As the regiment enters Paris on the morning of the 14 July and is greeted by the Parisian population, Ferdinand com-ments: 'On a passé la Porte Maillot le lendemain au petit jour. Ça changeait avec les grèves. Là, je peux dire qu'on était archipopulaire' (HER 1, 168).

The evolution of the narrator from the completely desolidarised Ferdinand of *Mort à crédit* and the first fragment of *Casse-pipe* to the acquiescent authoritarian is continued and accentuated in the short remaining fragment of the novel, again printed in the *Cahiers de l'Herne*. Once promoted to brigadier, Ferdinand undergoes a

9. An unpublished fragment, kindly communicated to the author by Henri Godard.
10. 'Inédit, deux lettres de Céline à Nimier'.

'conversion' (HER 1, 168): 'Dans la piaule où je commandais y avait plus de Bon Dieu ni de resquille. J'avais compris moi à la fin. Au coeur de la discipline tout ne doit être que tremblement' (HER 1, 168), and: 'Faut tout oublier, le civil, la ville, la campagne, éponger tout ça . . . Pas de regrets. Rien comme souvenir' (HER 1, 168). The narrator, who has already, along with the rest of the platoon on his first night in the barracks, attempted a search for a kind of non-being in Arcile's stable, now finds true non-existence in a complete acceptance of the military, anti-civilian ethic and total forgetfulness of the past. Such a discovery, however, is not purchased without some considerable expense. In the first place, Ferdinand is obliged to subscribe, at least tacitly, to the anti-proletarian, strike-breaking activities of the cavalry, and he records without comment the bloodthirsty anti-unionism of 'Leurbanne, le cantinier, le cocu, quand on parlait des grèves':

> Hardi les gars! Crevez-en un! Aux tripes: C'est du fainéant tous ces mecs-là! Du bidon! Y a qu'à piquer ça se degonfle!
> Il aimait pas les ouvriers. Il préférait comme tous les cadres les ploucs du Léon (HER 1, 168).

More importantly, Ferdinand, the disorientated *bleu* of the first fragment, has, as brigadier, become the terror of the regiment. As the liberal officer Lacadène comments: 'Alors, tu la fais sauter la bleusaille? . . . C'est toi il paraît qu'est le plus vache de l'escadron?, (HER 1, 168). In this final fragment of *Casse-pipe* begins a depressing cycle of repetition, which will be fully amplified in the pamphlets. Here, Céline has moved further on from the survival ethic propounded in *Mort à crédit*. In *Casse-pipe*, in order to survive, it is not sufficient to remain unobtrusive: survival is guaranteed only by supplanting and imitating those in authority and those who abuse authority. Thus, Ferdinand, the abject victim of brigadier Meheu and the *maréchal des logis* Rancotte, chooses to seek survival in the regiment by being even more brutal and exceeding even their abuses of authority. This process, which looks forward directly to the way in which Ferdinand, as narrator of *Bagatelles pour un massacre*, will imitate and outdo his tormentor Auguste's imprecations against the scapegoats of French society, establishes a depressing pattern by which the *victime* can only rebel against the *bourreau* and cease to be a *victime* by becoming a *bourreau* in his turn. The liberal middle ground, searched for so energetically by writers such as Camus in the years of the cold war, is totally absent from Céline's work, which is held in a narrow circle of punishment endured and punishment inflicted and of which the main dynamic force is not forgiveness but revenge. The last words of the fragment are: 'Moi, je pardonne jamais' (HER 1, 168).

Casse-pipe therefore, with its evolution to the state of *bourreau* from that of *victime*, looks forward to the settling of accounts which will be embodied in *Bagatelles pour un massacre* and which is supported by Céline's increasingly affectionate nostalgia for authoritarian and anti-Republican elements prior to 1914. In the same way, the eventual celebration of that most anachronistic of the branches of the army, the heavy cavalry, after the traumatic first night of Ferdinand in the barracks, connects with the implicit Bonapartism which surfaces from time to time in *Voyage au bout de la nuit* and which is directly present in the transposition of the *Chant de la Bérésina* into the 'Chanson des Gardes Suisses'. In addition, the evocation of the pre-war cavalry, with its elitism, its authoritarianism and its anti-Republicanism, accompanies the profound anti-humanism of *Mea culpa*: in the cavalry regiment, it is the horses which are paramount and the men of strictly secondary importance.

Whatever the stage eventually reached by the draft manuscript of *Casse-pipe*, the novel clearly never arrived at a publishable state and must be counted, along with the two plays, *Progrès* and *L'Eglise*, as one of Céline's failures. Even from the existing fragments, it is possible to detect some of the sources of the failure of the novel as a whole. In the first, major, fragment particularly, unlike *Mort à crédit* or *Voyage au bout de la nuit*, *Casse-pipe* is too dominated by its sources and its referential context: for all the side-glances at military novels by Hermant, Descaves and Courteline, it is by no means clear that the novel itself rises above them. In other words, rather than exploiting, transposing and reflecting the literary context, as happens in Céline's first two novels, it is doubtful whether *Casse-pipe* ever totally escapes from the constraints of the sub-genre of the military novel itself. At the same time, whilst the novel is clearly attempting to exploit a system of classical references, with Arcile's Augean stables and the description of Capitaine Dagomart as a centaur, the system is not sufficiently elaborated or sustained to enrich the work significantly, on the lines, say, of establishing Ferdinand as a debased and modern Theseus. Above all, it is probable that *Casse-pipe* should be seen as a casualty of a problem which afflicts, particularly, novelists who rely directly on a transposition of their biographical experience. After the exploitation of Céline's war experience and subsequent peacetime career in *Voyage au bout de la nuit*, transformed in the novel into a haunting fear of the present, and the evocation of his childhood in *Mort à crédit*, there is a kind of stultifying and inevitable logic which dictates that the next fictional endeavour must have as its subject one of the further remaining segments of his lived experience, the pre-war cavalry. It is no doubt this mechanical dictation of the subject-matter for the novel which inhibited its progress and imprisoned the author in a net of his own past. It is altogether logical, therefore, that he should attempt to renew himself by creating for himself a new present, which would be the conjuncture of a new persona, a new historical involvement and a new and more abrasive style. It is equally fitting that this attempt should take the form of a return to polemic, which has the effect of bringing the author back into the open from the camouflage of fiction and burning at least some of the boats which could take him back to the past.

Mea culpa

There exists no serious extended study of *Mea culpa*, doubtless because, due to its length, it is generally perceived as a slight, circumstantial work, an immediate reaction by Céline to his short visit to the Soviet Union in 1936. As Fred Kupferman notes, in his chronology of works on journeys to the USSR, in *Mea culpa* we find: 'l'URSS jugée et condamnée en 24 pages',[11] and this reputation of the work as a short dismissive essay based on the author's immediate experience has had the effect of diverting critics and readers to apparently more fruitful areas of Céline's work. *Mea culpa*'s importance in the Célinian canon, however, should not be underestimated. For all its shortness, it is by no means slight: rather, it is a dense and complex work, turning constantly around its subject and returning to its first premises in order to go further in the elaboration of its central theory. Stylistically it may be considered, with its fully confident manipulation of exclamations and *trois points*, as the first work of the mature Céline, opening the way to the pamphlets and the novels from *Guignol's Band* onwards. Most important of all, however, *Mea culpa* is a major statement of Céline's political and moral philosophy in transition from a tenuous, if modest faith, to almost blanket pessimism. As Kupferman remarks on Céline's journey to Russia: 'Il n'a pas eu beaucoup d'illusions à perdre',[12] and it is in his statement of how those

---

11. Fred Kupferman, *Au Pays des Soviets. Le Voyage français en Union Soviétique 1917–1939*, Paris, Julliard, coll. 'Archives', 1979, p. 180.
12. Ibid., p. 132.

illusions finally came to be lost that the truly desperate position of the author in the post-1914 world becomes apparent. In other words, *Mea culpa* is a crucial amplification of the medical writings and the novels and a vital precondition for the onslaught of the pamphlets.

In broad terms, *Mea culpa* transmits the same 'plague on both your houses' philosophy as that which motivates the two preceeding novels and the essays on social medicine: serious misgivings at the present and the recent past, coupled with a commensurate fear of the future, an alliance which has already led to a kind of conservative paralysis. *Mea culpa* begins with the statement of what is for Céline an unswerving position: an instinctive hatred of privilege and of the class, in Europe, who are its natural inheritors, the bourgeoisie, and a willingness to see that class meet a violent end: 'Les privilégiés, pour ma part, je n'irai pas, je le jure, m'embuer d'un seul petit oeil sur leur vache charogne! . . . Ah! Pas d'erreur! Délais? Basta! Pas un remords! Pas une larme! Pas un soupir!' (Mea, 8). In this context, he quotes a bloodthirsty revolutionary song:

> *Je te crèverai, charogne! un vilain soir!*
> *Je te ferai dans les mires deux grands trous noirs!*
> *Ton âme de vache dans la danse! Prendra du champ!*
> *Tu verras cette belle assistance! . . .*
> *Au Four-Cimetière des Bons-Enfants!*

Ces complets nouveaux me dansent au cassis. Je les offre à tous pardessus le marché, avec la musique! 'L'Hymne à l'Abbatoir', l'air en plus! C'est complet! . . . .

> *Tout va bien! Ca ira!*
> *L'un s'en va! Le joli un!*
> *Le deux qui vient . . .*

Ainsi de suite chantaient en cadence nos gais pontonniers d'autrefois! (Mea, 8–9).

The author is therefore at pains at the very beginning of his essay to situate himself in a truly revolutionary anti-bourgeois tradition, from Babeuf to Jehan-Rictus, to the extent that he is prepared to accept any political manifestation, be it authoritarian or anarchist, just so long as it is not bourgeois. Hence, the disparate list: 'Vive Pierre Ier! Vive Louis XIV! Vive Fouquet! Vive Gengis Khan! Vive Bonnot! la bande! et tous autres! Mais pour Landru pas d'excuses! Tous les bourgeois ont du Landru! C'est ça qu'est triste irrémédiable' (Mea, 9). Anything, for Céline, is preferable to the bourgeoisie, even the absolute monarchy, and for this reason, the

Revolution of 1789 and especially the Terror of 1793, the year of the bogus *Gardes Suisses* and the execution of Louis XVI, is a crucial event in the decline of the West: '93, pour ma pomme, c'est les larbins . . . larbins textuels, larbins de gueule! larbins de plume qui maîtrisent un soir le château, tous fous d'envie, délirants, jaloux, pillent, crèvent, s'installent et comptent les couverts et les draps . . .' (Mea, 9–10). At this early point in the essay, there enters into Céline's argument a concept which has been visible in his work since *Semmelweis* and which will profoundly colour his view of the events in Russia since 1917. *Semmelweis*, which similarly begins with an evocation of the Revolution of 1789, looks forward to the Hungarian Revolution of 1848 to point the moral that revolutions change nothing and, indeed, have a tendency to reinforce the state of affairs which existed before they started. In other words, Céline's doctoral thesis propounds a pessimistic theory of historical stasis in which human action is at best irrelevant and at worst uniformly harmful. In *Mea culpa*, this theory is moved to the forefront and is, moreover, underpinned by a sustained pessimistic reflection on human nature. In the light of 1789, and now 1917, Céline concludes that revolutions and pretensions to social progress, however well-meaning, break down on one irreducible fact: 'L'Homme est la pire des engeances! (Mea, 25), a fact which he is careful to nuance:

> L'Homme il est humain à peu prés autant que la poule vole. Quand elle prend un coup dur dans le pot, quand une auto la fait valser, elle s'enlève bien jusqu'au toit, mais elle repique tout de suite dans la bourbe, rebecqueter la fiente. C'est sa nature, son ambition. Pour nous, dans la société, c'est exactement du même. On cesse d'être si profond fumier que sur le coup d'une catastrophe. Quand tout se tasse à peu près, le naturel reprend le galop. Pour ça même, une Révolution faut la juger vingt ans plus tard (Mea, 25).

Céline's essay appears precisely twenty years after the October Revolution, and his examination of Soviet society has confirmed him in his pessimistic view of history and in his anti-humanism: in spite of the sincerity of the leaders of the Revolution — 'Ils étaient sincères au début' (Mea, 26) — human nature, in all its brutality and egoism, has reasserted itself, to the extent that there is now no difference between the Soviet and capitalist regimes, except that the former is more overt in its repression. Looking back at the poverty and violence of the Soviet experiment, Céline concludes that it is merely one of a long list of examples throughout history of the disastrous consequences of an Idea:

Combien ont fini au bûcher parmi les petits croyants têtus pendant les époques obscures? . . . Dans la gueule des lions? . . . Aux galères? . . . Inquisitionnés jusqu'aux moelles? Pour la Conception de Marie? ou trois versets du Testament? On peut même plus les compter! Les motifs? Facultatifs! . . . C'est même pas la peine qu'ils existent! . . . Les temps n'ont pas changé beaucoup à cet égard-là! (Mea, 27).

Yet, if these 'hommes à idéâs' ignore the principles of basic survival and suffer unnecessarily at the hands of a historical process which pays them no attention, they are none the less the agents of destruction: the men of ideas provoke '[des] guerres qu'on saura plus pourquoi! . . . De plus en plus formindables! Qui laisseront plus personne tranquille! . . . Que tout le monde en crèvera . . . deviendra des héros sur place . . . et poussière par-dessus le marché! . . . Qu'on débarrassera la Terre . . . Qu'on a jamais servi à rien . . . Le néttoyage par l'Idée . . .' (Mea, 27). In this way, Céline announces the pacifism and anti-intellectualism of the anti-Semitic pamphlets.

This ultimate rejection of revolutionary pretensions on the grounds of a belief in the irremediable baseness of human nature does not, however, automatically explain the choice of *Mea culpa* for the essay's title. In one sense, of course, the title signals the essay as part of a well-worn and recognisable genre of 1930s non-fiction writing: the journey to the 'pays des Soviets' and the subsequent realisation that the reality of Soviet Communism did not match up to the visitor's ideals and expectations. In such cases, the resulting 'mea culpa' was the product of a *voyage imaginaire* that went wrong. Of this genre, Gide's *Retour de l'URSS* of 1936 is undoubtedly the classic example, but the inter-war years in general saw a whole series of works in which writers, politicians and trade unionists, who had previously been favourable to the Soviet Union, expressed the disillusionment which followed a visit to the workers' paradise.[13] The problem with Céline's essay is that, whilst its title appears to signify the way in which experience of the Soviet Union has caused a revision in the author's previously held convictions, the work itself departs radically from the conventions of the genre by virtually excluding any first-hand eye-witness material. That personal account of Céline's 1936 visit to the Soviet Union appears, not in

13. For an extensive list of works published in France as a result of visits to the Soviet Union, see Kupferman, *Au Pays des Soviets*, pp. 172–82. For a useful detailed survey of French attitudes to Russia in general at this time, see: P. Gerbod, 'L'Union Soviétique dans l'opinion française 1917–1941', *Annales du C.E.S.E.R.E.*, 4, 1981, pp. 3–26.

Mea culpa, but, transposed into the experience of the narrator Ferdinand, in the final section of *Bagatelles pour un massacre*. *Mea culpa* itself constitutes an almost exclusively abstract study of the bankruptcy of Communism in the face of unalterable human nature. It is extremely difficult, therefore, from an initial reading of the text itself, to see why the author should be confessing to error.

In fact, this confessional side to the work can only really be explained by reference back to Céline's earlier works. The notion of guilt and bad conscience which dominate *Mort à crédit* have spilled out over into the succeeding title. More specifically, Céline's admission of guilt in the title of *Mea culpa* can only properly relate to his article in Henri Barbusse's periodical *Monde* in 1930, 'La Santé publique en France', and his memorandum to the League of Nations in 1932 on the 'cours des hautes études', where he concludes that: 'Il faudrait que cette société s'écroulât pour qu'on puisse parler véritablement d'hygiène généralisée qui ne s'accorde bien qu'avec une formule socialiste ou communiste d'Etat' (CC 3, 188). Looking at the state of the world's only Communist regime twenty years after its institution, Céline implies in the very title *Mea culpa* that his assumption of four years earlier is no longer applicable and that not only is there now no possible way of establishing a viable system of social hygiene, but that, more generally, all faith in progress is ultimately illusory.

For the Soviet Union strikes Céline in what is precisely his most vulnerable point: his distaste for and fear of the modern. 'I have been over to see the Future, and it works', crowed Lincoln Steffens after an early visit to post-Revolutionary Russia. It is precisely this aspect of the new regime, enshrined in Lenin's famous dictum that Communism was 'the Soviets plus electricity', that Céline dreaded. In observing the development of Russia under Soviet Communism, he noted the inevitable march of the modern world, the dangers of which he had already highlighted in his essays on Ford and 'les assurances sociales':

> Pour l'esprit, pour la joie, en Russie, y a la mécanique. La providentielle trouvaille! La vraie terre promise! Salut! Il faut etre 'Intellectuel' éperdu dans les Beaux-Arts, ensaché depuis des siècles, embusqué, ouaté, dans les plus beaux papiers du monde, petit raisin fragile et mur, au levant des treilles fonctionnaires, douillet fruit des contributions, délirant d'Irréalité, pour engendrer, aucune erreur, ce phénoménal barratin! La machine salit à vrai dire, condamne, tue tout ce qui l'approche! Mais c'est dans le 'bon ton' la Machine! Ça fait 'prolo', ça fait 'progrès', ça fait 'boulot', ça fait 'base' . . . (Mea, 14).

Yet this cult of the machine, which has now overrun Russia, as it has become a fashionable vogue in progressive circles in Paris, a phenomenon viciously lampooned in Marcel Aymé's novel *Travelingue*, of 1940, is deadly: it will destroy the Soviet experiment as surely as it has perverted Western society: 'Le principe du diable tient bon. Il avait raison comme toujours, en braquant l'Homme sur la matière. Ça n'a pas traîné. En deux siècles, tout fou d'orgueil, dilaté par la mécanique, il est devenu impossible' (Mea, 18). And Céline gloomily recognises in Russia the same miserable and corrupting domination by machines that he had observed in Detroit:

> La machine c'est l'infection même. La défaite supreme! Quel flanc! Quel bidon! La machine la mieux stylée n'a jamais délivré personne. Elle abrutit l'Homme plus cruellement et c'est tout! . . . J'ai été médecin chez Ford, je sais ce que je raconte. Tous les Ford se ressemblent, soviétiques ou non! . . . Se reposer sur la machine, c'est seulement une excuse de plus pour continuer les vacheries (Mea, 14–15).

In this central criticism, Céline was by no means exaggerating: so completely had the Soviet regime been won over to modern Western industrial philosophy that, not only had Stalin become a disciple of Taylor, but the Russians had, for a time, permitted the installation of a Ford plant on Soviet soil.[14] Nor was Céline alone in condemning the Soviets for embarking upon an industrial policy which appeared to owe so much to Taylor and Ford: indeed, so frequent had such criticism become that the Communist Georges Friedmann felt obliged to rebut it:

> Un des traits essentiels de la rationalisation soviétique est la participation active qu'y prennent les ouvriers. Lorsqu'il s'agit en 1930 de mécaniser l'extraction dans le bassin de Donetz, les ouvriers envoyèrent un flot de propositions dont plusieurs furent retenues et appliquées. Ici encore se marque une opposition fondamentale entre le taylorisme de l'usine capitaliste, où le consentement doit être acheté par des primes ou par la menace brutal du renvoi, et l'émulation socialiste.[15]

14. See Charles S. Maier, 'Between Taylorism and Technocracy', *Journal of Contemporary History*, V, 2, 1970.

15. Quoted in Kupferman, *Au Pays des Soviets*, p. 83. As Kupferman notes in his chronology, Ernest Mercier, the owner of the Compagnie Générale d'Electricité and the founder of a French corporatist movement, the Redressement Français, was deeply impressed by the possibilities presented to employers by the adoption of the Stalinist system. See Ernest Mercier, *Réflexions 1936*, Paris, Editions du Centre Polytechnique d'Etudes Economiques, 1936.

The corollary of this betrayal by the Soviet Union in its mission of providing an alternative to capitalism and machinism is the reappearance of the same inequalities which divide Western society. Céline asks:

Pourquoi le bel ingenieur il gagne les 7000 roubles par mois? Je parle de là-bas en Russie, la femme de ménage que 50? Magie! Magie! Qu'on est tous des fumiers! Là-bas comme ici! Pourquoi la paire de tatanes elle coûte déjà 900 francs? et un ressemelage bien précaire (j'ai vu) dans les 80? . . . Et les hôpitaux? . . . Celui, le beau du Kremlin à part et les salles pour 'l'Intourisme'. Les autres sont franchement sordides! Ils ne vivent guère qu'au 1/10e d'un budget normal. Toute la Russie vit au dixième du budget normal, sauf Police, Propagande, Armée . . . (Mea, 24).

In this way, after merely twenty years, the Soviet Union has become a caricature of bourgeois society: 'Ah! il est remplacé le patron! Ses violences, ses fadaises, ses ruses, toutes ses garceries publicitaires! On sait la farder la camelote! Ça n'a pas traîné bézef! Ils sont remontés sur l'estrade les nouveaux souteneurs . . . Voyez les nouveaux apôtres . . . Gras de bide et bien chantants! . . .' (Mea, 26). And it is only able to maintain its power over its citizens by brutal repression and the establishment of a police state. As Céline ruefully observes:

C'est lui qu'entretient, Prolovitch, la police (sur sa propre misère) la plus abondante, la plus soupçonneuse, la plus carne, la plus sadique de la planète. Ah! On le laisse pas seul! La vigilence est impeccable! On l'enlèvera pas, Prolovitch! . . . Il s'ennuie quand même! . . . Ça se voit bien ! Il s'en ferait crever de sortir! De se transformer en 'Ex-touriste' pour varier un peu! Il ne reviendrait jamais (Mea, 22).

It is important to avoid the temptation, accentuated by hindsight, of situating this kind of criticism exclusively on the Right. In fact, doubts about the exaggeratedly industrialised nature of Soviet man, epitomised by Gladkov's novel *Ciment*, and anger at the inequalities and repression rife in Soviet society, are at the heart of left-wing responses to visits to the 'pays des Soviets', from the English trade-union leader Walter Citrine to the French socialist miner Kléber Legay. What is important about *Mea culpa*, however, is that, in spite of the minor pieces of reportage, authenticated by the words: 'J'ai vu', the essay operates on a more abstract level and is less interested in immediate political conclusions that in the elaboration and reinforcement of a deeply pessimistic philosophical and moral theory which goes far beyond the purely political sphere.

This philosophy begins with a basic assumption which is so

absolute and so unamenable to modification that there are only the most vestigeal of possibilities of progress: Man is a non-humanist value, imprisoned in his own baseness: 'L'Homme n'a jamais eu, en l'air et sur terre, qu'un seul tyran: lui-même!' (Mea, 15). From this state of original sin, under the even more dehumanising power of materialism and the massively corrupting force of politics, Man has declined to a state in which he is irrecuperable: the Soviet experiment represented the chimerical possibility that this process of decline could be reversed and, with its blatant failure, the circle is now firmly closed. Yet, in this historical process, there was one moment when Man was in a vigorous and positive stage, the Middle Ages: 'La politique a pourri l'Homme encore plus profondément pendant ces trois derniers siècles que pendant toute la Préhistoire. Nous étions au Moyen Age plus prés d'être unis qu'aujourd'hui . . . un esprit commun prenait forme. Le bobard était bien meilleur "montée poésie", plus intime. Il existe plus' (Mea, 16). Connected with this nostalgia for the Middle Ages is an admiration for 'la supériorité pratique des grandes religions chrétiennes' (Mea, 16–17), which insist on the primacy of salvation over the search for *bonheur*. It is the search for salvation in the medieval context of national solidarity which leads to greatness; the pursuit of happiness leads inescapably to pettiness and alienation: 'Le monde entier tourne critique, donc effroyablement médiocre' (Mea, 18). This invocation of the Middle Ages, in which the mediocrity and hypocrisy of the modern world is confronted with the vigour, solidarity and faith of the old Christian Europe, is by no means an isolated example, either in Céline's own writing from 1936 onwards (we have already seen the significance of Caroline and Krogold in *Mort à crédit*) or in the general French intellectual and literary context of the inter-war years. Nor is it a rhetorical device which is exclusively the preserve of the Right: it is implicit in Malraux's cult of the adventurer or, even, in Saint-Exupéry's evocation of the pilot. Yet it is in his affinity with Bernanos and Drieu la Rochelle, who both look whistfully back to the unity and meaning of Europe in the Middle Ages, that Céline is most interesting. Bernanos, explicitly in his two pamphlets, *La Grande peur des bien-pensants* and *Les Grands cimetières sous la lune*, as well as implicitly in the novels, excorciates the system of bourgeois rule, which is divisive and materialistic, and harks back to the pre-bourgeois era in which a stable society, presided over by a strong king, devoted itself to its faith. Along similar lines, Drieu la Rochelle, notably in his *Notes pour comprendre le siècle* of 1940, but also in the preceeding essays and novels, sees the degeneration of Europe as due to the inexorable consequences of the split between mind and body, between intellect and action, which came into being and has widened increasingly since the decline of the Middle Ages, and which may yet be bridged by the institution of a strong vigorous anachronistic regime, be it Fascist or Communist. In this context, Céline's disappointment with the Soviet Union, which had for some European thinkers been a possible candidate for a renewal of the medieval ethos, becomes clearly explicable, as do his celebrations of the pre-war cavalry in *Casse-pipe* and the incipient Bonapartism which surfaces in his work for time to time. It is likely that Céline, like Drieu and Malraux, also owes his modest cult of the Middle Ages, which will become more explicit in the pamphlets, to the reading of Nietzsche which seems to be alluded to in the cyclical theory of history expressed in *Semmelweis* and the transposition of the German philosopher's last train journey into the return of Semmelweis to Vienna.

In fact, *Mea culpa* marks the continuation into the 1930s of the preoccupations which motivate *Semmelweis* and the medical pamphlets. The horror of the modern world depicted in the lecture on Ford and the article on social medicine emerges immeasurably strengthened from the author's witnessing of the Soviet regime's attempt to reverse the historical process and recreate the solidarity of the Middle Ages. Similarly, that irreducible human stupidity and cruelty which leads to the rejection and neutralising of Semmelweis's discovery is proclaimed in *Mea culpa* as the only constant. After the failed revolutions of 1789 and 1848, Céline regretfully adds that of 1917 to the list. It is entirely fitting, therefore, that *Mea culpa* appeared accompanied by the first published version of *La Vie et l'oeuvre de Philippe-Ignace Semmelweis*: not only do they depict the same world, with the same need for a valid system of social hygiene, with all that that implies politically, morally and philosophically, but they both recognise the need for the same recklessness, of an almost self-destructive kind, if the inevitable decline is to be reversed. Semmelweis, with his fatal lack of tact, abandons the comfortable career to which he appears destined in order to follow to the end the consequences of his discovery. Céline, too, has made a discovery: about human nature and human progress in general, and about the Soviet regime in particular; after cutting himself adrift from national and conservative myths in *Voyage au bout de la nuit* and from that of the family in *Mort à crédit*, he breaks away from a potent myth of progressivism by dissociating himself from the Soviet Union. As Sartre wrote in his obituary of Gide, it needed courage to break with Russia in 1936, the year of the Front Populaire.[16] In Céline's case, it was perhaps not so much a question of courage as of an almost perverse need for persecution. He notes, at the beginning of *Mea culpa*: 'Se faire voir aux côtés du peuple, par les temps qui courent, c'est prendre une "assurance-nougat". Pourvu qu'on se sente un peu juif, ça devient une "assurance-vie". Tout cela fort compréhensible' (Mea, 10). The 'assurance-nougat' is systematically destroyed by Céline in the course of *Mea culpa*, not specifically by the criticism of the Soviet Union or even by the refusal of the notions of human progress and human goodness, but by the deliberately provocative and insulting use of right-wing polemical terminology, like 'Prolo', 'Popu' and 'Prolovitch'. For the first time, Céline is going out of his way to bait his readers, and the process will continue with the termination of the 'assurance-vie' in the anti-Semitic pamphlets.

The last fragment of *Casse-pipe* ends with the words: 'Moi, je pardonne jamais'. *Mea culpa* uses as its *exergue* the tantalising comment: 'Il me manque encore quelques haines. Je suis certain qu'elles existent'. Not only do these comments shed light on the previous fiction as an elaborate settling of accounts with all the narrator's old enemies, the bourgeoisie, the Army, the war, the colonies, the family, all held tightly under the domination of money and time, they also propose the notion of writing as an activity fuelled principally by hatred and the desire for revenge. Up until 1936, however, that motive force was mitigated by the faint hope, expressed explicitly in the 1932 memorandum, that the circle was not entirely closed, that Man's progress to disaster was still reversible by a massive social reorganisation along Communist lines. With the visit to Russia in 1936, however, that hope disappears, and the modern world appears as one vast Ford plant. With this disappointment, Céline will devote his next works to an exaggerated and violent attack on that modern world which he so hates and which he perceives now as both symbolised and caused by the figure of the Jew. At the same time, Céline has learned his lesson from the wilder activities of Semmelweis, and if, on one level, the pamphlets constitute a definitive breaking of cover, an unambiguous flight from the protection of the insurance policy of left-wing rhetoric, they none the less demonstrate the perplexing chameleon-like ambition for survival and the disquieting operation of irony, often in the most unexpected places, which make the reading of the medical pamphlets far more difficult than would appear to be necessary. Momentarily blocked as a novelist and finally severed from any commitment to the future, Céline unearths the ghost of Drumont.

---

16. See: Jean-Paul Sartre, *Situations* IV, Paris, Gallimard, 1964, pp. 85–9.

[5]

Anti-Semitism
and the Ghost of Drumont

Even after the spirited refutation of the optimistic humanism at the basis of the theory of Communism, in *Mea culpa*, Céline's three anti-Semitic pamphlets, *Bagatelles pour un massacre*, of 1937, *L'Ecole des cadavres*, of 1938, and *Les Beaux draps*, of 1941, come as a considerable shock to the reader. The major problem is not essentially the exaggerated violence of the anti-Semitic denunciation, but rather the fact that there is little in the preceeding works of the 1920s and 1930s which announces it. Far more than *Mea culpa*, *Bagatelles pour un massacre* appears, and consciously so, as a glaring act of betrayal. It is true that, for the assiduous reader of the Céline canon, this new target of the author's distaste for the modern world is not totally unexpected. *Mort à crédit* contains a disparaging allusion to the 'Comptoir Judéo-Suisse' (MC, 671), a jibe which is by no means gratuitous but which refers directly back to Céline's play of 1926, *L'Eglise*. In the third act of this play, Bardamu, after his African and American adventures, is in Geneva working for the League of Nations, where his immediate superior is Yudenzweck (*Judenzweck*, in German, signifying 'aim of the Jews'), 'Directeur du Service des Compromis', with his two colleagues, Mosaic, 'Directeur des Affaires Transitoires', and Moise, 'Directeur du Service des Indiscrétions'.[1] This early attack on the 'Jewishness' of the League of Nations is transposed into *Bagatelles pour un massacre*, where Yudenzweck becomes 'Jubelblatt' (in German, 'jubilant

---

1. Interestingly, Céline is precise in noting the age of all these as forty-five years old, which, if the play were written in 1926, would place their date of birth as 1881, the year of the collapse of the Catholic-owned Union Générale bank, generally considered by the Right to be the result of a Jewish–Masonic plot. See Roger Magraw, *France 1815–1914: The Bourgeois Century*, London, Fontana, 1983, p. 264.

newspaper') (BM, 98–111), and constitutes a common enough grievance amongst anti-Semites during the inter-war years, one which, moreover, by no means conflicts with one possible reading of the medical writings of the 1920s: the way in which these texts propose an authoritarian approach to the fact and the metaphor of social hygiene.

This pattern, however, by which the authoritarianism of the medical writings is reinforced by an already pronounced anti-Semitism, was not visible to Céline's readers and critics of the 1930s, who had only the novels at their disposal. In this light, for most readers, the pamphlets caused considerable disarray, as much on the Right as on the Left, which still, broadly, saw Céline as one of its own. Thus, Marcel Arland, in the liberal *Nouvelle Revue Française*, hesitates as to what literary category *Bagatelles pour un massacre* is best suited: he notes that the review itself has called it a 'pamphlet', but feels that the term 'soliloque' may describe the work more accurately.[2] What this really translates is Arland's view that the work cannot be simply what it appears: either as pamphlet or as soliloquy, 'il ne se satisfait qu'en grossissant démesurément une donnée jusqu'à l'apparence d'un mythe monstrueux'.[3] For, 'l'événement initial, fictif ou vrai, fait boule de neige',[4] to the extent that '[cette] virulence laisse loin derrière elle toutes les attaques antisémitiques'.[5] This attempt to recuperate the work as a mythical treatment of anti-Semitism is not merely the result of a refusal on the part of the liberal or left-wing critic to acknowledge an apparent betrayal by one of his own side: it reflects a general sense of unease about how to approach the text itself, an unease shared by André Gide. Like Arland, Gide is unwilling to take *Bagatelles pour un massacre* at what appears to be face value and, like Arland, he prefers to see the work, not as a pamphlet but, rather, as the satirical transposition of a pamphlet. It is only at the end of his article that doubts assail him: 'S'il fallait voir dans *Bagatelles pour un massacre* autre chose qu'un jeu, Céline, en dépit de tout son génie, serait sans excuse de remuer les passions banales avec ce cynisme et cette désinvolte légèreté'.[6] Even then, the possibility that Céline might be in deadly earnest does not occur to Gide. Nor was the extreme Right any more

---

2. Marcel Arland, '*Bagatelles pour un massacre*, par Louis-Ferdinand Céline', *Nouvelle Revue Française*, 293, February 1938, p. 308.
   3. Ibid., p. 309.
   4. Ibid.
   5. Ibid.
   6. André Gide, 'Les Juifs, Céline et Maritain', *Nouvelle Revue Française*, 295, April 1938, p. 634.

comfortable with Céline's contributions to the anti-Semitic debate. Lucien Rebatet emphasises that: 'Je dois dire encore . . . pour être exact, que si nous autres fascistes nous avions dansé la pyrrhique en 1938 autour des *Bagatelles, L'Ecole des cadavres*, un an plus tard, nous cassa bras et jambes . . . Céline continuait à exagérer' (HER 1, 45). For readers on the Right and the Left, therefore, Céline's pamphlets presented considerable problems of reading and categorisation, problems which have tended to be repressed rather than elucidated by subsequent critics.

On the face of it, of course, these problems should have been considerably diminished in the light of twentieth-century literary and intellectual history. Not merely can they be read as a logical continuation of the social criticism embodied in *Semmelweis* and the medical writings of the 1920s, they also, on one level, appear to fit unproblematically into the category of extended, discursive right-wing pamphleteering, embodied in the works of Drumont, Léon Bloy and, of course, in Bernanos's two essays, *La Grande peur des bien-pensants* and *Les Grands cimetières sous la lune*. Yet, like the medical writings themselves, they fit uneasily into what appears to be their logical category, to the extent that they begin to subvert it. According to one interpretation, from *Bagatelles pour un massacre* to *Les Beaux draps*, Céline appears to be in a direct line of descendence from Drumont, the Drumont of *La France juive* and *La Fin d'un monde*, who was recognised in the 1930s as the fountain-head of the French anti-Semitic tradition. Why then, each time he refers to the master in all three of these pamphlets, should he choose to write his name as 'Drummont', with two *m*s? It can only have the effect of, at best, devaluing the reference and, at worst, of subverting the entire tradition. In the same context, Emmanuel Mounier's attack on *Bagatelles pour un massacre* in *Esprit* discovers not merely acts of plagiarism on Céline's part, but deliberate falsification of data. Thus, whilst indicating Céline's unacknowledged pillaging of de Vries's *Israël, son passé, son avenir* and contemporary pamphlets such as *Le Règne des Juifs* and *La Prochaine Révolution des travailleurs*, Mounier draws attention to his systematic deformation of the original facts, supposedly for polemical purposes. Whereas *Le Règne des Juifs* puts the Jewish population of Paris in 1914 at 70,000 and in 1936 at 174,000, Céline blatantly exaggerates by increasing the figures to 90,000 and 400,000 respectively (HER 2, 342). Similarly, whilst *La Prochaine Révolution des travailleurs*, puts the Jewish population of France at 650,000, Céline gives a figure for 'Juifs et matinés' of 2 million, and sets the number of Frenchmen mobilised in 1914 at 9.95 million, as opposed to his model's more cautious figure of 4.95 million (HER 2, 342). Clearly, this procedure goes beyond a purely polemical desire to convince, and Mounier joins Arland, Gide and Rebatet in a state of general perplexity: 'Où finit la plaisanterie? Où commence l'indélicatesse? Céline est-il un sceptique qui s'amuse ou un obsédé soumis à son délire?' (HER 2, 342). This hesitation on Mounier's part raises two important issues. In the first place, the wilful subversion of factual data is a common enough procedure in Céline's work and is at the heart of his supposedly factual doctoral thesis on Semmelweis. Secondly, the effect of this transformation of data is to reinforce Céline's fictional world at the expense of the real one, a procedure crucial to the work of the novelist, but counter-productive, if discovered, to the aims of the polemicist.

A further factor which undoubtedly contributed to the disorientation of contemporary readers is the fact that there appears to be a marked gap between the fictional stances of the author and his polemic, a gap which constitutes a repetition of the divide between the treatment of the Ford factory in Detroit in *Voyage au bout de la nuit* and the 1928 lecture. Not only is anti-Semitism virtually absent from Céline's two novels of the 1930s, as it is from the manuscript of *Casse-pipe*, it is also explicitly mocked, under the general guise of racism, in Bardamu's opening conversation with Arthur Ganate:

La race, ce que t'appelles comme ça, c'est seulement ce grand ramassis de miteux dans mon genre, chassieux, puceux, transis, qui ont échoué ici poursuivis par la faim, la peste, les tumeurs et le froid, venus vaincus des quatre coins du monde. Ils ne pouvaient pas aller plus loin à cause de la mer. C'est ça la France et puis c'est ça les Français (V, 8).

Similarly, 'le Président Poincaré qui s'en allait inaugurer . . . une exposition de petits chiens' (V, 7–8) is transformed into a revered saviour-figure in the pamphlets. This poses exactly the same problem as that posed by the apparent contradiction of the views of Dr Destouches on Ford by the author of *Voyage au bout de la nuit*: either the two views are simply, and unsatisfactorily, irreconcilable, or Céline has changed his mind between 1932 and 1937. Or, as in the case of the medical writings, the procedures of polemic in Céline are considerably more elusive and ambiguous than has hitherto been assumed.

This hypothesis is connected to the fact that, in addition to its polemical content, Céline's anti-Semitic writing possesses definite fictional qualities, highlighted by the presence in *Bagatelles pour un massacre* of the three ballets and the narration of the idyll with

Nathalie, the Molly of the Russian journey, by the episode of the *sirène* which introduces *L'Ecole des cadavres*, and the bizarre tale of the disappearance of the narrator's elderly patient in the Parisian industrial suburbs which concludes *Les Beaux draps*. The sheer presence of the fictional elements, which, significantly, often open or close the works, in the body of the polemical texts is enough to at least question their status. Furthermore, the fact that Céline's excursion into anti-Semitism begins with a ballet and ends with an opera, at the end of *Les Beaux draps*, prompts the suspicion that the three pamphlets in fact constitute a self-contained trilogy within Céline's work in which fictional procedures, together with the creation and sustaining of a narrator, are essential.

None of this complexity is to imply, however, that Céline can or should be absolved from responsibility for the clear anti-Semitic stances he adopted before and during the Occupation. Both Paul Bleton and Paul Kingston[7] have amply demonstrated the place occupied by Céline's writings in the tradition of French anti-Semitism, as have Jean-Dominique Poli and Philippe Bourdrel.[8] At the same time, Pascal Ory notes the publication 'sous occupation et en zone nord . . . [de] *L'Ecole des cadavres*, assorti d'une préface raciste et "européenne" sans équivoque et [de] *Bagatelles pour un massacre*, agrémenté cette fois de vingt photographies antisémites légendées par Céline avec un sens de l'humour très personnel',[9] whilst Colin Nettlebeck has scrupulously charted all the minor collaborationist pieces of writing undertaken by Céline from 1940 to 1944, including those articles which appeared under the guise of letters to the collaborationist press:

> on remarquera qu'il ne les adresse pas à n'importe qui: les destinataires sont un Pierre Costantini, un Jacques Doriot, un Jean Drault, un Alain Laubreaux, un Jean Lestandi; et elles paraissent dans des organes comme *L'Appel*, *Les Cahiers de l'émancipation nationale*, *La Gerbe*, *Je suis partout* et *Au pilori*. D'une note à l'autre, Céline joue sur toute la gamme de la presse collaborationniste la plus scabreuse et la plus fatigante.[10]

7. See Paul Bleton, 'Maximes, phrases et efficace d'un pamphlet', BLFC 3, 249–71; Paul Kingston, 'Céline et l'antisémitisme de son époque: aspects de *Bagatelles pour un massacre*', BLFC 5, 49–66.
8. See Jean-Dominique Poli, 'Les Données de mentalité dans les romans et les pamphlets', BLFC 1, 167–84; Philippe Bourdrel, *Histoire des Juifs de France*, Paris, Albin Michel, coll. 'H comme Histoire', 1974, p. 317.
9. Pascal Ory, *Les Collaborateurs 1940–1945*, Paris, Seuil, coll. 'Points', 1980, p. 232.
10. Colin W. Nettlebeck, 'Céline devant l'an 40. *Les Beaux draps* et le début de *Guignol's Band*', BLFC 5, 68–9.

There is therefore a wealth of material to testify to a consistent expression of racism on Céline's part, both in his pamphlets and in his contributions to the collaborationist press, and to counter the by now tedious assertions of Céline's contemporaries that his sole aim was to prevent war.

Nevertheless, although these recent analyses have served to invalidate partisan defences of Céline on pacifist grounds, they are by no means sufficient to provide an adequate explanation of the dynamics of the pamphlets themselves. Indeed, Pascal Ory's reference to the photographs, with their 'sens de l'humour très personnel' which accompany the republication of *Bagatelles pour un massacre* in 1942, testifies to the same perplexity as that which inhibits Arland, Gide, Mounier and Rebatet. In fact, the photographs, with their bizarre captions, constitute a prime subversive device in relation to both *Bagatelles pour un massacre* and *L'Ecole des cadavres*, of the same status as the exaggeration, misquotation and mixing of genres which characterise the works. For the problem which faces the reader is not, as most critics would have it, the simple *identification* of anti-Semitic thematic elements within the pamphlets, but the attempt to ascertain and elucidate the mechanics and meaning of the way in which they are manipulated. The pamphlets pose exactly the same problem as the medical writings, to which they are linked by the republication, in 1942, of the Ford lecture, and which describe the same world: the *ideas* alone do not necessarily convey the entire meaning, which is found, rather, in the use to which Céline puts them and the light in which he makes them appear. It is only then that it is possible, in both sets of interlinked pamphlets, to explore the question of Céline's seriousness or irony or, even further, the extent to which he attempts to protect himself through the use of ambiguity and camouflage. In order to do this, it is necessary to avoid the synthetic approach to Céline's pamphlets which, although yielding interesting results, as in the case of Albert Chesneau's *Psychocritique de Louis-Ferdinand Céline*, necessarily denies the works their individual status as texts and therefore their specific qualities. Merlin Thomas is the only critic to have written extensively on each of the three anti-Semitic pamphlets and to have attempted to point out the characteristics, successes and failures of each component in the trilogy. Each of these works possesses a different emphasis in its preoccupations and a different literary format. It is from the interaction between these two quantities and from the evolution within the three texts that it is possible to establish their real significance in the broad pattern of Céline's work in the inter-war years and a more accurate understanding of their author's relationship to the modern world in which he lives and the world before the First World War, his Golden Age.

Bagatelles pour un massacre

In a very concrete sense, *Bagatelles pour un massacre* constitutes a sequel to *Mea culpa*: it contains references to the criticism to which the author has been subjected as a result of his 'betrayal' of Russia (BM, 45, 46) and, on numerous occasions, presents the retrospective documentary evidence of which the earlier theoretical denunciation was based: the appalling social conditions prevailing in the Soviet Union, the inequalities in Soviet society, its backwardness, all summed up in the lengthy description of the Leningrad venereal disease clinic.[11] Finally, the pamphlet ends on a wistful and rigorously non-anti-Semitic evocation of the narrator's half-love affair with his Intourist guide Nathalie and his final attempt to have a ballet produced: *Van Bagaden*. In other words, whereas *Mea culpa* provides the philosophical refutation of the optimism inherent in Communist theory, *Bagatelles pour un massacre* is Céline's real *Retour de l'URSS* a journey for which, unlike Gide, but like Bardamu on the *Amiral Bragueton*, he paid the price himself, both literally and metaphorically.

At the same time, *Bagatelles pour un massacre* is carefully established as a sequel to *Mort à crédit*, with the same narrator, Ferdinand, and the same interlocutor, his cousin Gustin. In addition, the work looks forward to procedures used in the later fiction, notably in the *D'un château l'autre* trilogy, by which the author's name, Céline, is explicitly introduced and joined to that of the fictional narrator of the preceeding works, and by which real figures are included in the fiction: the use of the painter Popaul, Gen Paul in *Bagatelles pour un massacre*, looks forward to the presence of that other Montmartre figure, the actor Le Vigan, and of the entire

---

11. See BM, 113–22. This episode is interesting, however, for more than its documentary value. If 'tous les Ford se ressemblent, soviétiques ou non', then all clinics do as well, and the Leningrad hospital is a mere reflection of the main work of Gustin's practise and Ferdinand's *dispensaire* in *Mort à crédit*. The narrator's outrage at conditions in the Leningrad clinic constitutes a repetition of that of Semmelweis in Klin's *pavillon* in Vienna. And the fact that the doctor who acts as Ferdinand's guide in Leningrad shouts 'en baryton' (BM, 118–19) refers the reader back to Bardamu's employer in Vigny-sur-Seine in *Voyage au bout de la nuit*. In other words, Céline is concerned, not merely to maintain a pattern of sexuality being linked to disease and death rather than to life and birth, but also with the construction of a totally fictional universe.

Vichy cabinet in *D'un château l'autre*. All of this must at least prompt the speculation as to whether *Bagatelles pour un massacre* is not more intimately connected to the evolution of Céline's fictional production than might at first sight appear.

On the face of it, of course, as most commentators have pointed out, Céline's pamphlets are the vehicle for the common fund of French inter-war anti-Semitism: the view that, since the First World War, in which they allegedly suffered fewer casualties proportionally than the native French population, the Jews had taken control of France, which they were running through international finance and undermining by the proliferation of the distribution of alcohol; the paranoid assertion of the existence of an international Jewish conspiracy, operated through the government of the Soviet Union, the 'Jewish' government of the United States, the American financiers who, like the Loeb-Warburg Bank, allegedly funded the October Revolution, and the sinister power of England, with its 'Jewish' City and its shadowy but omnipotent Intelligence Service. In *Bagatelles pour un massacre* the common phobias of the French anti-Semite emerge clearly: hatred of America and Russia, the confidence-trickster behind the *Emprunts Russes* débâcle, combine with traditional Anglophobia to construct a vision of a world-wide plot to destroy the Aryan race, enshrined in the hoax of the *Protocols of the Elders of Zion*, from which Céline quotes liberally. Nor is the apparent suddenness of the narrator's conversion to anti-Semitism particularly unusual, though on this specific point some doubts begin to emerge as to what Céline's real purpose is. One such example of a sudden and apparently inexplicable onset of anti-Semitism is that of Marcel Jouhandeau. In *Le Péril Juif*, of 1936, he recalls: 'Le jour que parut mon premier article contre les Juifs, Marcel Aymé, pour qui j'éprouve une profonde sympathie, m'avouait son étonnement de me voir devenu tout d'un coup si acharné xénophobe',[12] and he offers as an explanation to the bemused Aymé the number of Jews involved in the running of the Gallimard publishing-house,[13] concluding: 'ce troupeau bien humble (the poor Jews of the rue des Rosiers), installé dans la ville, ne présenterait en lui-même aucun danger pour nous, s'il n'était la pépinière du juif intellectuel qui tentera demain de nous détruire'. Ferdinand's own conversion to anti-Semitism in *Bagatelles pour un massacre* is equally sudden, shocks his audience by its virulence, and

---

12. Marcel Jouhandeau, *Le Péril juif*, Paris, Fernand Sarlat, 1936, p. 19.
13. Ibid., p. 19. Marcel Aymé, of course, was a friend of Céline's and a fellow inhabitant of Montmartre.

is based on a sense of anti-intellectual professional outrage analogous to that of Jouhandeau: the refusal of the Opéra and the 1937 Exposition, both allegedly under the control of the Jews, to perform his ballets, *La Naissance d'une fée* and *Voyou Paul, brave Virginie*.

It is indeed the presence of the three ballets in the text which alerts the reader to something which is occurring which does not precisely fit the conventional anti-Semitic tract or pamphlet. In fact, like the ballets themselves, the anti-Semitism of the narrator Ferdinand is transitory, almost arbitrary: it emerges with the rejection of the first ballet because no Jewish musician will provide a score for it, and it vanishes, unexplained, before the long final episode recounting Ferdinand's exploration, in the company of Nathalie, of Moscow and Leningrad. The presence of the ballets and the sudden upsurge and disappearance of the narrator's anti-Semitism highlight the self-consciously literary characteristics and preoccupations of what is masquerading as an unambiguous polemic. For, in addition to the conscious stylisation of the ballets, *Bagatelles pour un massacre* contains an unusual number of purely literary concerns. Thus, set against Ferdinand's dictum that: 'Un style c'est une émotion, d'abord' (BM, 164), is the threat of the Jewish 'style robot' (BM, 166), which looks forward to Bernanos's *La France contre les robots* of 1940 and constitutes the legacy of the Renaissance and the Enlightenment and of their more recent manifestations, Naturalism and Surrealism. Similarly, like Jouhandeau in 1936, Ferdinand attacks the Jews for their alleged grip upon international culture and their attempts to diminish French culture by the imposition on France of foreign authors: it is the Jews who are snuffing out the rare glimmers of emotion in French literature through their massive distribution of foreign works in translation, particularly from the Anglo-Saxon countries, and through their attempt to 'standardise' (with connotations of conformity and the assembly line) the production of literature (BM, 195–8). Against this tide of Jewish cultural influence and subversion, Ferdinand sets the small number of authors who are still cultivating the values of emotion and musicality in literature which alone constitute a barrier to the rise of decadence: Simenon, Aymé, the Malraux of *Les Conquérants*, Elie Faure, Dabit, Paul Morand and Pierre Mac Orlan, the great precursor: 'il avait tout prévu, tout mis en musique, trente ans d'avance' (BM, 216), to whom he adds the figures of Claude Farrère, Barbusse and Léon Daudet in literature, and Vlamminck, Gen Paul and Henri Mahé in painting. Through a quite conscious series of artistic digressions — 'Je divague comme une vieille chaisière', (BM, 217) — *Bagatelles pour un massacre* subverts itself as a work of polemic and becomes an *art poétique*. Nor is it negligible, in this context, that the work should contain an abundant use of what is essentially a dramatic or fictional element, namely, dialogue: Ferdinand's anti-Semitic quest, which echoes that of Bardamu throughout *Voyage au bout de la nuit*, takes place through increasingly heated dialogue with Gustin, Léo Gutman and Popaul.

It is this essential, dramatic ingredient of the work which is conveyed by the title itself. To read the title of *Bagatelles pour un massacre*, as Mounier does, as signifying simply: 'Petit travail sans valeur pour exciter les gens au meurtre' (HER 2, 341), is not merely unjustifiably to limit the meaning of a highly complex text, but to miss both the main argument of the narrator and the framework in which Céline, as author, places him. It is more illuminating, rather, to explore the possibilities of the artistic or musical implications of the term 'Bagatelle': 'Composition légère, petite pièce agréable et facile, destinée à plaire plutôt qu'à édifier', and 'Morceau de musique légère et de courte durée, sans forme précise'.[14] This particular perspective highlights the formless quality of the work, but also, in support of the Gidean interpretation of the essay as a satire, its occasional, amusing, rather than seriously instructive, nature. More revealing, however, is a further, archaic meaning of the word 'Bagatelles': 'Bonniments que débitent les forains à l'entrée de leur porte pour inciter les gens à assister au spectacle',[15] a meaning which in itself explains the second *dédicace*: 'A mes potes du "Théâtre en Toile"'. The precise meaning of the work as a whole is now thrown into relief: Céline is not, in *Bagatelles pour un massacre*, inciting the French to murder the Jews; on the contrary, he is asking his audience to watch the imminent massacre of the French by the Jews and the vain efforts of his narrator Ferdinand to prevent it. None of the thrust of the work goes in the direction of even envisaging physical retaliation: the whole work is narrated in the light of French powerlessness and vulnerability in the face of the international Jewish menace. At the same time, it is readily apparent what kind of theatrical performance is being laid on for the audience: it is fairground theatre, the drama of 'jeu de massacre' and 'Grand Guignol' in which, in highly exaggerated form, the narrator will take on the Jews and, inevitably, lose.

The pamphlet, therefore, becomes a grotesque and exaggerated theatrical representation of Ferdinand's anti-Semitic quest, in which he undertakes to defend, specifically, French literature. The prob-

14. See: *Trésor de la Langue Française*.
15. See: ibid.

lem, however, is that this quest is doomed to failure *because* it only takes the theatrical form of dialogue, because it is purely verbal and rhetorical. Real power and the real forces of destruction are to be found in more absolute and more concrete forms: 'Les Juifs sont nos maîtres' (BM, 49) because 'L'or devient par ce passe-passe la toute propriété des Juifs' (BM, 63) — 'ils ont saisi tout l'or' (BM, 66). The same stumbling-block to survival, let alone progress, of the petite bourgeoisie, the lack of gold, of real economic and verbal credit, is magnified and racialised in *Bagatelles pour un massacre*. It is for this reason that the pamphlet has the same narrator-protagonist as the novel and the same interlocutor: it constitutes the repetition of the same drama, except that now the agents of modernity, only fleetingly alluded to in *Mort à crédit* through the 'Comptoir Judéo-Suisse', are fully exteriorised. It is also for this reason that the pamphlet maintains the connection established in the novel between gold and excrement: Ferdinand, deprived of the gold which has now become the exclusive property of the Jews, is reduced to its counterpart in the deployment of excremential imagery and excremential language in the form of abuse.

Yet the crucial importance of this language is that it is, ultimately, useless, and here again the pamphlet reflects accurately the pattern of the novel. The writer-narrator of *Mort à crédit* is unable to move his cousin Gustin by his reading of the Krogold Legend and so hypothesises a literature, not of transcendence, but of auto-destruction, which will guarantee survival in non-being. In *Bagatelles pour un massacre*, the relationship with Gustin and the other interlocutors, Gutman and Popaul, is more complicated but ultimately expresses the same pessimism. Gustin already shares Ferdinand's anti-Semitism, to the extent that he is willing to envisage an alliance with Hitler: 'Ferdinand, quand c'est la bataille, le fascisme vaut le communisme' (BM, 316), and: 'Moi je voudrais bien faire une alliance avec Hitler. Pourquoi pas? Il a rien dit contre les Bretons, contre les Flamands ... Rien du tout ... Il a dit seulement sur les Juifs' (BM, 317), which draws from the narrator the more cautious comment: 'Je veux pas faire la guerre pour Hitler, moi je le dis, mais je veux pas la faire contre lui, pour les Juifs' (BM, 317). The difference between the two characters is that Gustin, unlike Ferdinand, is operating on a political level, and in this context it is worth recalling that during the Occupation it was precisely the nationalist movements in Flanders and Brittany who were the most in favour of integration into the Reich.[16] Ferdinand,

16. See Ory, *Les Collaborateurs*, Chapter 9.

however, is working on a level which is ultimately not political at all, but which is absolute, aesthetic and, perhaps, fully conscious that there is no future for him anyway. The racist diatribe, therefore, which constitutes the bulk of *Bagatelles pour un massacre*, has the effect, neither of convincing nor of reassuring his listeners but, on the contrary, of boring or worrying them. Thus, after Ferdinand has rehearsed his attacks upon Jewish trusts, the Jews and the Freemasons, the Jews as a zoological phenomenon and Jewish psychoanalysis, all the well-worn clichés of conventional anti-Semitism, Gustin merely comments with some exasperation: 'Mais je sais bien que t'aimes pas les Juifs!' (BM, 309), and, throughout their arguments, it is Gustin, Gutman and Popaul, as *reasonable* people, who constantly recommend caution and show disquiet at Ferdinand's crusade. As Gutman sums up: 'Si tu sors pas du désert, tu sors des cavernes, c'est bien pire' (BM, 322), and he warns: 'T'auras le monde entier contre toi!' (BM, 325). In other words, Ferdinand as a latter-day John the Baptist, arising from the prehistoric caves or from the dark recesses of the human mind, terrifies and perplexes his closest collaborators in exactly the same way that Céline will disorientate Rebatet and the *Je suis partout* team with the publication of his second pamphlet, *L'Ecole des cadavres*.

This ambiguous effect on his hearers, however, is not there merely to demonstrate the vulnerability of Ferdinand's rhetorical crusade. By the very conventional formulae employed and by the lack of progression in the argument — the fact that the work is a series of repetitive and unevolving *bagatelles* — Ferdinand is imprisoned in a linguistic, social and psychological world which is severely limited and from which there is no escape. It is a limitation which is rendered all the more poignant and complex by the fact that it echoes, exactly, not the situation and responses of Ferdinand, in *Mort à crédit*, but the frustration of his father Auguste. In some respects, *Bagatelles pour un massacre* is no more than an extended amplification of Auguste's imprecations throughout the novel, against 'Le Destin . . . Les Juifs . . . La Poisse . . . L'Exposition . . . La Providence . . . Les Francs-Maçons'. In the light of the close bonds between Ferdinand and Auguste in *Mort à crédit*, to the extent that the entire novel may be read as an extended *Mea culpa* directed at the father through the person of the cousin, Gustin, this repetition of the father's phobias becomes highly significant. The attempt to murder Auguste with the typewriter, the symbol of mechanised language, reveals a desire, not merely to supplant the father but to *become* the father, and it is this ambition which is realised in the theft of the father's language in *Bagatelles pour un massacre.* This theft also explains more fully the necessity of the presence of Gustin in both the novel and the pamphlet: Ferdinand the son, by borrowing and exaggerating the father's language at extraordinary length, finally surpasses the racism of the father's representative in the pamphlet. The work therefore shows a complex duality: the narrator Ferdinand, in the grip of the same uncontrollable frustration as that which had previously driven Auguste into paroxysms of rage, is driven to imitate his father; but, in an attempt finally to exorcise the ghost of Auguste, he strives throughout the pamphlet to surpass him both emotionally and rhetorically. *Bagatelles pour un massacre* possesses a strong psychological, even psychoanalytical component, which is connected to the drama of *Mort à crédit*, and if *Guignol's Band*, written after the pamphlets, testifies to a new confidence and serenity on the part of its narrator, it is likely that it owes that to the way in which, in *Bagatelles pour un massacre*, the narrator can finally exorcise the *mauvaise conscience* of the novel.

This process is undoubtedly facilitated by the way in which, for Céline, history in the 1930s appears to be conforming to the Nietzschean cyclical vision of eternal recurrence, visible in *Semmelweis*. And, as in the medical thesis, repetition signifies not merely imprisonment but decline. In the late 1930s, a war is threatening which will definitively complete the process begun in 1914. At the same time, whereas the defeat and erosion of the Parisian petite bourgeoisie is signalled and consecrated in 1900 by the Universal Exposition which dominates *Mort à crédit*, itself the culmination of an entire cycle of exhibitions, the destruction of what remains of that class is heralded in *Bagatelles pour un massacre* by the 'Exposition Poly-Juive-Maçonnique 37' (BM, 232), the Front Populaire International Exposition of 1937. Not only does this event confirm Jewish control of France, but its real crime is in the fact that it is a pale reflection of the event of 1900. It is 'la plus sale foire, la plus toc, et la plus couteuse que le peuple aura jamais vue' (BM, 235), a miserable fairground theatre, far inferior to Ferdinand's own, played out on the stage of *Bagatelles pour un massacre.* Yet this 1937 Exposition is not merely a further example in Céline's work of history repeating itself as farce: commenting on the pathetic unoriginality of the Front Populaire's Exposition, he notes: 'C'est suranné, c'est mesquin, ça fait pour toujours 1900' (BM, 234). Céline's terminology is important here, for it implies, not merely that 1937 is a pale imitation of 1900, so that history repeats itself with ever-diminishing returns, but that, since 1900, French, if not Western society in general, has become stuck and fixed, so that there is no real progression or movement possible. In the same way that Bardamu, in spite of all his journeyings, never really leaves the Place Clichy in 1914, Céline's social world is constantly and unalterably that of 1900, when the great betrayal of his class was consecrated. The fact that Nino Frank notes an upsurge in a 'mode 1900' in the 1930s merely confirms this constancy. *Bagatelles pour un massacre*, therefore, takes over from *Mort à crédit*, with its two historical polarities of the 1900 Exposition and the 1934 riots. The agents and profiteers of the destruction of the artisanal petite bourgeoisie are no longer the shadowy bourgeois who constitute the clientele of Clémence, nor the *baron* who heads the insurance company, *La Coccinelle*, nor even the faintly alluded-to Comptoir Judéo-Suisse; this time, they are the international Jewish conspiracy, which dealt the death-blow to the French petite bourgeoisie through the contrivance of the First World War and the enormity of the Soviet confidence-trick over the *Emprunts Russes*. Above all, the Jews in *Bagatelles pour un massacre* are both the agents and a symbol of a modern, cosmopolitan, industrialised world, in which Ferdinand and his like have no place and where even their cries of outrage are increasingly irrelevant — of the same irrelevance as Auguste's outpourings in *Mort à crédit* which are merely the rhetorical equivalent of hiding in the cellar. For this reason, linguistically, Ferdinand is imprisoned in a tight circle of imitation, repetition and digression, with all progression rigorously denied him.

It is at this point that two different, but by no means totally irreconcilable readings of the text present themselves. On one level, *Bagatelles pour un massacre* is an act of revenge for the imprisonment to which Ferdinand finds himself condemned, a revenge announced by the *exergue*: 'Il est vilain, il n'ira pas au Paradis celui qui décède sans avoir réglé tous ses comptes (Almanach des Bons-Enfants)', which in its turn echoes the conclusion of the final fragment of *Casse-pipe*: 'Moi, je ne pardonne jamais'. What is perplexing about this desire for revenge is that it should lead, not merely to the inescapable rhetorical repetition and exaggeration of the pamphlet, but to a situation in which Ferdinand is willing to enlist the support of those who, only recently, have been his deepest enemies. Thus, when he justifies his attacks on the Jews, he does so by invoking 'Ford qui les a en horreur' (BM, 62), that same Ford who has poisoned Bardamu's existence in Detroit and even the Soviet Union in *Mea culpa*: 'Ford qui les a en horreur' is written less than a year after 'Tous les Ford se ressemblent . . .'. More bizarre is his recourse to the English polemical writer, Nesta Helen Webster, who, in *The Surrender of an Empire*, chronicles the subversion of the British Empire by the Jews, a process which is now occurring in France itself.[17] Yet, on the evidence of the rest of the pamphlet, the collapse of Britain and its Empire should cause Ferdinand no grief at all. Moreover, Mrs Webster was the very archetypal chauvinist, the author during the First World War of a pamphlet, *Britain's Call to Arms: an Appeal to our Women*,[18] which is a glaring example of all those received ideas which, through the character of Lola, strove to push Bardamu to his death at the Front. In other words, so great apparently is Ferdinand's thirst for revenge on the Jews that it leads to the same logical contradictions in relation to the other texts as are presented by the medical pamphlets and to the same internal inconsistency, signalled neatly in *Bagatelles pour un massacre* by the way in which the little quotations which serve as chapter headings in fact relate in no way whatsoever to the chapters' subject-matter, a technique fully exploited in the 1940s by Boris Vian in *L'Automne à Pékin*.

Alongside this reading based on obsession with revenge, however, there operates a different one, which picks up a whole strain of references in both *Voyage au bout de la nuit* and *Mort à crédit* and which is based on the notion of the text as a vehicle for self-destruction. Indeed, at this point, one of the chapter headings at least takes on a profound significance. At the beginning of the thirty-eighth section, Céline gives a quotation from Agrippa d'Aubigné: 'Que voulez-vous que j'espère parmi ces coeurs abâtardis, sinon de voir mon livre jeté aux ordures' (BM, 185), a quotation which might pass unnoticed, if it did not recall certain references in *Mort à crédit* or look forward to Ferdinand's meeting with the anarchist Borokrom in Leningrad, who, in his turn, looks forward to *Guignol's Band*. In Leningrad, Borokrom confides to Ferdinand his strange ambition to be a hated and hateful despot, with the result that: 'J'aurais fait, moi leur monarque, l'accord de toutes les haines de mon royaume, je les aurais centralisées, magnétisées, fanatisées sur ma propre royale personne' (BM, 368), a confidence which serves as a *mise en abyme* for the entire work. For Borokrom, it is only by making oneself into an object of utter hatred that the nation can be both infused with life and unified. Within the context of *Bagatelles pour un massacre*, it is not so much the Jew who is to fulfil this function as the narrator Ferdinand himself, through his own text: the ultimate victim of the *massacre*

17. Nesta Helen Webster, *The Surrender of an Empire*, London, 1931.
18. Nesta Helen Webster, *Britain's Call to Arms: an Appeal to our Women*, London, 1914.

and the central character of the play the audience is invited to watch is none other than Ferdinand himself. Thus, *Bagatelles pour un massacre* joins *Mort à crédit* as an example in Céline's work of the ideal of the auto-destructive text which serves to bring down the author into oblivion at the same time. As the narrator of *Mort à crédit* muses: 'J'aime mieux raconter des histoires. J'en raconterai de telles qu'ils reviendront, exprès, pour me tuer, des quatre coins du monde. Alors ce sera fini et je serai bien content'. Quite clearly, the 'ils' are the characters of the novel, the figures from Ferdinand's past, and their return, to avenge themselves on their creator, will signify the sought-after oblivion in the ending of the novel.

But, if Céline can write: 'ils reviendront', then these characters are also, literally, 'revenants', part of Céline's consistent evocation of the world of ghosts, and here again the pamphlet rejoins the very deep preoccupations of the novels. At the very end of his reminiscences on Leningrad, when the narrator interestingly intermingles his memories of the Grand Duke Nicholas in Nice in 1910 with more recent references to Borokrom and Nathalie, he comments on all his characters: 'Il n'échappe rien au temps . . . Ils deviendront tous fantômes . . .' (BM, 373), to the extent that the entire conclusion is permeated with the presence of ghosts. Because of the danger to the traveller from the *fantômes*, Ferdinand states: 'Je ne veux plus partir nulle part' (BM, 374), and, just before he introduces his final ballet, *Van Bagaden*, he amplifies the comment revealingly: 'Je veux rester ici pour voir . . . tout voir' (BM, 374): Ferdinand himself has become an invisible, all-seeing *fantôme*, with one of the main prerogatives of the ghost, that of being able to take revenge with impunity. The entire process of the text, therefore, is that by which the narrator Ferdinand is progressively revealed as a ghost, finally able to satisfy his desire for revenge and who reaches this status by inciting his audience to destroy him. *Bagatelles pour un massacre* therefore goes further than *Voyage au bout de la nuit*, although it starts from the same premises: the narrator has no purpose in the world which he is describing and exists in it as a ghost. It is for this reason that, whereas *Voyage au bout de la nuit* begins with the 'Chanson des Gardes Suisses 1793', *Bagatelles pour un massacre*, published in 1937, is dedicated, not only to 'mes potes du "Théâtre en Toile"', but also to Eugène Dabit who died in Russia a year earlier. Both works are dedicated to ghosts.

As the narrator explains about his final ballet: 'voici qui danse exactement entre la mort et l'existence' (BM, 374). Between the dedication to the ghost Dabit and Céline's auto-destructive *Grand Guignol* theatre, hovers the pure world of *féerie* which, it must be recalled, is part, with Utopias, of the same literary sub-genre as the *voyages imaginaires*. Thus, Ferdinand, before deciding to emigrate to anti-British and mystical Celtic Ireland, decides to give the reader some more chapters, a 'grande féerie' (BM, 330), and he provides a definition of ballet as 'Ballet veut dire féerie' (BM, 347). Yet that final ballet, *Van Bagaden*, reunites the two disparate elements of the pamphlet's title. When the Russian *directeur* commissions the ballet, he wants something more modern than *La Naissance d'une fée*: 'Les Russes raffolent de la violence. L'ignorais-je? . . . Il leur en faut! . . . Ils l'exigent! . . . Quelques batailles! . . . de l'émeute! . . . pourquoi pas? . . . des meutres! . . . d'amples massacres bien amenés . . .' (BM, 350). And, when the script is complete, the narrator concludes his long address to the reader with the words: 'Je vais vous lire le début de ce long divertissement . . . une bagatelle!' (BM, 374).

We are now in a position to isolate and identify the different elements which combine in the construction of *Bagatelles pour un massacre*. At the centre of the work are quite clearly the three hundred or so pages of anti-Semitic vituperation. Yet this bulk is counterbalanced to a certain extent by a significant portion of the text, some seventy-five pages, which has no overt anti-Semitic content at all and is taken up with the three ballets and the narration of the Russian idyll with Nathalie. At the same time, the anti-Semitism is not conveyed by pure authorial declaration, but through the intermediary of a narrator, Ferdinand Céline, the author and narrator of *Mort à crédit* who continues his literary preoccupations in *Bagatelles pour un massacre*. Not only that, but, *as a character*, he moves far closer to the centre of the stage than is conventional in the French tradition of pamphleteering from Drumont to Bernanos, to the extent that he concretises the ambiguous relationship between narrator and father in *Mort à crédit* by imitating Auguste's outpourings and finding himself, like his father before him, imprisoned in the same narrow world of repetition and limitation to which the only response is equally futile exaggeration. The narrator remains as much in his father's world of 1900 as in the threatened world of the inter-war years. Yet, the more the pamphlet becomes the property of an idiosyncratic narrator, the more internal and external contradictions, first seen in the medical polemic, emerge. The perplexity of contemporary reviewers becomes more comprehensible therefore in the light of these different elements, which appear to fail to match up completely and raise important questions. Chief amongst these is the entire problem of the status of the anti-Semitic context: no one could dispute its presence, nor its debt to historical and contemporary French anti-Semitism, but, as seen clearly in the similarity between Céline's conversion to anti-Semitism and that of Jouhandeau, the nagging possibility exists of parody, a procedure which is, after all, one of Céline's favourite devices in his fiction. Furthermore, quite apart from the status of the anti-Semitism as authentic, parodic, or both, there is also the suggestion that it may constitute, not an end in itself, but a pretext: the exorcism of the father's presence which alone can open the way to the real centre of the work, the *grande féerie* at its end. To a large extent, these competing elements and interpretations remain irreconcilable if *Bagatelles pour un massacre* is consulted in isolation. Fortunately, Céline's second pamphlet, *L'Ecole des cadavres*, appears to present a simplified schema and permit a less ambiguous evaluation of its pure anti-Semitic content.

L'Ecole des cadavres

It is in his second pamphlet that Céline appears to let the mask of ambiguity drop, so that the unequivocal authorial standpoint becomes clear. It is undoubtedly for this very reason that the work has attracted less individual discussion than the other two pamphlets, most critics agreeing with Merlin Thomas that 'it is Céline's one real incursion into what one might call journalism, and it is by a very considerable distance his feeblest and least interesting book'.[19] Later, after discussing the disparity of the material covered in the pamphlet, he concludes:

> What on earth can Céline have thought was going to be the effect of all this material — and on whom? Even in the wildest pages of *Bagatelles* there is a discernable degree of aesthetic control of material that is often lacking in the second pamphlet: it is as though, exasperated by the relative lack of response to his earlier outburst, and even more aware of the approach of war, he writes not only hastily but petulently and without any real attempt at persuasion.[20]

In contrast with *Bagatelles pour un massacre*, *L'Ecole des cadavres* has little recourse to any overtly literary or specifically fictional procedures. There is a short introduction which establishes a narrator in the person of the recurrent Ferdinand, but this device is

19. Merlin Thomas, *Louis-Ferdinand Céline*, London, Faber and Faber, 1979, p. 156.
20. Ibid., p. 160.

nowhere exploited fully as the text progresses: the work does not return to the narrator when it comes to the end, as it does in the first pamphlet, and there is no attempt to establish an interlocutor who will permit the manipulation of dialogue. Instead, after the short scene in which Ferdinand and the *sirène* trade insults on the Seine between Courbevoie and La Jatte, the work consists of a long series of independent fragments of apparently pure and extreme anti-Semitism: a succession of genuine *bagatelles* in the technical sense.

Nevertheless, repetitive and disjointed as these *bagatelles* may appear, they are grouped into a certain number of common anti-Semitic preoccupations of the 1930s. The first of these, which accords ill with the ostensible admiration of Americanism in the medical pamphlets and with the idyllic evocation of London during the First World War in *Guignol's Band*, is a sustained Anglophobia which extends to the entire Anglo-Saxon world. On his last visit to the United States, Ferdinand has been frightened by the massive power of Jewish propaganda, particularly through the cinema, which, in the guise of anti-Fascism, is in fact pushing the French towards war with Germany: 'La gangsterie américaine nous ordonne aux tranchées pour avril!' (EC, 41). America is now under the complete domination of the Jews, to the extent that 'Uncle Sam' is in reality 'Samuel Cohen' (EC, 43), who exhibits all the ruthless philistine qualities of Sinclair Lewis's Babbitt (EC, 44), and the President, Roosevelt, is really a Jew who has changed his name from 'Rosenfeld' (EC, 50). The American deification of money, which Bardamu has observed in the New York bank in *Voyage au bout de la nuit*, has now taken on a more precise and sinister meaning: it is Jewish gold, through which the Jews will come to destroy the West and dominate the world. It is for this reason that the implicit contempt in *Voyage au bout de la nuit* of the American for the European, of Lola for the *miteux* Bardamu, is rendered explicit in *L'Ecole des cadavres* through the description of the New York burlesque houses which specialise in 'séances françaises' (EC, 51). Here, the Americans come to witness the degeneracy of the French in exactly the same way that the French go to see the 'singes, au Jardin des Plantes' (EC, 52) or Ferdinand's family in *Mort à crédit* go to gawp at the *indigènes* at the Exposition (MC, 580). Yet there is a final sting in the tail of this contempt: 'les judéo-américains . . . ne nous rendent l'estime . . . qu'au moment où le clairon rallie nos viandes' (EC, 53).

The real threat comes, however, not from America but from England: 'Tous déclics, de la Guere, de la Paix, sont à Londres' (EC, 59). It is London, with its City, dominated by Jewish gold, its

Court and, especially, its Intelligence Service, which is the centre of the Jewish world-conspiracy. Thus, the Prime Minister, Chamberlain, has his policy dictated to him by the City: 'Très bien, Monsieur Or!' (EC, 130), and even the English throne is the agent of Zionism. Commenting on the recent visit of George VI to Paris, to cement the alliance with France which will place her at England's mercy, Ferdinand cries: 'Vive les Sages de Sion!' (EC, 123). Yet, more than the Court or the City, it is the mysterious Intelligence Service which is the embodiment of British power and which is used to subvert the world order in the interests of the Jews. Here, Céline is subscribing to a potent myth in Europe in the inter-war years, by which the British Intelligence Service was viewed as a sinister, all-pervading naked instrument of British imperial power. In Drieu la Rochelle's *Notes pour comprendre le siècle*, for example, agents of the Intelligence Service figure, alongside German Nazis, Russian commissars and adventurers and colonialists of all types, as vestigial representatives of will and energy in an otherwise decadent Europe. More significantly, in Malraux's *Les Conquérants*, one of the works singled out for specific praise in *Bagatelles pour un massacre*, the hero's biography is conveyed to the reader in the form of extracts from a stolen British Intelligence Service dossier, and Britain and the Intelligence Service come to represent the values which the hero, Garine, holds most dear: 'Diriger. Determiner. Contraindre. La vie est là'.[21] The sources of this myth are not difficult to find: they clearly have their origins in European fears at the extent and efficiency of British imperialism in the nineteenth century, which seemed to be confirmed in patriotic colonial fiction, such as the *Sanders of the River* tales by Edgar Wallace or, more importantly, Rudyard Kipling's *Kim*, in which the whole course of world-history is 'the Great Game', to be played and won by the agents of the Intelligence Service. From these fictional origins, it is not surprising that a myth of world-wide conspiracy, centred on London, could be elaborated which fed an already traditional French Anglophobia stretching back to the Napoleonic Wars and which re-emerged powerfully during the *belle époque* and could easily be combined with fear and envy of the City of London to produce a specifically Jewish threat.

Where *L'Ecole des cadavres* differs strongly from *Bagatelles pour un massacre* is that, whereas the first pamphlet concentrates on the Soviet Union, financed by the American Jewish banks, as the

21. André Malraux, *Les Conquérants*, in *Romans*, Paris, Gallimard, coll. 'La Pléiade', 1947, p. 161.

heartland of the international Jewish plot, its successor sees the West as more dangerous than the East, and contains very little direct anti-Soviet polemic. It is interesting that, in the course of the three pamphlets, Céline is not as repetitive as he might appear, and the objects of his attacks are complementary: Russia in *Bagatelles pour un massacre*, Britain and America in *L'Ecole des cadavres*, France itself in *Les Beaux draps*. In fact, Communism emerges in the second pamphlet as an ideal, admirable in itself, but which is debased in practice. In this way, *L'Ecole des cadavres* is a direct continuation of *Mea culpa* and a further bitter renunciation of the Communist idealism glimpsed in the memorandum of 1932 on the 'cours des hautes études'. Thus, in the second pamphlet, Ferdinand draws a distinction between 'le communisme raisonnable' and real Communism. He begins one important section: 'On ne devient pas communiste. Il faut naître communiste, ou renoncer à le devenir jamais. Le communisme est une qualité d'âme' (EC, 101). It is precisely this spiritual quality which gives to Communism its grandeur and nobility: 'le Communisme dans la pratique c'est unanimité des âmes, des âmes toutes communistes, toutes altruistes, toutes embrasées de passion unanime' (EC, 101). Yet this vision of the Golden Age is cruelly rebutted by reality: 'D'où vont surgir ces sublimes effectifs? Imposture grotesque dans l'état actuel des hommes' (EC, 101). The ideal is Communism become poetry: 'Le Communisme doit être folie, avant tout, par-dessus tout, poésie' (EC, 102), but is killed by fanaticism, rationalism and the mechanical age:

> Le Communisme sans poète, à la juive, à la scientifique, à la raison raisonnante, matérialiste, marxiste, à l'administrative, au mufle, au peigne-cul, au 600 kilos par phrase, n'est plus qu'un très emmerdant procédé de tyrannie prosaïque, absolument sans essor, une imposture juive satrapique absolument atroce, immangeable, inhumaine, une très dégueulasse forcerie d'esclaves, une infernale gageure, un remède pire que le mal (EC, 102).

At the same time, whereas the ideal of Communism, spiritual solidarity, is tempting, although lost, its practical procedure, revolution, is merely the occasion for the unleashing of the worst of human passions, envy. The people wish to supplant the bourgeois, simply because the bourgeois is 'le frère envié . . . le frère qui a réussi!' (EC, 98). Hence the succession of revolutions in France, dedicated in reality to the propagation of the self-interest of the masses: '93! 71! 36! grandes messes démocratiques à la gloire du Peuple-Dieu!' (EC, 98). Revolution in practise, therefore, is by no means the way to a spiritual heightening, but rather the maintenance of humanity at its lowest level, a process which, even worse for Céline, is accompanied by uncontrollable violence, and in this discussion, he returns repeatedly to the image of the slaughterhouse of La Villette (EC, 97), the potent metaphor of destruction in *Voyage au bout de la nuit*.

As an alternative to this vision of debased Communism and a debilitating revolutionary process, Ferdinand turns to the real embodiment of socialism and Communism in Europe, Hitler's Germany: 'Hitler est un bon éleveur des peuples, il est du côté de la Vie, il est soucieux de la vie des peuples, et même de la nôtre. C'est un Aryen' (EC, 108). This is a discovery which will lead Ferdinand in the course of the work to what Merlin Thomas calls 'a number of very compromising remarks about Hitler'.[22] Interestingly enough, with what seems like extraordinary prescience, Céline is able specifically to counter the sort of charges made by Sartre in 'Portrait de l'antisémite' after the Liberation: 'Si Céline a pu soutenir les thèses socialistes des nazis, c'est qu'il était payé'.[23] At the end of *L'Ecole des cadavres*, Céline devotes an entire *bagatelle* to this subject: 'Je vais couper les ailes d'un canard. Il volera quand même. De tous les côtés l'on m'annonce que j'ai touché des sommes formidables d'Hitler' (EC, 222). But:

> Ce que j'écris je le pense, tout seul, et nul ne me paye pour le penser, ne me stimule. Personne, ou presque personne, ne peut se vanter d'en faire autant, de se payer ce luxe. Moi je peux. C'est mon luxe. Mon seul luxe. Et ce n'est pas terminé! Je n'ai pas fini de travailler. Ma mère, à 71 ans, insiste encore pour ne dépendre de personne. Elle continue à travailler, elle gagne sa vie. Je suis pareil. Je ferai de même. Pas de fainéants dans la famille. A 71 ans j'emmerderai encore les juifs, et les maçons, et les éditeurs, et Hitler par dessus le marché, s'il me provoque. Qu'on se le dise. Je dois être, je crois bien, l'homme le moins achetable du monde (EC, 222).

Quite apart from the way in which this passage looks back to the petit-bourgeois morality of *Mort à crédit* and forward to the imprecations of the narrator of *Guignol's Band* and the trilogy against his publisher, it constitutes a further example of Céline's insistence on the fate befalling the 'seul payant du voyage'.

What attracts Ferdinand to Hitler is that the Hitlerian solution alone can remedy the disastrous state of the France of the inter-war

---

22. Thomas, *Louis-Ferdinand Céline*, p. 160.
23. Jean-Paul Sartre, *Réflexions sur la question juive*, Paris, Gallimard, coll. 'Idées', pp. 47–8.

years. Under the influence of the Jews, the French have become decadent, materialist and false: 'Spirituellement, nous sommes retombés à zéro . . . Tous nos arts le prouvent' (EC, 79). And: 'N'ont en France jamais réussi que les traîtres, les saltimbanques, et les donneurs. Peuple creux' (EC, 69). What is lacking in the French is any sense of lyricism and vigour, and it is here that Ferdinand's message coincides with the polemical style of the pamphlet itself: his aim is to 'retrouver une confiance, un rythme, une musique à ce peuple, un lyrisme qui le sorte du baragouin juif' (EC, 73), and it is precisely the 'music' of *L'Ecole des cadavres* itself which points the way. The decadence, however, is almost too all-embracing and it is most unlikely that the French will avoid the drift to war which will wipe them all out: 'Nous périrons sous les vainqueurs si c'est les fascistes qui gagnent . . . Nous périrons sous nos alliés si c'est leur victoire' (EC, 73). And the medium for this self-destruction will be the ever-faithful victims of Republican power, the petite bourgeoisie. It is the French petit bourgeois, with his constant fear of 'escroqueries' (EC, 111), with his traditional virtues: 'du "très bien savoir se priver", du "jamais rien prendre à crédit", de la "prévoyance du lendemain", de la "féroce économie", de "l'existence pauvre mais honnête", du "faire honneur à ses affaires"' (EC, 112), who can be relied upon to staff the coming cataclysm as he did the war of 1914: 'Toutes les concessions doctrinales pourvu que Petit Bourgeois laisse pas tomber l'armée française, reprenne sa place aux effectifs, qu'il bondisse à la gare de l'Est, qu'il saute sur les marchepieds, aux premiers roulements du tambour, qu'il fournisse, encore une fois, les cadres à la pipe!' (EC, 111). So essential is the petit bourgeois to the French war effort that '[on] irait jusqu'a rembourser Petit Bourgeois l'Emprunt Russe pour qu'il retrouve sa vaillance, tout son cran, tout son moral avec ses coupons, son patriotisme exultant, toute sa combativité, sa joyeuse furia de 14!' (EC, 111). In other words, whilst invoking his own petit bourgeois values as a defence against the charge of being bought by Hitler, Ferdinand merely establishes himself as a perennial dupe and victim along with the rest of his class.

With the mass of the French population irremediably weakened by the Jewish 'microbes' (EC, 194) and in a state of irreversible decadence, and with France's only 'moral' class, the petite bourgeoisie, unconsciously acting in the direction of the nation's destruction, France is doomed to vanish under the combined machinations of the Jews and the Freemasons, who exercise, and have always exercised, unlimited power because of their singleminded acquisition and manipulation of gold. Against this unstoppable force, Ferdinand makes one final attempt, by having recourse, not to mere anti-Semitism, but to the much more potent racism. As he comments on Italian Fascism, in a passage which is significant for its use of a bacteriological metaphor which specifically invokes Pasteur, and implicitly Semmelweis, with its references to surgery and antisepsis (EC, 195), Mussolini's Italy will eventually be subverted by the Jews, in the first place because the Italians 'croient aux mots, ils ne croient qu'aux mots' (EC, 196), and secondly because, whereas the regime has a policy of anti-Semitism, it stops short of racism, a fatal error, for: 'Les Juifs n'ont peur que du racisme' (EC, 197). To avoid this fate for France, Ferdinand sounds his warning: 'Racisme d'abord!' (EC, 161) and 'Vive le Racisme! On a compris à force de cadavres' (EC, 166). The message of the 'école des cadavres', the dead Frenchmen of the First World War, is that only racism will preserve France from the Jewish threat. Yet there is a conspiracy to hide this clear and obvious truth: the British deny the very existence of French racism because, like Bardamu, in *Voyage au bout de la nuit*, they dispute the existence of a French race (EC, 170–2); few official scientists will admit the possibility of race, one of the major exceptions being that major figure in traditional anti-Semitism, Georges Mantandon (EC, 167).

Yet the question is not simply one of 'scientific' racism, it is connected to the entire course of European history since the Dark Ages and to the steady decline of Europe since the partition of the Holy Roman Empire of Charlemagne by the Treaty of Verdun in 843. Hence, Ferdinand, at the beginning of one of the *bagatelles*, quotes from a deliberately vague source, 'Les Journaux, 31 octobre 1938', to the effect that: 'Le Gouvernement du Reich a inauguré hier le canal Rhin-Danube commencé par Charlemagne' (EC, 204), and this introduces an entire series of reflections upon the glories of the United Europe under Charlemagne, when there was no artificial division between France and Germany, and the decline since that unity was fragmented. For Ferdinand, this is not an event confined to the past: 'Je la trouve crépitante, embrasante d'actualité ma petite histoire du débonnaire' (EC, 204), for 'La catastrophe de Verdun, c'est la catastrophe permanente' (EC, 205). The division and distrust between France and Germany, maintained by and benefiting the Jews and the British, is the direct cause of Europe's decadence and recurrent wars. The solution is to redraw the map of Europe by repealing, after 1100 years, the Treaty of Verdun and forging an alliance between France and Germany: 'Moi, je veux qu'on fasse une alliance avec l'Allemagne . . .' (EC, 211). This alliance and the re-establishment of the old Europe will have the effect of excluding

Britain and America from intervention in European affairs, of thwarting the international Jewish plot and of enforcing permanent peace by eradicating artificial problems like Czechoslovakia, which is merely the repetition in the late 1930s of the problem of Serbia in 1914 (EC, 36) and Belgium in the nineteenth century (EC, 50). It must be emphasised that, in his evocation of the re-establishment of the Europe of Charlemagne, Céline is by no means going beyond the bounds of right-wing intellectual orthodoxy: not only was the founding of a new European order, with its origins in the old Holy Roman Empire, an article of faith of German Nazi ideologists and of French fascists and anti-Bolsheviks, it was also, often through the mediation of Nietzsche, with his recurrent emphasis on 'good Europeans', a central tenet of a number of French intellectuals, from Giraudoux, with his constant reflections on the complementary nature of French and German temperaments, to Drieu la Rochelle who, in *Notes pour comprendre le siècle*, analyses French decadence and European fragmentation in identical terms to those employed by Céline and with the same nostalgic evocation of the ideal of Charlemagne and the Middle Ages.

It is easy to see, therefore, why critics should spend so little time on *L'Ecole des cadavres*, since it appears to fit so comfortably into a tradition of 1930s French anti-Semitism. What is less easy, in fact, at the outset, is to understand why Céline's right-wing readers, such as Rebatet and the *Je suis partout* team, should have been so dismayed by the work, considering that 'Céline continuait à exagérer'. On closer inspection, however, the second pamphlet is considerably less non-problematical that it appears, although pure exaggeration, as in the case of *Bagatelles pour un massacre*, is not perhaps the primary difficulty. First of all, the title of the work, as with the preceeding pamphlet, is deliberately ambiguous, consciously designed to tease the reader. On one level, a perfectly coherent meaning is given by the exclamation: 'Vive le Racisme! On a compris à force de cadavres': the reader of 1939 is instructed by the victims of the previous cataclysm. At the same time, the work itself presents a different meaning. At the end of the pamphlet, Ferdinand cries:

> Puisqu'ils veulent rien comprendre, puisqu'ils veulent rien apprendre, puisqu'ils veulent rabâcher toujours, toujours les mêmes conneries, très bien! Très bien! Ils seront gâtés! Ils passeront l'examen quand même! à la grande kermesse des Têtus! C'est un monde! d'une façon toute fantastique, par prodigieux écartelements, feux gregais munificents . . . L'école mirifique! Tout le monde sera reçu (EC, 221).

This threat, which is a direct echo of the *école primaire* in *Mort à crédit*, where all the pupils, whatever their capabilities, pass the *certificat* examination, proposes a reading of the title by which Céline's readers will only understand the truth of what he has been writing when they become *cadavres* themselves. The pamphlet is therefore both teaching the French how to become *cadavres* and, indeed, also looking forward to the time when they will *be* corpses: a ghost readership to accompany the ghostly cast of *Voyage au bout de la nuit*.

From this point of ambiguity onwards, it becomes more understandable why Rebatet should be disturbed by the text, since it constantly appears to be trying to escape the limits and constraints of pure polemic. This is apparent at the very beginning of the work, with the dialogue between Ferdinand and the *sirène*. At the outset, Céline is careful to place Ferdinand between La Jatte and Courbevoie: the industrial suburbs of Paris, where Ferdinand himself is born and where most of Céline's work is set. The *sirène* is known to Ferdinand: 'Je la connaissais comme sirène . . . je l'avais déjà rencontrée assez souvent . . . en des estuaires bien différentes . . . de Copenhague à Saint-Laurent' (EC, 15), a description which places her both in the fairy-tale world of the ballets, particularly *Scandale aux abysses*, but also in the tradition of waterfront adventure-literature exemplified by Pierre Mac Orlan's *Filles et ports d'Europe*. What is important, however, is that both Ferdinand and the *sirène* are in decline: the *sirène* is 'déchue' (EC, 16) and taunts the narrator:

> — Tu vas être grand-père . . .
> — T'es bien renseignée, chère morue! que je lui reponds, tac au toc
> (EC, 16),

to which the *sirène* replies: 'Cadavre vous-même!' (EC, 16). Ferdinand is back in his favourite role as ghost, sermonising his readers from beyond the grave. Thus the notion of decline is present from the very beginning of the pamphlet and is accentuated in the case of the *sirène* by the fact that it is due to the pollution of the Seine from distilleries: again at the outset, the theme of alcoholism and decadence is announced which will be amplified in the course of the pamphlet. Stung by Ferdinand's insults, the *sirène* replies with accusations of cowardice: 'Qu'as-tu donc fait dis à Clichy?' (EC, 17), and the question: 'T'as plus du tout rien à dire?' (EC, 18), to which the narrator riposte: 'Passe-moi donc l'encre de la Seine . . . tu vas voir comment j'ai à dire . . .' (EC, 18). In this very condensed introduction, a number of complex points are being made. The writer-narrator is with a populist, debased version of his muse, who is taunting him with both social and political ineffectualness and with artistic sterility. In other words, that block encountered by Céline in the composition of *Casse-pipe* is about to be surmounted by an incursion into polemic, in which the narrator will use the 'encre de la Seine', the corrupt waste of modern society, in order to take on that same society. At the same time, the question: 'T'as plus du tout rien à dire?' looks forward to the pamphlet's concluding section, 'Tout est dit', in the same way that the 'Moi j'avais jamais rien dit' which introduces *Voyage au bout de la nuit* looks forward to *its* conclusion, 'Qu'on n'en parle plus'. What this raises in its turn is not merely the nineteenth-century ambition identified by Philippe Roussin as 'tout dire',[24] but an entire theme within the pamphlet connected with speech, writing and the effectiveness of language.

This preoccupation is confirmed by the second section of the work which takes the form of an abusive letter received by Ferdinand from 'Salvador, juif', 'A Céline le dégueulasse' (EC, 19). What is important about this letter is not its formal content, its disputing of the statistics of Jewish servicemen involved in the First World War, so much as the fact that it is a *bagatelle* (EC, 19) which presents a mirror-image of the style or the previous pamphlet and which automatically shifts the level of preoccupation of *L'Ecole des cadavres* from the political to the stylistic. Ferdinand is worried by the fact that Salvador, one or the recurrent figures in the legend surrounding the *Protocols of the Elders of Zion*, has imitated his style almost perfectly but without conveying the essential qualities. Thus, as a professional stylist, Céline analyses: 'Il me froisse, il m'agace, il ne m'excite pas' (EC, 20), for: 'La passion le rend impossible' (EC, 20). Salvador has not read Céline carefully enough:

Qu'il me lise.
Qu'il me décalque gentiment (EC, 20),

and so is reprimanded by his master: 'Salvador, vous me bouzillez!' (EC, 20). The rest of the pamphlet appears, therefore, as a demonstration to an ineffectual disciple, showing how passion is to be kept under control in order for the music, and the message, to be heard. In this way, *L'Ecole de cadavres*, like *Bagatelles pour un massacre*, becomes in a sense an *exercice du style*, or a *défense et illustration*, with the anti-Semitism as the pretext.

24. Philippe Roussin, 'Tout dire', BLFC 8.

It is therefore the status of the anti-Semitic content in relation to the stylistic considerations which becomes problematical and which remains so throughout the text which, at certain points, becomes a general reflection on the effectiveness of writing. Thus, Ferdinand compares implicitly the writing of polemic with the work of the doctor:

> On se fait des petites illusions, on pense que l'on vous a compris. Et puis pas du tout.
> Sans prétentions, tout bonnement, consciencieusement, on a rédigé dans sa vie des milliers, milliers d'ordonnances . . . Et l'on ne saura jamais, jamais, tout le bien qu'elles ont pu faire, à la ronde . . . Ça n'a pas beaucoup d'importance. On vous a sûrement compris, toujours, toujours, de travers (EC, 159),

and, by intervening directly, by addressing the reader, he again calls into question the effectiveness of his own text:

> Peut-être vais-je vous fasciner vous aussi? Peut-être que je vais vous faire rendre? Peut-être allez-vous me trouver odieux? assomant au possible? Peut-être allez-vous me honnir? Si vous m'avez lu jusqu'ici c'est déjà du tempérament, c'est déjà la preuve d'une haine solide. Mais la suite est admirable.
> Je vous préviens tres courtoisement. L'émouvant récapitulatif de toutes les tergiversations des 50 chapitres liminaires . . . Vous n'aurez pas à vous plaindre! . . . Avec toutes conclusions 'ad hoc!' 'extra fortes!' . . . architecturales! . . .
> Mais c'est vers la fin que je triomphe, dans l'envol pathétique, le surpassement du bouquet!
> Je suis de ces auteurs qui ont du souffle, du répondant, du biscato.
> J'emmerde le genre entier humain à cause de mon répondant terrible, de ma paire de burnes fantastiques (et bordel de dieu je le prouve!). Je jute, je conclus, je triomphe, je trempe la page de pleine génie . . .' (EC, 160).

Not only does this passage recuperate references to Semmelweis ('Mais Semmelweis a du souffle, dieu merci') and to Bardamu ('un héros juteux'), but it attempts to sow doubt in the mind of what should be a naive polemical reader. It is deliberately dispersive, but it is also, quite literally, a *non sequitur*: unlike *Bagatelles pour un massacre* and *Les Beaux draps*, *L'Ecole des cadavres* does not contain an impressive conclusion: the series of isolated *bagatelles* runs on right to the end with no noticeable attempt to draw them together into any kind of synthesis. Indeed, the concluding section 'Tout est dit' merely takes the form of a blatantly false report of a motion voted by the equally spurious 'Front Populaire de la Région

Parisienne', according to which, if the Jew is more gifted than the native Frenchman: 'Il est juste qu'il commande et dirige les Français inférieurs à leur tâche' (EC, 227).

This doubt in the mind of the reader is maintained by the way in which Ferdinand begins to turn against his own side. The attacks on Colonel de la Roque and Doriot could be justified on the basis of their anti-German stance and their readiness to accept Jewish recruits. But what is the reader to make of Maurras' 'Jewish' style and the consistent deformation of Drumont to 'Drummont' (EC, 32)? Or, for that matter, the obligingly helpful list of anti-Semitic nonentities, together with useful addresses and acceptable anti-Semitic journals (EC, 31–2)? The naive reader may be prepared to believe that the British Intelligence Service is pushing France into a war for its own devious purposes, even if he is puzzled by its leaders, 'Moses Sieff, Mark Spencer et Sassoon' (EC, 152), but will he place the same credibility in 'les agents trop voyants de l'I.S., tels Mirabeau, Danton, Robespierre, Borodine, Trotsky, Lawrence, etc. . . . etc. . . .' (EC, 152)? Finally, from the mouth of a self-proclaimed doctor, what is he to make of the assertion that Jewish hatred of the Aryan is due to a faulty chromosome (EC, 87) or that: 'Les Juifs, racialement, sont des monstres, des hybrides loupés, tiraillés, qui doivent disparaître' (EC, 84)? And, even if he is prepared to accept this personal vision of a Jewish plot, can he possibly follow Ferdinand in his counter measures?. How seriously can Ferdinand's proposed *décrets* be taken:

1er, L'expulsion de tous les Juifs
2e, Interdiction, fermeture de touts les Loges et Sociétés Secrètes
3e, Travaux forcés à perpétuité pour toutes les personnes peu satisfaites, dures d'oreilles, etc. . . . (EC, 77)?

Like *Bagatelles pour un massacre*, though less obviously, *L'Ecole des cadavres* turns away from polemic towards a more personal concern and leaves the unpleasant doubt with its reader that it may, after all, constitute no more than a latter-day *Dictionnaire des idées reçues*.

In fact, *L'Ecole des cadavres* pursues some of the familiar Célinian preoccupations more than is necessary for purely polemical effect. One example of this is the obsession with gold. Whilst it is true that the Jewish monopoly of gold is a recurrent theme of anti-Semitic literature, the emphasis which is placed on it in *L'Ecole des cadavres* is more idiosyncratic and reinforces a continuing reflection on the symbolism and function of gold throughout

Céline's work. This additional emphasis is seen clearly in Céline's evocation of the liner *Normandie*. This description rapidly outstrips its polemical purpose, which is to show the luxury of the vessel, a luxury which only Jews can afford, and its symbolic value as a refuge in times of trouble. Instead, it becomes the very embodiment of the gold-principle:

> L'on s'en nourrit d'or, l'on s'en bâfre, l'on s'en regorge, l'on s'en dégueule, l'on s'en évanouit.
>
> *Va petit mousse*
> *Tout l'or te pousse!*
>
> Il en gicle partout, ça pisse l'or, les bienheureux embarqués tombent malades d'or. Ils vont, surgorgés, crever d'or (EC, 55–6).

Yet:

> C'est mince, c'est tout mince quand même la coque d'un si gros, si géant transatlantique . . . Ça frémit, ça grince, ça trembloche, ça joue . . . ça finit . . . C'est pas très solide . . . et puis là-dedans c'est plein de juifs . . . dans tout cet or . . . et puis ça flotte sur des abîmes . . . si profonds . . . sur des nuits et des nuits d'oubli . . . (EC, 57).

The writing in this *bagatelle* is unusually complex for *L'Ecole des cadavres*, but it points the reader in several directions other than the ostensible anti-Semitic message. On one level, the preoccupation is with a, literally, Golden Boat, or Golden Ark, the ultimate refuge from time and disaster and from which the narrator, as ever, is excluded. In addition, Ferdinand plays upon the notion of gold as food which will recur in the Van Claben episode of *Guignol's Band*: the ingurgitation and evacuation of gold which is implied by the earlier comment: 'Tout juif est un préposé de l'or et du Diable' (EC, 32), and which is connected to the Freudian association of the Devil's gold with excrement. Céline has already shown, in *Mort à crédit*, how the symbolism of gold and excrement places the narrator in an ambiguous relationship towards authority and the Father, and this ambiguity is continued in the obsession with gold in the pamphlets. Finally, in the evocation of the frailty of the liner's hull, Céline is returning to an image employed in *Voyage au bout de la nuit* to denote the various layers of the text of the novel itself: the various 'couches de peinture', like 'pelures d'oignon'. Here, the image of the vessel, all in gold, floating with great vulnerability over the depths of forgetfulness, becomes literally a *mise en abyme* of the text itself: equally vulnerable and threatened with oblivion.

For Ferdinand is conscious that, for all the apparent vigour of the text, the *musique* of *L'Ecole des cadavres* is fragile and its ultimate ambition is doomed to failure. The text is about the evocation of a Golden Age which will serve as an antidote to the music-less, emotionless, mechanical present. It is for this reason that *L'Ecole des cadavres* moves towards the nostalgic reconstruction of the Empire of Charlemagne before the fatal fragmentation of Europe in 843, the age of Krogold and Gwendor, when emotion and life were guaranteed by the symbolism of gold. Thus, 843 becomes one of those key dates in Céline's work, like 1793 and 1914, which mark the end of an era and beyond which mankind lives out a ghostly existence. The *cadavres* of the second pamphlet have the same status as the *Gardes Suisses* in *Voyage au bout de la nuit*: they are part of Céline's collection of *fantômes*. Not that this in itself contradicts the anti-Semitism of the text. The ideal of a Golden Age in the past and fear of an imminent Apocalypse are the two components of a mystical millenarian philosophy which traditionally goes hand in hand with anti-Semitism.

What is ultimately significant about *L'Ecole des cadavres*, however, is that Ferdinand has little faith in the effectiveness of his warning. By denouncing the soullessness of the present, by following Nietzsche and Elie Faure in his prescription of dance as the antidote, by invoking the glories of the age of Charlemagne, Ferdinand is aware that he is merely trying to turn back the clock with little chance of success. It is for this reason that the work is dedicated to Julian the Apostate, the Roman Emperor who attempted to turn back the tide of Christianity and restore the Empire to the, golden, cult of Mithras, but who failed and was murdered by his enemies. At the very end of the experiment, *L'Ecole des cadavres*, like *Bagatelles pour un massacre* and *Mort à crédit* before it, is a further example of the self-destructive text in which permanent salvation is to be sought in silence and the oblivion of the 'abîmes': 'Voici Ferdinand au poil. Il faudra le tuer. Je ne vois pas d'autre moyen' (EC, 223).

Les Beaux draps

Céline's third and final pamphlet, published during the war in 1941, uses the same format as its two predecessors: a series of apparently isolated *bagatelles* which, upon closer inspection, are more carefully structured and are grouped around a number of thematic preoccupations. Similarly, as in the transition from *Bagatelles pour un massacre* to *L'Ecole des cadavres*, the shift to the final work entails a continuation of themes, but also a change in emphasis. Finally, as in the two previous pamphlets, Céline is able to deploy a considerable amount of ambiguity through his use of references, his manipulation of irony and, above all, his establishment at the end of *Les Beaux draps* of the common narrator Ferdinand.

In its ostensible polemical material, *Les Beaux draps* is immediately disconcerting because of a kind of historical schizophrenia which seems to pervade the work. On one level, the title of the pamphlet itself and the opening sections freely acknowledge the dominant factor in France's historical circumstances: its catastrophic military defeat in June 1940. Hence, the work begins with a traditional *ancien combattant's* contempt for the French Army of 1940: 'J'ai pourchassé l'Armée Française de Bezons jusqu'à La Rochelle, j'ai jamais pu la rattraper' (BD, 11), and with the jibe:

> Hé! qu'as-tu fait de ton fusil?
> Il est resté au champ d'honneur! (BD, 13).

It is worth emphasising at the outset that this attitude is by no means unambiguous, and that comments like: 'Ça devient curieux les soldats quand ça veut plus du tout mourir' (BD, 13), square ill with the anti-militarism of *Voyage au bout de la nuit* nine years earlier, as does the pious invocation of Poincaré: 'S'il était encore vivant ça se serait pas passé comme ça' (BD, 35). This kind of statement begins to read already like prevalent clichés of the moment of defeat rather than an effective polemical response to events: the question of a Célinian *Dictionnaire des idées reçues* poses itself early on in the work.

However ambiguous this kind of comment may be, however, it undoubtedly recognised that the 'draps fort douteux' (BD, 19) in which the French find themselves are the consequences of military defeat and Occupation. What comes as a surprise throughout the work, however, is the fact that Céline rarely acknowledges the reality of the Occupation itself and never refers to Hitler or Pétain. In other words, the pamphlet is constructed upon a strange *non sequitur*, by which there is certainly military defeat, but followed by a vacuum rather than by a specific new regime. Clearly, it could be argued that such an omission serves the German aim of giving the impression of a rapid return to normality and of keeping a low profile in general, although other polemical works of the time, notably Rebatet's *Les Décombres*, were not similarly inhibited. With more justification, it could be asserted that Céline is indulging in his favourite pastime of blending together historical periods, so that here he is writing not only about 1940, but also about 1870. Whatever the reason for this lack of emphasis on the Occupation itself, Céline chooses to follow up his gloating references to France's defeat with a picture of French society, which in spite of the new regimes in both northern and southern zones, has not changed one iota since *L'Ecole des cadavres*:

> Plus de juifs que jamais dans les rues, plus de juifs que jamais dans la presse, plus de juifs que jamais au Barreau, plus de juifs que jamais en Sorbonne, plus de juifs que jamais en Médecine, plus de juifs que jamais au Théâtre, à l'Opéra, aux Français, dans l'industrie, dans les Banques. Paris, la France plus que jamais livrés aux maçons et aux juifs plus insolents que jamais (BD, 44).

Plainly, none of these assertions is true: the *Statut sur les Juifs* was not promulgated until 2 June 1941, but already by the publication of *Les Beaux draps* in February, anti-Jewish policies were in operation in both zones, particularly in the north, under the German military government in Paris: only pro-collaborationist and racist newspapers and periodicals were allowed to reappear and the same anti-Semitic policies were operating at all levels of society.[25] Nevertheless, Céline continues to write as if Jewish influence is stronger than ever, rather than having been eliminated: his latter-day Rastignac can only succeed through 'Jewish' education, Free-masonry and entry into a 'Jewish' career: 'On est à la cour à Mammon, à la cour du grand Caca d'or!' (BD, 53). Céline finally makes explicit the connection between gold and excrement which is implicit throughout his work. In addition, he returns obsessively to his well-worn accusation of international Jewish domination: Jewish direction of the Russian Revolutions of 1917, a process which began in 1789 with the principle: 'Pas d'or, pas de revolution' (BD, 92); the Fall of the Bastille was due to 'les Banques, les démons de Londres' (BD, 96) under Pitt. In the Bolshevik Revolution, like any other: 'Qui ouvre les crédits, mène la danse' (BD, 100), the tsarist regime and the Kerensky interregnum were the victims of the revolutionary leaders' personal desire for money (BD, 99–100) and, more specifically, of the Loeb-Warburg Bank conspiracy, already alluded to in *L'Ecole des cadavres*: 'Il se sont entendus illico, Warburg, la Banque et Trotsky. Tout ça c'était dans les présages . . . un chèque présenté par le Temps, New York faisait la couverture,

25. See: Ory, *Les Collaborateurs*, Chapters 4 and 10.

200 millions de dollars-or pour foutre en l'air l'empire du Tzar . . .'
(BD, 103)

Against this increasingly unreal international Jewish conspiracy,
Céline emphasises the need for genuinely racist attitudes:

> Une nation . . . se relève admirablement des plus grands torchons mili-
> taires, des plus cruelles occupations, mais seulement à une condition,
> cette condition très essentielle, mystique, celle d'être demeurée fidèle à
> travers victoires et revers aux mêmes groupes, à la même éthnie, au même
> sang, aux mêmes souches raciales, non abâtardies . . . (BD, 68).

And it is here, in *Les Beaux draps*, that he becomes open in his
threats against the Jews. Using a racial definition of the Jew which is
considerably more rigorous than that embodied in the Vichy anti-
Jewish laws: 'J'entends par juif, tout homme qui compte parmi ses
grands-parents un juif, un seul' (BD, 115),[26] he moves for the first
time towards encouragement of violence against the Jews: 'Luxez le
juif au poteau! y a plus une seconde à perdre!' (BD, 197). Yet his
main weapon against the Jews is a policy of forestalling them in
their revolutionary projects, and it is in this context that Céline
introduces his famous concept of 'Communisme Labiche' (BD, 197).

The reasoning behind this is simple: 'Le juif il a peur de rien . . . Il
a peur seulement que d'une chose: du Communisme sans les Juifs'
(BD, 144). Hence: 'Le Communisme Labiche ou la mort! Voilà
comme je cause! Et pas dans vingt ans, mais tout de suite! Si on en
arrange pas un nous, un communisme à notre maniere, qui con-
vienne à nos genres d'esprit, les juifs imposeront le leur . . .' (BD,
197). This 'Communisme Labiche', or 'Communisme petit-bourgeois' (BD, 137), ushered in by 'La Révolution moyenneuse!' (BD,
135), with its policy of a maximum daily salary of 100 francs,
no unemployment and global nationalisation, is often read as an
Utopian statement, which could be connected to the later *féeries*
and the *voyage imaginaire* of *Voyage au bout de la nuit*. What is
more important, however, is the fact that this is not the first time
that Céline has invoked the strategy of pre-emption in his polemical
writing: it appears first in the preamble to the 1928 article, 'Les
Assurances sociales et une politique économique de la santé publique', where Céline recommends the Disraelian policy of pre-
empting the demands of the Left by implementing watered-down

26. The first article of the Vichy *Statut des Juifs* read: 'Est regardé (*sic*) comme
Juif, par l'application de la présente loi, toute personne issue de trois grands-parents
de race juive, ou de deux grands-parents de la même race, si son conjoint lui-même
est juif'. See François de Fontette, 'Eléments pour une définition du Juif', *Annales du
C.E.S.E.R.E.*, 5, 1982, p. 21.

socialist policies before more vigorous ones are imposed by force (CC 3, 157). Yet in this case the strategy of pre-emption served an ironic purpose, to the extent that the model set up, the vision of a totally industrialised society policed by a medical surveillance team, became in its turn rebarbative. In the pamphlet *Les Beaux draps*, the same procedure operates: as Céline comments on the various components of his 'Communisme Labiche': 'Voyons mesquin, voyons médiocre' (BD, 137). It is a Communism which is the logical extension of the ambition of every Frenchman to be a *fonctionnaire*, the epitome, the accession to power of those petit-bourgeois values derided in *Mort à crédit* and *L'Ecole des cadavres*, and miles apart from the vision of spiritual Communism evoked in the second pamphlet. The effect of this device, therefore, as in the article on 'Les Assurances sociales', is ultimately not to look forward towards a credible alternative in the future but, through the very implausible nature of that alternative — Clémence and Auguste as Commissars — to indicate the bleakness of the present: out of 'le Communisme Labiche ou la mort', it is 'la mort' which is the only real alternative.

In fact, the main thrust of the pamphlet is towards exploring ways of remedying France's decline, of finding antidotes to the dessication and mediocrity epitomised in the concept of 'Communisme Labiche'. Like *L'Ecole des cadavres*, therefore, *Les Beaux draps* is an attempt to 'remonter le courant' (BD, 168) to an age when mediocrity and materialism did not hold sway. 'La France est juive et maçonnique, une fois pour toutes!' (BD, 78); but France is also, like the France of the medical pamphlets, in the grip of modernisation and materialism of which the embodiment is the factory: 'L'usine c'est un mal comme les chiots, c'est pas plus beau, pas moins utile, c'est une triste nécessité de la condition matérielle' (BD, 146). No idealism of Fordism here, yet no possibility of escape either: the factory remains for Céline the one inescapable fact of modern existence, the true source of all his pessimism. It is the factory which has created the modern world and has suffused it with the blanket of mediocrity, to the extent that even the magic of childhood has been stifled by the school system, that 'désastre de féerie' (BD, 160) which has as its mission to 'tourner en plomb leur vif argent' (BD, 161). Céline's France, therefore, poised between literal death and a living death in 'Communisme Labiche', is spiritually and emotionally bankrupt: '*Crédit est morte une fois pour toutes*' (BD, 151), for 'Nous crevons d'être sans légende, sans mystère, sans grandeur. Les cieux nous vomissent. Nous périssons d'arrière-boutique' (BD, 162). The *Passage des Bérésinas* of *Mort à crédit* now symbolises the entire nation.

Yet the principle of arid intelligence and utilitarianism embodied in the factory can be surmounted by a number of opposing values, chief amongst which is the dream life which permits 'legend, mystery and grandeur'. They open the door to an appreciation of existence which is not intellectual, but emotional and physical, and which may be obtained less through orthodox literature than through music and dance: 'Il faudra rapprendre à danser. La France est demeurée heureuse jusqu'au rigodon. On dansera jamais en usine, on chantera plus jamais non plus . . .' (BD, 148), and: 'Tout homme ayant un coeur qui bat possède aussi sa chanson, sa petite musique personnelle . . .' (BD, 171). For Céline, it is necessary to reestablish the conditions for dance and music, and this entails a return to an appreciation of the human body. Thus, Céline, celebrating the 'secrets de danse et musique', emphasises: 'Que le corps reprenne goût de vivre . . .' (BD, 175). Like the anti-intellectualism and anti-modernism of *L'Ecole des cadavres*, this emphasis on the body, dance and music is part of a tradition of French thought in the inter-war years which owes much to Nietzsche and finds its clearest expression in Drieu la Rochelle's *Notes pour comprendre le siècle*, with its evocations of France's medieval greatness, and in Bernanos's assertions of the literal need for Saints, which Céline himself picks up in *Les Beaux draps*: 'On est pas des Saints! Mais justement! Il en faut!' (BD, 187).

Whereas for Drieu and Bernanos the medieval ideal was essentially an intellectual and political entity, however, for Céline its application is really aesthetic. One of the most important sections of *Les Beaux draps* begins with a quotation: 'Malédiction sur la France! LAMARTINE (Dernières paroles)' (BD, 174), which could equally well apply to Céline himself: both the quotation and the pamphlet constitute the last words of an author in the form of a curse on his country. Yet, if Céline is pessimistic about the future of France, he is curiously optimistic about the role of the artist:

Une fois le coeur consacré au don de soi-même, la vie ne peut plus grand'chose sur votre belle heureuse humeur. C'est un genre de lampe d'Aladin qui trouve toujours de nouvelles joies en lieux les plus sombres.
Ça s'arrange toujours plus ou moins, on ne foudroye pas un artiste. C'est lui qui juge l'univers, qui se fait marrer à sa guise, tantôt en bien, tantôt en mal, comme ci, comme ça, à petites astuces, au petit bonheur.
On peut plus grand'chose contre lui, ni les éléments, ni les hommes . . . (BD, 174).

And this new-found invulnerability contains not merely a salvation for the artist, but also a means of renewal for the nation as a whole through art and a certain kind of education which will minimise the teaching of 'les choses utiles' (BD, 175) in favour of 'la danse, les ports, les beaux-arts' (BD, 175). In this way, by the cultivation of the body, the cultivation of the mind will follow, and not through the 'accablants grimoires, marmonnerie de textes, contextes, bâfreries d'analyses de poux . . .' (BD, 175–6) found in the school curriculum. This art, however, which will ultimately renovate the French school system, is a national racial art:

> L'art ne connaît point de patrie! Quelle sottise! Quel mensonge! Quelle hérésie! Quel dicton juif!
> L'art n'est que Race et Patrie! Voici le roc où construire! Roc et nuages en vérité, paysage d'âme.
> Que trouvons-nous en ce pays, des Flandres au Béarn? . . . Chansonniers et peintres, contrées de légère musique, sans insister . . . peut-être un fraîcheur de danse, un châtoyement de gaîté au bord des palettes, et d'esprit en tout ceci, preste de verve et badinant . . . et puis doux et mélancolique . . . (BD, 177).

And Céline moves on from this evocation of French art, which would do credit to Giraudoux or to the Morand of *Doulce France*, by concluding:

> Tout est sacré de ces miracles . . . les plus infinis accents . . . trois vers, deux notes, un soupir . . .
> De cy l'on peut tout recréer! les hommes, leurs races, et leurs ferveurs . . . (BD, 177),

a resurrection which can come about only through the school: 'Si la France doit reprendre l'âme, cette âme jaillira de l'école. L'âme revenue, naîtra Légende, tout naturellement' (BD, 178).

This speculation goes further than the similar writings of Drieu la Rochelle or Bernanos in that, whilst it points to a spiritual rebirth of France through the inculcation of 'medieval' values to children in school, it also constitutes an *art poétique*, minimising intellectuality in art and emphasising the importance of supposedly specifically French characteristics. For Céline, racism is ultimately aesthetic and linguistic: hence his periodic recourse to snatches of Old French in the text itself. In other words, yet again the political polemic serves as a pretext for a more complicated aesthetic reflection, a complexity compounded in *Les Beaux draps* by an unusual level of textual awareness. This takes the form of a succession of direct references to other writers or anti-Semitic authorities: Balzac, Gobineau, Michelet, Montandon, Montaigne, the by now obligatory deformation of Drumont to 'Drummont' (BD, 80), and a number of allusions in the text to a contemporary intellectual context established by figures such as Bernanos, Conrad, Drieu la Rochelle, Malraux, Nietzsche and Vallès. This textual awareness of the final pamphlet is confirmed by the long concluding section, which is one of the single most remarkable pieces of writing produced by Céline, and which constitutes both a practical demonstration of the *art poétique* contained in the body of the text and a careful musical conclusion, not just to *Les Beaux draps* but to the entire trilogy of the pamphlets.

This conclusion has the effect, first of all, of, belatedly, establishing a narrator for the pamphlet. After two hundred pages of what appears to be a direct address to the reader from the author, Céline himself slips away and introduces the mediating figure common to all the pamphlets, the doctor Ferdinand (BD, 209). He is also careful, again, to establish an interlocutor, this time Ferdinand's medical colleague Divetot who, if transcribed as 'D'Yvetot', introduces a further Flaubertian element into the pamphlets. Finally, Céline is careful to provide both seasonal and topographical precision:

Ah! C'est un hiver rigoureux... ça on peut le dire... la Seine va charrier des glaçons... On s' attend... J'ai vu ça du Pont de Bruyères... si ça siffle!... la nature n'est pas clémente pour les personnes dans le besoin... Une bise!... Une rigueur!... la petite montagne d'Argenteuil en est toute gelée... avec son moulin... Elle arbore grand manteau de neige... la traîne éparpille... enveloppe les maisons, poudre les toits... trempe à la rive... émiette à l'eau... à grands remous passant à voltes autour des arches... Ah! c'est un hiver rigoureux! la plaine en nappe jusqu'aux remblais loin, loin là-bas tout son blanc... joue à la russe au vent des steppes... à sifflants tourbillons dansants et flocons et poudres... (BD, 205).

It is the first winter of the Occupation, but evoked in such a way that it echoes the beginning of Villon's *Le Testament*, thus continuing the Old French element in the text, and establishes an Impressionist imprecision through the *tourbillons* of the snowflakes. At the same time, through the precise use of topographical details, Céline fixes *Les Beaux draps* in his traditional landscape: the industrial suburbs of the north-west of central Paris, contained in the loop of the Seine between Neuilly and Bezons which Céline recognised as his heartland in the preface to *Bezons à travers les ages*. It is within this loop of the Seine that La Garenne-Rancy is situated in *Voyage au bout de la nuit* and that Gustin's *dispensaire* is to be found in *Mort à crédit*; moreover, in the second novel, Ferdinand's family move to central Paris from Courbevoie and Caroline still owns property in Asnières. The connection between *Les Beaux draps* and the rest of Céline's work is even stronger, however: *L'Ecole des cadavres* begins with Ferdinand walking by the Seine 'entre La Jatte and Courbevoie' (EC, 15); similarly, the final episode of *Les Beaux draps* opens with Ferdinand crossing the Seine on the Pont de Bruyères, which links Paris, via de Ile de la Grande Jatte, with Bécon-les-Bruyères and Courbevoie. In both pamphlets, the Seine fulfils a major role, and the starting place and end point are identical geographically. In addition, the covert geographical allusion in the epilogue of *Les Beaux draps* gives greater significance to the opening statement of the pamphlet: 'Je suis parti de Courbevoie, au poil, le 13 au matin' (BD, 11). The pamphlet is therefore a circular work, but also imprisoned in the same geographical context as that which informs all of Céline's writing, the same context, incidentally, as that of the Impressionist painters. Thus, the epilogue, like the whole of *Les Beaux draps*, is dominated by the image of the factory: 'L'usine tout au froid brandit au ciel ses quatre tours, effilées, plus hautes que les nuages, en plein flamboyement...' (BD, 205), and evokes a precise topography: Argenteuil, the Mont Valérien, La Folie, Charlebourg and Gennevilliers, before taking the reader further, into an imaginary warren of significant street names: 'rue des Bouleux-Verts', 'rue des Michaux', 'Venelle des Trois-Soeurs', 'Impasse du Trou-de-Sable', 'Ruelle des Bergères' (BD, 213).

Within this precise and significant geographical setting, Céline provides a short narrative which has two components. The first half of the epilogue recounts Ferdinand's journey to his clinic and his consultations. In describing the journey, Céline is careful to insert his narrative into the general context of his fiction. Ferdinand notices a cyclist of the bridge who is so overcome with cold that he is obliged to dismount and stop, but he reflects that in his own case: 'Ah! il faut passer quand même! Moi, j'ai mes fonctions de l'autre côté, j'ai des choses à faire...' (BD, 206) — a direct echo of Bardamu's reluctance to cross the Seine and return to Bébert and Rancy in *Voyage au bout de la nuit*: 'Tout le monde n'est pas César!' In his treatment of the patients, he meets the same problems as those encountered by Bardamu in Rancy and detailed in the 1920s medical writings: the problems are less medical than social and economic, the cold and the hunger, and orthodox medicine is useless: 'bonne volonté ne suffit pas!... ni la science, ni les connaissances... y a des fatalités qu'arrivent... qui sont rigoureuses et terribles...' (BD, 208). In fact, far more of the doctor's time is spent in giving out fuel and food coupons than in prescribing

medical treatment: 'c'est le rythme ... un ... deux ... trois
Bons ... une ordonnance! ... C'est la cadence depuis l'hiver ... de
moins en moins d'ordonnances ... de plus en plus de bons ...'
(BD, 210). In other words, the crisis of the Occupation and the
hardships of the Winter of 1940–1 have confirmed Ferdinand's
belief in the redundancy of 'bourgeois' medicine, and this is neatly
conveyed by the fact that his main task is delivering death certifi-
cates: 'Je suis Dieu assermenté ...' (BD, 212). He has also become
the 'grand auxiliaire de la Mort'.[27]

This primary role of Ferdinand as a suburban doctor in a period
of hardship introduces the second component of Céline's narrative:
Ferdinand's journey 'Tout aux confins de la commune' (BD, 212–13)
to issue a death-certificate for an old lady. On arriving, however, he
discovers that: 'Elle est pas morte ... elle est partie ...' (BD, 214).
This patient, aged eighty-six, therefore born in 1855, the year of the
first Universal Exposition, is 'une personne originale' (BD, 214)
who periodically vanishes, allegedly to visit friends in Gennevilliers.
What is important about her is that she is a representative of
'fantaisie' (BD, 216) and, more significantly, an encapsulation of
traits found in *Voyage au bout de la nuit* and *Mort à crédit*. Like
Bardamu: 'Elle a beaucoup voyagè d'après ce qu'elle raconte ...'
(BD, 215); like Robinson, 'elle suivait son idée' (BD, 215); finally,
like the narrator of *Mort à crédit*, 'elle en racontait des histoires'
(BD, 216). In other words, she is as much an alter ego to the
narrator of *Les Beaux draps* as Robinson is to Bardamu in *Voyage
au bout de la nuit*, and this emphasised by the central role of music
in the epilogue. The old lady is periodically spirited away by music:
'C'est la musique qui l'entraîne ... qu'elle raconte!' (BD, 214); 'son
air lui chante et c'est fini!' (BD, 215); 'elle entendait sa musique ...
d'après son idée ...' (BD, 215); 'du moment que sa musique lui
passe, elle file on dirait une jeunesse!' (BD, 216). Yet even before he
knows of the old lady's existence, Ferdinand has picked up a strange
music on the Parisian air. He asks Divetot:

> Vous entendez pas? ... Taa! ... too! ... too! ... too! ... too ... too
> ... Taa! ... Taa! ... comme le vent d'hiver rapporte? ... Je lui chante

27. It is worth noting to what extent *Les Beaux draps* is under the sway of *Mort à
crédit*: not only do the two works share a common suburban geography, but also a
common fear of communication. Whereas, in *Mort à crédit*, 'tous les chagrins
viennent dans les lettres' (MC, 511), in *Les Beaux draps*, 'Enfin grêle le téléphone ...
je tréssaute! Je bondis! ... C'est la catastrophe! ... C'est rien! ... les noms seulement des defunts ...' (BD, 212). Similarly, the interlocutors share similar literary
tastes: Gustin Sabayot is 'expert en joli style' (MC, 515); Divetot is 'sensible aux
Belles Lettres' (BD, 208).

pour qu'il entende mieux . . . la! fa! sol! la si do! la! Do! qu'il entend bien
tout l'appel! . . . do dièze! . . . sol dièze! . . . bien entendu! . . . fa dièze
mineur! C'est le ton! Le charme des Cygnes! . . . l'appel, ami, l'appel!
(BD, 208–9).

This precise technical notation of the 'appel des Cygnes' is picked
up later, when Ferdinand recounts his visit to the old lady to
Divetot: 'Vous entendez ça comme des ondes . . . des avis qui
passent . . . des symphonies . . .' (BD, 217), and 'l'appel des Cygnes
c'est une chose qui vous saisit!' (BD, 217). In this way, it announces
the entirely musical structure of the end of the epilogue.

Yet the music is part of a complex web of references, all ultimately connected with death. The 'appel des Cygnes' is clearly a
reference to a swan-song and, more precisely, to the social and
historical death outlined in Baudelaire's *Le Cygne*. Ferdinand ac-
cedes to the music of the old lady by coming to deliver her
death-certificate, and his visit is followed by: 'des morts . . . vraiment des morts, des morts' (BD, 217). Finally, it is clearly stated
that the realm of music lies beyond death, beyond life and beyond
time:

c'est fait! la chose est faite! La vie partie! . . .
   Diaphanes emules partons ailleurs nos entrechats! . . . en sejours
d'aériennes grâces ou s'achèvent nos melodies . . . aux fontaines du grand
mirage! . . . Ah! Sans être! Diaphanes de danse! Désincarnés rigodo-
dants! tout allégresse! heureux de mort! gentils godelureaux! A vous
toutes fées et le souffle! . . . Elançons-nous! Aux cendres le calendrier!
Plus rien ne pèse! plumes d'envol! Au diable lourds cadrans et lunes!
plumes de nous! tout poids dissous! âmes au vol! âmes aux joies! . . . au
ciel éparse à bouquets . . . fleurettes partout luisantes, pimpantes scin-
tillent! Volée d'etoiles! . . . tout alentour tintent clochettes! . . . c'est le
ballet! . . . et tout s'enlace et tout depasse, pirouette, farandole à ravir! . . .
ritournelles argentines . . . musique de fées! (BD, 220–1).

Ferdinand has at last gone beyond time to a point where *calendriers* and
cadrans no longer have any meaning, and his apotheosis is described
and conceived of it balletic and operatic terms, which recall Verlaine
and, behind him, the Baudelaire of the last section of 'Le Voyage'.
The pamphlet itself, therefore, ends in a pure music: 'Que tout se
dissipe! ensorcelle! virevole! à nuées guillerettes! Enchanteresses! ne
sommes plus . . . écho menu dansant d'espace! fa! mi! re! do! si! . . .
plus frêle encore et nous enlace . . . et nous déporte en tout ceci! . . .
à grand vent rugit et qui passe!" (BD, 222). Nor is it merely *Les
Beaux draps* which has moved from polemic to Utopia and then on
to *féerie* in music and ballet, it is the whole cycle of the anti-Semitic

trilogy, which begins with a ballet, significantly called *La Naissance d'une fée*, and which finally returns to its origins at the end of the final pamphlet.

How, though, does Ferdinand come to this privileged state 'où mélodie nous a conduits . . .' (BD, 221–2)? On one level, it is the *cliente* who, like Robinson, is the narrator's mirror-image, who shows the way to the 'grand air d'Opéra' (BD, 220). On another level, it is connected to a notion of collective defeat: 'N'échapperons! notre défaite s'accomplit! . . . charges de joies ensorcelantes! à derobades! prestes retours! mieux vaut nous rendre! . . . nous fumes défaits aux lieux des Cygnes . . .' (BD, 221). The music is perceived, therefore, when not only the narrator but also France herself admit that they are finished and struggle no more. Finally, the metaphorical death of the narrator comes from a precise reflection on betrayal, suicide and the power of satanic forces. In an image which takes up the final lines of *Voyage au bout de la nuit* and looks forward to the ghostly *bateau-mouche*, *La Publique*, of *D'un château l'autre*, Céline writes:

A la berge péniche malmène, chasses aux remous, rafle, drosse, amarre . . . Oh, ça finira pas comme ça! . . . C'est pas moi qui vendrai la mèche! . . . Mais je connais des malfamants, des quidams en perversité, des gens qu'ont les esprits torves, des ambitieux tout hermétiques, inouïs de reluisances diaboliques qui sont en véritables pactes avec les puissances d'outre-là! . . . Ah! Pour ces possédés rien ne compte! . . . ni de coeur, ni délicatesse! tout à l'abîme des mauvaises Foi . . . Ah! des terribles aux damnations! . . . Voilà! je n'en dirai pas plus! Tel blême pendu de son vivant se resuicide à peine au sol pour dérouter les succubes! . . . Ah! que voici de vilaines morts! . . . L'infâmant mystère. Trépas de rats calamiteux! . . . Je n'en dirai pas davanatage! . . .' (BD, 218).

This passage introduces in its turn an extended reflection on traitors and the power of malevolent forces. The pamphlet ends, not merely with a ballet, but also with a nightmare ghost-story in which 'remontent des ténèbres les suicides, les gestes très affreux, les viols, les contrefaçons, les félonies scorpionimiques des personnes vouées lucifèrement! . . . (BD, 219), and this reign of diabolical ghosts is summoned up by the last anti-Semitic reference in the text: 'Lorsque la Kabale brûle les ambres . . . buboneux crapauds gobent l'encens! du coup toutes les marmites culbutent! Et c'est la fin du rizotto!' (BD, 220). Céline has already asked the question in *L'Ecole des cadavres*: 'Ça serait intéressant de savoir combien il y a eu de suicides de soldats . . . pendant la dernière semi-mobilisation' (EC,

109). The Jews have provoked the suicide of France and have summoned up all the diabolical forces in the earth. Yet, in order to undertake a mission of exorcism, Ferdinand is willing to commit suicide himself: the 'fantôme burlesque' of bourgeois medicine has become the 'blême pendu de son vivant' who 'se resuicide à peine au sol pour dérouter les succubes'. Hence the dedication of the work to 'la corde sans pendu'. In this light, the narrator appears conscious that his work, and the anti-Semitic trilogy in particular, represents a form of repeated suicide, a sacrifice in order to halt the decline of France. It is for this reason that the text itself is so conscious of the previous corpus, which constitutes a kind of textual *fantôme*, and that it refers back continually to *Voyage au bout de la nuit*, 'Le seul livre vraiment méchant de tous mes livres',[28] and the origin of the narrator's problems. Yet, in its reflection of *Voyage au bout de la nuit*, *Les Beaux draps* finally announces the sense of an ending: the 'Ça a débuté comme ça' of the novel becomes the 'ça finira pas comme ça' of the final pamphlet; 'Qu'on n'en parle plus' is reflected by 'Je n'en dirai pas davantage!'. According to the German legend of the *Doppelgänger*, when the victim comes face to face with his double, he dies and all is ended. There is very much the sense in *Les Beaux draps* of Céline having come face to face with himself and that this is his last literary suicide, which ushers him into the permanently ethereal world of the ballet. What goes on beyond, like *Guignol's Band*, will lead to *féerie*.

Drumont or 'Drummont'?

The debate on whether the anti-Semitic pamphlets should be republished has always been an integral part of the process of rehabilitation of Céline as a writer and has often been unduly confused by partisan political considerations. Nevertheless, even though many critics oppose republication on tactical political grounds, few of them now deny the pamphlets' importance in the corpus of his work. The problem, as François Gibault points out, is that, whilst on the one hand: 'Il est certain que les pamphlets sont des oeuvres intéressantes pour les chercheurs et les gens qui s'intéressent à Céline et que, sur le plan littéraire, ce sont des textes importants', 'D'un autre côté, ce sont tout de même des oeuvres de circonstance qui doivent être replacées dans leur temps, c'est-à-dire avant la

---

28. 'Préface à une réédition de *Voyage au bout de la nuit*', *Romans* 1, ed. Henri Godard, Paris, Gallimard, coll. 'La Pléïade', pp. 1113–14.

guerre . . .'.[29] The problem, however, is that it is in practice very difficult to divide Céline's work into two categories, the circumstantial and the timeless, precisely because the fiction itself is conscious of and subject to the same historical context as the polemical writing. *Voyage au bout de la nuit*, *Mort à crédit*, and *Casse-pipe* constitute the fictional transposition of the world and the historical process evoked in the medical writings and the anti-Semitic pamphlets which bracket them.

In this respect, the trilogy of the pamphlets is not merely an 'interesting' adjunct to the main body of Céline's work, but plays a major role in the expression of his stylistic and thematic preoccupations. Stylistically, as Philippine Muray observes, 'l'antisémitisme de Céline a été logiquement et paradoxalement mené par sa révolution d'écriture':[30] not merely does the 'outrageous' subject-matter of the pamphlets follow on from the 'outrageousness' of Céline's stylistic innovation, but, inversely, it appears at moments in the pamphlets to serve as a pretext for that innovation, to such an extent that, as we have seen, the pamphlets may be read in part as a latter-day *défense et illustration* of an innovative *français parlé*. Thematically, the world-view of the novels on the one hand, and of the pamphlets on the other, are identical, concentrated on the same narrow spectrum of threats, all of which, from *Semmelweis* onwards, may be expressed at any time through the metaphor of the Jew, who encapsulates all the principles of intelligence, modernity, and cosmopolitanism from which Céline instinctively distances himself. In particular, however, the Jew traditionally represents two forces which profoundly threaten Céline and of which he is perennially aware: time and money, the twin motive-forces of *Mort à crédit*. Lionel Kochan, in *The Jew and his History*, introduces Rosenzweig's theory of anti-Semitism as a metaphysical phenomenon, based upon resentment at the Jew's privileged position beyond history and beyond time: 'If the Jew belongs to eternity, then the Christian belongs to time'.[31] In other words, whilst Ferdinand and his class are the victims of time and condemned to disappearance, the Jew, historically, is free from such constraints and becomes triumphant. At the same time, the difference between 'Temps chrétien' and 'Temps juif' is the historical precondition for the Jews' role of userers, a profession from which Christians were rigorously excluded. Hence, the Jew dominates, not merely time, but money as

29. 'Tout Céline?', *Le Bulletin Célinien*, 27, November 1984, p. 4.
30. Philippe Muray, 'Le Siècle de Céline', *L'Infini*, 8, Autumn 1984, pp. 34–5.
31. Lionel Kochan, *The Jew and his History*, London, Macmillan, 1977, p. 111.

well: that other, constant, threat to Céline's existence. Thus, the 'cochon aux ailes en or' which presides over *Voyage au bout de la nuit*, and of which the 'ailes' are the phonetic rendering of the '£' of the pound sterling, is also the Aryanisation of the Jewish golden calf, the recurring symbol of Jewish power in anti-Semitic propaganda. In other words, the French have exchanged a calf for a pig, but are no less subject to the 'Jewish' money-principle. As Léon Bloy writes in his anti-Drumont pamphlet, *Le Salut par les Juifs*: 'Quelques profanes, il est vrai, se sont demandés quelle victoire essentielle résidait, pour la morale — *même pratique* — dans l'indéniable fait d'avoir entrepris de substituer au fameux Veau d'or un cochon du même métal . . .'.[32] Thus, the Jew, as controller of time and money, as the monopolist of gold which encapsulates both time and money, is, throughout Céline's work a potential metaphor of threat which becomes real when the last faint hope in a Communist system is snuffed out by the visit to Russia in 1936. *Mea culpa*, therefore, is the essential link between the writings on social medicine, the two novels and the anti-Semitic pamphlets.

At the same time, anti-Semitism is an integral part of the literary and philosophical tradition in which Céline produces, not merely his polemical work, but also his fiction. The debt of the pamphlets to Nietzshe, Bloy and Bernanos, all of whom look back nostalgically to a Golden Age in the Middle Ages in order to castigate the 'Jewish' domination of the modern world, is by now apparent, as are the close links with writings such as Drieu la Rochelle's *Notes pour comprendre le siècle*. Yet other influences on Céline's writing as a whole have explicit anti-Semitic connotations. That of Shakespeare is not confined to *The Tempest*, which dominates *Guignol's Band*, or *Pericles*, which provides the title and the model for Céline's first play; it also takes the form of Shylock in *The Merchant of Venice*. Similarly, echoes of Dickens are not restricted to the reflection of *Nicholas Nickleby* in the Meanwell College episode of *Mort à crédit*; there are also those of Fagin in *Oliver Twist*. Finally, it is worth recalling that Balzac, one of the great precursors of Céline in nostalgic representations of Paris, centred his analysis upon a detailed and acute study of the role of money in modern society which, already in the early nineteenth century, was perceived to be in the hands of the Jews. As Monsieur Crevel reminds the *baronne* Hulot, in *La Cousine Bette*:

---

32. Léon Bloy, *Le Salut par les Juifs* Paris, Librairie Adrien Demay, 1892, p. 7.

Vous vous abusez, cher ange, si vous croyez que c'est le roi Louis-Philippe qui règne, et il ne s'abuse pas là-dessus. Il sait, comme nous tous, qu'au-dessus de la Charte il y a la sainte, la vénérée, la solide, l'aimable, la gracieuse, la belle, la noble, la jeune, la toute-puissante pièce de cent sous! Or, mon bel ange, l'argent exige des intérêts, et il est toujours occupé à les percevoir! 'Dieu des Juifs, tu l'emportes!' a dit le grand Racine. Enfin, l'éternel allégorie du veau d'or . . .[33]

This reference serves to remind us, in its turn, that, on one level, Céline's racism is not enough to distinguish him from other writers of the inter-war years. As a racist, he is in the company of Maurras and Action Française, Jouhandeau, and the younger polemicists of *Je suis partout*, including Rebatet. Similarly, Céline's emphasis on European racism in his pamphlets serves to situate him in a broad category of French thought in the inter-war years which concentrated on the threat to European civilisation from the East and was centred on the conflict between Malraux's *La Tentation de l'Occident* and Henri Massis's *Défense de l'Occident*. This theme of the threat from the East re-emerges in Céline's *D'un château l'autre* trilogy in the form of the vision of the Chinese at Meudon, but it is also connected, through the writings of Bernanos and Drieu, with a particular view of Western civilisation, by which there was a Golden Age in Europe, situated either in the time of Charlemagne or in the High Middle Ages, when money had not yet destroyed spirituality and vigour. Finally, as Philippe Muray indicates, mild anti-Semitism was by no means unusual amongst a large number of respected French writers including, obviously the Giraudoux of *Pleins pouvoirs*, but also Gide, Morand and Duhamel.[34]

Yet the case of Céline's anti-Semitic writing cannot be fully explained or resolved by recourse either to the remarkable consistency of his views or to the clearly visible tradition in which he is writing. In one respect, the problem comes down again to the style and the apparently gratuitously abusive and exaggerated quality of it. Whereas the refined, literary expression of anti-Semitic thought was tolerated and went largely unpunished after the Liberation, the racism of a Caliban, speaking, unlike Guehenno's Caliban, in the

---

33. Honoré de Balzac, *La Cousine Bette*, Paris, Garnier, 1959, pp. 285–86. The same novel contains a reference to Clichy which emphasises the suburb's role in nineteenth-century Paris as a debtors' prison and associates it to Anglophobia: 'Mon cher Wenceslas, Je suis venu te voir ce matin, à dix heures, pour te présenter à une altesse royale qui désirait te connaître. Là, j'ai su que les Anglais t'avaient emmené dans une de leurs petites îles dont la capitale s'appelle *Clichy's Castle*' (pp. 125–6).
34. Muray, 'Le Siècle de Céline', p. 34.

apparently demotic, was unforgivable. At this point, the problem of
Voyage au bout de la nuit is posed even more acutely: the *miteux*
and the language of *misère* are always unacceptable, precisely because politically and aesthetically they contradict liberal bourgeois
norms of expression and behaviour.[35] It is through the deliberate
miteux style in the pamphlets, therefore, that Céline places himself
at risk and in a situation where he will have to pay. *Les Beaux draps*
ends with the evocation of the 'trépas de rats calamiteux' which
echoes the 'On était fait comme des rats' and the 'miteux' of the
beginning of *Voyage au bout de la nuit*. It is not the language alone
which is the problem, however: there is an irreducible, unclassifi-
able quality about the pamphlets which has the effect of perplexing
even the most racist of Céline's supporters. Whilst the bulk of the
anti-Semitic material is easily assimilated into the corpus of Céline's
work, there remain a number of perverse contradictions. One of
these concerns the status of Henry Ford. Much of the ambiguity of
the medical writings stems from the exaggerated praise of Ford
immediately after a rebarbative description of his plant in Detroit
which conflicts with the unambigously satirical treatment of the
same plant in *Voyage au bout de la nuit*. The invocation of Ford in
Bagatelles pour un massacre as an example of anti-Semitic thought is
in a similarly contradictory relationship to Bardamu's experience
and to the much more recent denunciation in *Mea culpa*. Similarly,
whilst England is vilified in the pamphlets as the epicentre of Jewish
power, it appears as the idyllic capital of *féerie* in *Guignol's Band*.
As with the medical pamphlets, these procedures, like those of
Defoe and Swift, point ultimately to one hidden target, the corrup-
tion of modern France, whilst rendering ambiguous the status of the
ostensible target, the Jews themselves. And nowhere does this
ambiguity emerge more strongly and more disconcertingly than in
Céline's references to the High Priest of French anti-Semitism,
Drumont.

A reading of *Bagatelles pour un massacre*, *L'Ecole des cadavres*
and *Les Beaux draps* in the light of Drumont's *La France juive* and
La Fin d'un monde shows little progression on Céline's part from
French anti-Semitism of the 1890s. All the elements are already
there in Drumont: the decline of France as a major power, her
subservience to England, the control exerted in all walks of life by
the Jews, a control which, for Drumont, becomes a veritable per-

---

35. See Frédéric Vitoux, *Louis-Ferdinand Céline Misère et parole*, Paris, Gallimard, 1973.

secution, a *massacre* of the Gentiles. It is true that Céline now has the evidence of the First World War and the Front Populaire government to confirm his fears, but essentially his anti-Semitism is that of Drumont, that of the Dreyfus Affair, which was perceived at the time as a British plot. As Hannah Arendt writes: 'Ils (Catholic politicians) furent donc les premiers à lier l'antisémitisme à l'Impérialisme, à declarer que les Juifs étaient les agents de l'Angleterre, donc à faire passer leur antisémitisme pour de l'anglophobie'.[36] Yet, for the same writer, the Dreyfus Case, with its pent-up frustration at the defeat of France in 1870, the collapse of the Catholic-owned Union Générale bank, the scandal over the Panama Canal, was resolved by a *deus ex machina*, the 1900 Universal Exposition which diverted the French from their internecine political struggles.[37] It is apparent, however, since *Mort à crédit*, that Céline stands on the wrong side of 1900, cut off from a Golden Age by the Exposition. It is entirely fitting, therefore, that whilst Céline may calque his own anti-Semitism on to that of the epic strugglë of the *belle époque*, when apparently the battle could still be won, he should do so ironically, now that the battle has been irretrievably lost and that the world ushered in by the Exposition has gained universal dominance. In such a case there is nothing more natural than that Céline should call upon Drumont, but should code the hopelessness of the invocation by deforming the name.

This ambiguous relationship to Drumont, which yet again establishes the essential time-span in Céline's work between 1900 and the 1930s, is compounded by two further factors. Firstly, Céline makes some use in his pamphlets of *The Protocols of the Elders of Zion*, a popular anti-Semitic document of the inter-war years in Europe, which originated in tsarist Russia and which purported to be firm evidence of an international Jewish conspiracy to take over the world.[38] Yet this work was in reality a carefully doctored forgery which relied upon a number of myths of a Jewish world-conspiracy, one of which began, interestingly enough in the light of Céline's use of Disraeli in his work, with the English politician's novel *Conningsby*, and was a rewriting of a satire on Napoleon III by Maurice

---

36. Hannah Arendt, *Sur l'antisémitisme*, Paris, Calmann-Lévy, coll. 'Diaspora', 1973, p. 253.

37. See ibid., p. 258.

38. See Norman Cohn, *Warrant for Genocide. The Myth of the Jewish World-Conspiracy and the Protocols of the Elders of Zion*, London, Eyre and Spottiswoode, 1967. One French edition is that edited by Mgr Jouin, *Le Péril Judéo-Maçonnique*, 1: *Les 'Protocoles' des Sages de Sion*, Paris, Revue Internationale des Sociétés Secrètes/Emile-Paul Frères, 1920.

Joly entitled *Dialogue aux Enfers entre Montesquieu et Machiavel*. The *Protocols* were shown to be a forgery as early as 1921, with three articles in *The Times* proving their derivation from the Joly satire,[39] and there were two trials in 1934–5, one in South Africa, the other in Switzerland, to contest the validity of the documents.[40] The problem, of course, is that confirmed anti-Semites merely saw these actions as proof of Jewish power and as additional evidence for the truth of the *Protocols* themselves. Nevertheless, by making slavish and unquestioning use of the *Protocols* in his pamphlets, Céline is using a problematic model which may be designed to point to the ambiguity of his own texts. More important, he is using a document which has its real origins in the nineteenth century, not the twentieth, and whose real title, *Dialogue aux Enfers . . .*, looks forward directly to Céline's consistent preoccupation with Hades and ghosts.

In the second place, the oscillation in the pamphlets between the present and a past which lies beyond the First World War is continued in the 'Photographies antisémites légendées par Céline avec un sens de l'humour très personnel',[41] which accompany the editions of *Bagatelles pour un massacre* and *L'Ecole des cadavres* published during the Occupation. The illustrations to *Bagatelles pour un massacre* concentrate on the tsarist regime in Russia and the Russian Royal Family in prison in Ekaterinburg just before their execution, yet another *massacre*. Those included in the new edition of *L'Ecole des cadavres* are more interesting, precisely because they appear to relate so little to the apparently transparent and contemporary anti-Semitism of the text. The vast majority of the photographs are taken from press sources prior to 1918, and whilst some of these invoke the war and the Russian Revolution (one photograph is of the 'Premier Commissariat du Peuple en URSS', as non-existent an organisation as the 'Front Populaire de la Région Parisienne' whose minute ends the text itself), the rest are strangely oblique and stylised images, relating to the Dreyfus Case, 1900s racism, monarchism, and one significant picture: a female cyclist, with the caption: 'Une Précurseuse, 1900'. Once again, Céline's magic date is mentioned, this time in a way which combines anti-Semitism, anti-feminism and anti-modernism. Whilst the last two photographs contrast a banqueting Lord Castleross, as a metaphor for a buoyant self-confident England, with an insouciant

39. See Norman Cohn, *Warrant for Genocide*, p. 155.
40. See ibid., Chapter X, 'Forgery Pushers on Trial'.
41. Ory, *Les Collaborateurs*, p. 232.

group of Frenchmen in a bar, little suspecting what is about to happen to them, the centre of gravity of the illustrations is very much the *belle époque*, epitomised by the picture entitled: 'M. Fallières se laisse aimablement photographier par l'aide de camp du prince de Monaco'. Not only is this a literal *mise en abîme*, a photograph within a photograph, but it connects with the semi-nostalgic, semi-satirical account of the 14 July parade in *Casse-pipe*: the world of the *belle époque*, for Céline, as for Proust, gone for ever.

The photographs, therefore, by their very inconsequentiality, have a disruptive purpose, and emphasise the gap between 1900 and the present. At the same time, they point to something else: many of them are taken from a review called *Je sais tout*. Whilst this title bears a sinister resemblance to *Je suis partout*, it was in fact a 'magazine encyclopédique illustré', appearing monthly and catering specifically for a petit-bourgeois audience trying to gain knowledge: the world of *Mort à crédit*. The images therefore come from a precise historical and sociological origin. They are part of that deluded attempt on the part of the post-1900 petite bourgeoisie to keep afloat in the modern world by the acquisition of knowledge. The title of the magazine, however, has an added significance. Philippe Roussin has emphasised the way in which Céline attempts to fulfil the nineteenth-century writer's ambition of 'tout dire'. Yet, in order to be able to say: 'Je dis tout', it is necessary first to say: 'Je sais tout': the entire notion of anti-Semitic polemic depends, not just on saying the unacceptable, the mission which Céline identifies with Zola and the Naturalists, but also on a pact between reader and polemicist based upon the faith that the latter possesses special knowledge, indeed a *total* knowledge of the innermost workings of the world. The problem with Céline is that he both plays on this pact and subverts it in his pamphlets: the reader is forced by the narrator to believe what he is saying, yet at the same time prevented from doing so by inconsistency, exaggeration and repetition. We are asked to believe in the message of Drumont, but then diverted by the misspelling of his name.

It is this procedure which links the anti-Semitic pamphlets with the earlier medical polemic and which furnishes Céline not merely with a polemical stance derived from eighteenth-century English satire but also with a means of camouflage and self-protection. The ambiguity, irony, exaggeration and inconsistency in the pamphlets have the effect of allowing Céline to say the outrageous, whilst at the same time providing an in-built escape clause, in the same way that the use of a narrator deflects the responsibility from the author.

This is further compounded by Céline's use of the epithet 'Jew' to describe those who are manifestly not Jewish, such as Maurras. This forms part of a standard procedure of anti-Semitism which is to claim that attacks are mounted against the Jew as metaphor and not against the Jew as a person. Thus, Léon Poliakov quotes Matthieu-Daurivaell: 'Je n'en veux aucunement aux Juifs que je considère comme mes frères . . . J'en veux à ceux que j'appelle Juifs',[42] and Robert Soucy refers to Barrès' notion that 'Antisemitism joins hands with Socialism' in similar terms: 'Deep down in our hearts, Jewish is only an adjective we use to designate usurers, hoarders and speculators on the stock-market — all those who abuse the omnipotence of money . . . Each of us has a Jew he refers to for purposes of reprobation . . . Conversely, we have Christians whom we treat as Jews . . .'.[43]

This technique of 'playful' anti-Semitism has a deeper purpose, however, that of merely providing camouflage for the author. In his essay on Baudelaire, Walter Benjamin refers to a short statement which comes at the end of *Mon coeur mis à nu*: 'Belle conspiration à organiser pour l'extermination de la Race Juive. Les Juifs, *Bibliothécaires* et témoins de la *Rédemption*',[44] and categorises it as part of the technique known as the *culte de la blague*, an essential component of Fascist propaganda, which consists in stating the outrageous in such a way that it appears as a joke, but has in fact a deadly serious meaning.[45] If the same statement were delivered formally, it would be rejected, whereas in 'playful' form, it is insidiously convincing. At the same time, for Baudelaire, like Céline, watching his gradual exclusion from the new Paris, the *culte de la blague* is part of a general search for a scapegoat which, in his case, takes the ultimate form of a diatribe, not against the Jews, but against the Belgians, in *Pauvre Belgique* and the *Amoenitates Belgae*, and in which there is more than a hint of a pretext for an *exercice du style*.

Yet, as Arnold Mandel observes, the very playfulness of the literary *culte de la blague* is psychologically extremely significant. He writes:

42. Léon Poliakov, *Histoire de l'antisémitisme*, II, *De Voltaire à Wagner*, Paris, Calmann-Lévy, 1968, p. 357.

43. Robert Soucy, *Fascism in France. The Case of Maurice Barrès*, Berkeley, Los Angeles and London, University of California Press, 1972, p. 134.

44. Charles Baudelaire, 'Mon coeur mis à nu', in *Oeuvres complètes*, p. 1300.

45. Walter Benjamin, *Charles Baudelaire. A Lyric Poet in an Age of High Capitalism*, London, New Left Books, 1973.

Dans la première partie de *D'un château l'autre*, Céline décrit le chaotique Berlin dés ruines de la toute proche débâcle hitlérienne. Il apperçoit, entre autres, dans ce grouillement d'épaves, des Juifs intrigants en quête de trafics. Or, depuis bien longtemps, il n'y a pas de Juifs du tout dans la capitale du Reich, sauf peut-être quelques fantômes de troglodytes, omis par hasard de l'appel a l'incinération, quelques morts vivants, claque-murés dans les caves et les greniers. Céline a-t-il menti? Pas exactement, mais il a eu la berlue, parce que cette berlue était absolument indispensable à la bonne preservation de la vision et du champ optique qu'il s'était aménagés pour déployer sa verve.[46]

Céline's anti-Semitism, therefore, is part of a complex system of doublethink:

On pourrait qualifier le processus en question de recours à l'amnésie. Le meurtrier oublie qu'il a tué, non pas pour échapper au sentiment de culpabilité et pour ne pas se faire horreur à lui-même, mais parce qu'il a toujours besoin de celui-là même qu'il occit ou fait occire. Donc il faut que ce mort soit encore vivant. En conséquence, ce mort n'est pas mort et il ne l'a jamais tué. L'antisémite hait le Juif, l'antisemite excessif le hait très fort, et s'il le peut, il l'extermine. Sa haine n'est pas assouvie pour autant. Comme elle se nourrit d'elle-même, elle est le buisson ardent qui flambe et ne se consume pas. L'objet de cet inimité ayant disparu et étant irremplaçable, on passe outre au fait de sa disparition en croyant — et non pas en faisant semblant de croire — qu'il est toujours là. S'il était permis à cet égard d'établir une comparaison sur le ton plaisant, il faudrait comparer — mais à rebours ce 'jeu' à celui de certains enfants jouant à la guerre avec des fusils-jouets. L'un des garçonnets brandit son arme visant son petit camarade, appuie sur la gachette — s'il y en a une — puis s'écrie: 'Pan-pan t'es mort'. L'antijuif judéocide, lui, s'approche du Juif avec une arme authentique et chargée. Il tire à bout portant et l'abat, puis dit: 'Pan-pan t'es pas mort'.[47]

Céline needs the constant presence of the victim, even after the excessive imprecations directed at him, and it is for this reason that the trilogy of pamphlets is centered on the device of repetition.

Yet, if this repetitiveness is part of the 'playful' *culte de la blague* and guarantees the continuing ability of the anti-Semitic writer to write, it is also, like all Freudian repetition, ultimately directed towards death. Undeniably, Céline's pamphlets have a positive effect on the course of his work: they liberate him from the ideological and literary 'block' constituted by *Mea culpa* and *Casse-pipe*; they have the effect, through imitation, of exorcising the ghost of Auguste haunting Ferdinand; and they break the claustro-

46. Arnold Mandel, *Nous autres Juifs*, Paris, Hachette, 1978, p. 64.
47. Ibid., pp. 63–4.

phobic dome of the modern world which oppresses Céline's entire output until the onset of the Second World War. Yet they do so at the price of self-immolation. Even more than *Mort à crédit*, the pamphlets are self-destructive texts and, literally, suicidal for the author. Yet, with this 'suicide', it is as if a barrier has been lifted: no longer is Ferdinand the *fantôme burlesque* condemned to wander through the limbo of the inter-war years, the path is open back to the last manifestation of Céline's Golden Age: the imperial might of London, in *Guignol's Band*.

[6]

Guignol's Band
and the Ghost of Shakespeare

The two volumes of *Guignol's Band* constitute the last extended attempt by Céline to recapture the world before the end of the First World War. That this should be so is undoubtedly due to the way in which history provided Céline with other preoccupations from the Liberation onwards. Yet even without the fact that the Second World War came to impose itself as an inescapable theme and base for the subsequent fiction, *Guignol's Band* has about it very much the sense of an ending, as if the problems which have preoccupied Céline so deeply in the interrelation between the inter-war years and the *belle époque* had finally been solved and the old ghosts exorcised.

Specifically, the novel is an evocation of London during the First World War, a London which has not yet become the menacing, all-powerful Jewish City of the pamphlets, but which is still a fairy-tale town, acceded to by an association of one bombardment with another, and one bridge with another: the German bombardment of the bridge over the Loire at Orléans during the rout of June 1940 which opens the first volume, and the air-raid by zeppelins which looms over the last part of the second volume and which precedes the narrator's final crossing of London Bridge: 'd'un bombardement l'autre; d'un pont l'autre'.[1] This repetition, however, which in Céline's preceding work has merely imprisoned him in an inescapable stasis, operates in a different way in *Guignol's Band*: it is liberating, and it owes its liberation to the fact that the London Céline chooses to depict is a fantasy city, half-grotesque and frightening, half *féerie*, but always unreal and, like the sailing-

---

1. It is, of course, just possible that the depiction of a group of exiled French criminals in London would have quite specific anti-Gaullist polemical connotations after 18 June 1940.

ship on which Ferdinand is to escape to South America, the *Kong Hamsun*,[2] ultimately anachronistic.

The creation of this fantasy city of London in *Guignol's Band* is achieved through two procedures: the by now familiar dislocation and invention of the topography of the city, as seen already in *Voyage au bout de la nuit*, *Mort à crédit* and *Les Beaux draps*, and a considerable use in the text of reflections of other literary works, many of which deal specifically with the English capital.

Céline is careful, in *Guignol's Band*, to establish a paradoxical relationship between the narrator's pretensions to complete veracity and his falsification of the topographical data in order to create an autonomous fictional city. As the narrator of what is, essentially, a memoir or historical novel, Ferdinand is aware that he will only achieve and maintain credibility in the eyes of his reader through the proven accuracy of his account: once more, the precondition of 'tout dire' is 'tout savoir' and the reader must be made confident that this is so. Hence, where he cannot prove, the narrator asserts: 'C'est exact tout ce que je vous raconte . . .' (GB 1, 12), and: 'J'ai vu cela! Je peux causer!' (GB 1, 182). At the same time, the narrator is aware that this pretension to veracity is undermined by the passage of time and the fallibility of memory. Thus, recognising that he will never be able to return to London to verify his impressions, Ferdinand subtly changes tack during his evocation of the house of Van Claben: 'C'est fini tout ça! . . . C'est du rêve . . . C'est comme un autre monde à present . . . Je les reverrai jamais sans doute les endroits réels . . . Je suis obligé d'imaginer . . . Je vais vous faire un petit effet d'art . . . j'avais pas voulu être réduit á un mélodrame . . .' (GB 1, 211).

In this way, the narrator is making two important assertions. Firstly, the world he has chosen to evoke, like all Céline's pre-First World War settings, is dead and gone and cannot be resuscitated. Nor can it be accurately recreated by memory: falsification and error are inherent to the entire act of transposition from past to present. Yet, whereas the documentary remains on the level of the real, it is precisely through falsification and invention that the way to art is opened up. In other words, although Ferdinand can claim confidently to Sosthène de Rodiencourt that 'Les cartes ça me

2. A sailing clipper during the First World War, whilst not quite as anachronistic as the *galère* in *Voyage au bout de la nuit*, is nevertheless fairly dated and serves, like so much in Céline's fiction, to push the centre of gravity of the novel further back into the nineteenth century and into the realm of the imagination. This latter aspect is reinforced by the dual connotations of the name of the vessel: 'Kong' from the Fay Wray film *King Kong*, 'Hamsun' from the Swedish adventure-writer Knut Hamsun.

connait!' (GB 1, 337), the maps he draws for his reader are more like the mythological and magical maps of his employer than a Naturalist account of London, and they are established through the presentation of an accumulation of topographical detail which, on closer inspection, is either invented or compressed and dislocated in order to recreate, not a real city, but an autonomous world.

Céline's falsification of the topography of London is continued throughout the two volumes of *Guignol's Band*, but affects the first volume more deeply. This subversion takes the form initially of a technique of compression of topographical details, so that the city becomes smaller and limited to a small number of areas. Thus, for the narrator, Mile End Road, with the London Hospital and the public house, 'La Vaillance', are next door to Wapping and its docklands, and just on the other side of the river from Greenwich, the fief of Van Claben. In fact, the 'Croisière de Dingby' is one kilometre from the London Hospital and five or six kilometres from Greenwich. Similarly, Ferdinand makes a point of remembering 'tout l'East End, de Highgate aux Docks' (GB 1, 119), although in reality Highgate, in north London, is not part of the East End at all and is some ten kilometres from the river.[3] In addition to this technique of compression of the topography, Céline employs place names, accurate in themselves, but in the wrong location, for purely poetic effect. Thus, 'L'Eléphant' and 'Le Castle' which, as Elephant and Castle denote an area of south-east London, become in *Guignol's Band*: 'les deux extrêmes du Mile End' (GB 1, 114), and, when La Joconde is taken to the London Hospital, the taxicab passes Fleet Street and the Bank, perfectly accurately, only to end up in 'Seven Sisters' (GB 1, 114), to the north and not the east of the city centre.

This initial compression and dislocation of the topography of London is the first stage in Céline's attempt to fashion a legendary and not a real city, whilst nevertheless maintaining and asserting the fiction of nineteenth-century Naturalist veracity. It is highly appropriate, therefore, that this personal, phantasmagorical city should appear through the most extreme topographical disruption which occurs whenever Ferdinand, like his predecessor in *Mort à crédit*, is obliged to flee for his life. After the explosion of Borokrom's grenade in the 'Croisière de Dingby', for example, the band takes flight by way of: 'High Way Lambeth! . . . Moorgate, le Square, les Docks, Marylebone, Mint Place . . .' (GB 1, 152–4). A similar random selection of names, drawn from all over London, occurs

---

3. In this context, see also the faulty geography in Delphine's journey from Greenwich to Wapping (GB 1, 214).

after Ferdinand's supposed murder of Mille-Pattes, when he runs through: 'Bond Street, Marylebourne, Fenchurch Street, Wardow, l'Avenue, Straftsbury, Victoria . . . (GB 1, 291), a list which goes further than an attempt to establish local colour by any means, with characteristic French misspellings of English place names, and which translates the paranoia and panic of the narrator by a topographical delirium in which London itself appears to spin round and fragment.

Clearly, this kind of falsification of the geography of London seriously calls into question Ferdinand's pretension to be a credible guide to the city. Paradoxically, however, the more he attempts to establish his credentials by providing a proliferation and accumulation of place names and street names, the more he compounds the factual errors and dislocation. In the same way that the narrator of the pamphlets compensates for the weakness of his argument by exaggeration and repetition, Ferdinand in *Guignol's Band* attempts to guarantee the veracity of his account by the accumulation of detail, true or false, in the same way that London itself guarantees its position of power in the world through the same process of accumulation.

At the same time, however, the accumulation of place names paradoxically leads the novel away from the reality it is allegedly attempting to evoke to the purely imaginative, aesthetic pleasure in the place names themselves. The pleasure taken in the 'Noms de pays. Le Nom' depends not at all upon the ultimate reality which the name denotes, but instead upon the liberation and imaginative possibilities afforded by the names themselves. Thus, many of Céline's lists of streets and places in *Guignol's Band* are established less with a view to guiding the reader through the geography of the real London than with the construction of a series of patterns in the novel which operate on a purely imaginative and poetic level. Many of the street names, for example, are introduced simply because of their sound. Others, even though they do not exist in reality, form part of whole systems of allusions which motivate the novel. In this way, names like: 'Blossom Avenue', 'Orchard Alley' (GB 1, 39), 'Lavender Street', 'Daffodil Place' (GB 1, 42), introduce a whole system based on flowers, which culminates in the appearance of Sosthène's wife Pépé, 'la Fleur merveilleuse' (GB 1, 350). Similarly, 'Plymouth Street' (GB 1, 39), 'Falmouth Cottage' (GB 1, 42) and 'Neptune Commons' (GB 1, 39) underline the constant presence of the sea in the novel, whilst 'Hollander Place' (GB 1, 42) looks forward to the entry of Van Claben, whilst also introducing the theme of the *Fliegender Holländer*, the Flying Dutchman. Nor, in this context, should an unusually playful, almost Joycean manipulation of place names be ignored: the famous public house, 'The Prospect of Whitby', appears as 'La Croisière de Dingby', and a brand of beer, 'Courage', becomes a public house in its own right, 'La Vaillance'.

This disruption of the topography of London has the effect of creating a mythological city which is both immense: 'C'est grand, Londres' (GB 1, 114), and curiously limited to a small number of key districts. Thus, in the first volume, the town is described through an axis which, with Wapping and the port as its centre, extends towards Soho in the north-west and Greenwich in the south-east. Wapping *is* the port, the centre of the mythical richness of London, where the accumulation of wealth and exoticism gives rise to dreams; further north is Mile End, with its public house 'La Vaillance' and, especially, the London Hospital which catered throughout two world wars to the needs of the inhabitants of the East End and whose courageous reputation is faithfully evoked in the novel.[4] Soho is the fief of Cascade and defined solely in terms of crime, prostitution and the French *milieu*; Greenwich, at the other extremity of the axis, between its park and the port, between land and sea, is the domain of Van Claben, but it is also the site of the Greenwich Observatory, the home of the first meridian, in other words, the very centre of time. After Céline's constant and repetitious defeat at the hands of time throughout his writing in the inter-war years, it is fitting that his final work of the cycle that evokes the *belle époque* should take place at the epicentre of time, just as the Port of London and the City are perceived as the centre of the world's wealth. In *Guignol's Band*, by travelling to London, Ferdinand has finally reached the centre of the operation of time and money, of *mort* and *crédit*.

Nor does the second volume of the novel radically alter the axis established in the first part, except for the addition of the O'Colloghan household in Willesden, in the north of London, and Prospero Jim's new inn, the 'Moor and Cheese', in Blackfriars, due south of the City, on the other side of the Thames. It becomes clear, therefore, that, in spite of the narrator's insistence on his role as a *chroniqueur*, his natural role is imaginative and poetic and concerned with the construction of a legendary city, rich in sounds and

4. For a detailed study of the London Hospital, see A.E. Clarke-Kennedy, *London Pride. The Story of a Voluntary Hospital*, London, Hutchinson-Benham, 1979. The Hospital records make no mention of any possible involvement, either in the medical school or the hospital itself, of Céline or anyone who may have served as a model for Clodovitz.

connotations, in which the same preoccupations with time, money and the lost world of the past can once more be deployed and, perhaps, finally resolved.

It is for this reason that the novel relies so heavily on a pre-existent literary base. As Jill Forbes points out,[5] Céline is writing in a rich tradition of French evocations of the English capital which includes Paul Féval's *Les Mystères de Londres*, Jules Vallès's *La Rue à Londres* and Paul Morand's *Londres*, as well as the *Promenades dans Londres* by Flora Tristan, Taine's *Notes sur l'Angleterre* and Villiers de l'Isle-Adam's *Le Sadisme anglais*. Of all these works, however, it is undoubtedly to Vallès's *La Rue à Londres* that Céline owes a direct debt, as he does to *Jacques Vingtras* in the writing of *Mort à crédit*.[6] Indeed, he singles Vallès's work out in a letter from Denmark after the war to the Swedish writer Ernst Bendz:

> je vous recommande un livre étonnant, peu connu et admirable de Jules Vallès (membre de la Commune 71, exilé à Londres): 'La Rue à Londres'.
> Et j'aime l'Angleterre vous savez— beaucoup. Je la choisirais volontiers pour exil (HER 1, 127).

It is interesting that Céline should carry the identification with Vallès to the point of envisaging himself in the same place of exile: Vallès, driven out by the *Versaillais* in 1871, becomes Céline, exiled by the Resistance in 1944. The political stances of the two writers are, at least in appearance, diametrically opposed, yet their situations are remarkably similar: both are victims of a petit-bourgeois upbringing; both invite hostility from their audience through an uncompromising use of the first-person narrator and a close coincidence of biographical and imagined material in their fiction; both take political risks and are punished; both are considered unreadable by the new orthodoxy. Certainly, in large measure, Céline expresses his admiration for London in identical terms to those used by Vallès: it is the music which captivates them both. Vallès asks: 'Ne grince-t-elle pas?',[7] to which Ferdinand replies: 'C'est grêle

---

5. Jill Forbes, 'Symbolique de l'espace': le "Londres" célinien', BLFC 1, 27–40.
6. Assertions are often made regarding the similarity between *Guignol's Band* and Morand's *Londres*, of 1930. The problem is that, as with the same author's *1900* and *New York*, there are undoubtedly areas of common preoccupation. These do not, however, extend any further than a certain parallelism of observation and, for this reason, the relationship between Céline and Morand presents less interest than that between Céline and Vallès, where there are similarities of background, social thought, political unacceptability and style.
7. Jules Vallés, *La Rue à Londres*, Paris, Les Editeurs Français Réunis, 1951, p. 58.

ainsi les airs anglais' (GB 1, 35). Similarly, they are both obliged to invent a new style in order to introduce the musicality of London into their work. Thus, Vallès inserts a series of onomatopeoic exclamations: 'Zim! malaboum, boum, boum',[8] just as Céline uses 'Braoum! Vraoum!' (GB 1, 7) to convey the explosions on the bridge at Orléans or the effects of Borokrom's grenades.

At the same time, although there is considerable similarity between the two writers' evocations of London, they differ in that, uncharacteristically, Céline appears more mellow in his descriptions. Whilst, like Céline, Vallès sees Soho only as the centre of prostitution in London, dominated by the French *milieu* already in the 1870s, that 'bande de faiseurs, qui tend ses filets dans l'eau trouble',[9] who 'rode en marge de la Cité',[10] where 'le soir, on traîne dans Regent Street'[11] and which is 'plein de policiers',[12] he is uniformly more severe. Céline is willing to recognise the relaxation, the freedom, the music and the magic of Soho: as Ferdinand recalls, 'Je trouvais la condition magique après ce que j'avais connu' (GB 1, 91). In Vallès, it is always the ex-Communard writing:

> Il faut avouer qu'il était fait pour nous déshonorer, ce Leicester Square tout gros de la fange de France.
> Le Soho — l'infâme Soho![13]

It is interesting to note that this is exactly the same kind of criticism levelled by Céline at his own countrymen in his description of the burlesque-houses in New York in the anti-Semitic pamphlets; yet, in *Guignol's Band*, perhaps uniquely in Céline's work, that stringency has been relaxed, to give way to an innocent appreciation of the Marvellous. A similar distinction is present between the two writers' depictions of the Port of London. In *Guignol's Band*, Céline emphasises the exotic and fairy-tale quality of the goods brought from the four corners of the earth and which constitute the basis of England's fabulous wealth. In the chapter of *La Rue à Londres* entitled 'Le Wapping', however, Vallès sees in this accumulation of riches only the external signs of a brutal and sordid aggression. Yet, even so, it is an oppression and power which can still excite the imagination: for Vallès, England becomes a vast

8. Ibid., p. 33.
9. Ibid., p. 107.
10. Ibid.
11. Ibid., p. 106.
12. Ibid.
13. Ibid., p. 103.

pirate ship: 'Il y a là, amarrée au milieu de l'Océan, une machine terrible, qui coupe le bois, lamine le fer, vomit l'or, écrase les pauvres',[14] and he concludes: 'J'ai cherché à pénétrer l'âme de cette nation dure, et elle m'a paru redoutable et haute'.[15]

From this blend of brutality, strength and nobility comes, for Vallès, a peculiarly British aesthetic, based upon the person of the clown: 'Le clown représente l'ironie et la force. L'Angleterre est toute entière là-dedans',[16] and the clown's costume, all golden, is 'une revanche contre la fatalité grise, contre le climat noir!'[17] This conclusion is clearly of considerable importance in the context of the *Grand Guignol* aspect of Céline's novel as a whole and the work's concluding lines in particular: 'C'est moi le pitre maintenant!' (GB 2, 499). The novel, by its very form, assumes English aesthetic qualities and, by the end, Ferdinand has become an English clown, assimilated totally into the atmosphere in which he has been residing since the novel began, and imbued with the values of gold. And this is made even clear by Vallès' final comment: 'La pantomime d'Angleterre est devenue, à vrai dire, la féerie classique de notre pays'.[18] *Guignol's Band* is, precisely, a *féerie*, in the same tradition as the 'Utopia' and the *voyage imaginaire*, which chooses to adopt the form of an English pantomime and even, as Jill Forbes observes, alludes constantly to the English pantomime tradition.[19] It is highly appropriate therefore, in the light of Vallès's definition, that Céline's first excursion into *féeries* after the pamphlets should take the form of a novel set in London.

Vallès's depiction of London in *La Rue à Londres*, therefore, although more acerbic in its criticism and less relaxed in its evocation than *Guignol's Band*, concentrates on the same subject-matter and, from a documentary base, proceeds to the world of *féerie*. Céline's novel, in its imaginary evocation of the London of a generation later, follows the same path and arrives at the same result. In so doing, the novel distances itself from the historical reality of London even further by choosing, not a documentary base, but a literary one, constituted in part by the Vallès text and in part by Joseph Conrad's novel of 1907, *The Secret Agent*.

Conrad's high reputation in France before and immediately after

14. Ibid., p. 112. The image of vomiting gold looks forward strikingly to Céline's description of the death of Van Claben.
15. Ibid., p. 113.
16. Ibid., p. 136.
17. Ibid., p. 137.
18. Ibid.
19. See Forbes, 'Symbolique de l'espace'.

the First World War and the affinites between *Voyage au bout de la nuit* and his adventure fiction, particularly *Heart of Darkness*, have already been explored. Nor does it seem that Céline was ignorant of *The Secret Agent*: its most famous line, Winnie Verloc's reiterated statement of faith: 'She was aware that it did not stand looking into very much',[20] has already emerged in *Lex Beaux draps* and, most revealingly, in the company of a 'Guignol': 'le drame commence, le Grand Guignol ... Faut pas voir trop au fond des choses ...' (BD, 74–5). Céline's knowledge of British Edwardian fiction, the great literary expression of the *belle époque*, appears therefore as more detailed than generally thought, and encompasses not merely Kipling, to whom he refers directly in his letters from Africa, but also the novels of Wells and Conrad.

Conrad's novel, written in 1907 but set in the 1880s, describes the career of Adolf Verloc, a French anarchist now living in London, who has become an *agent provocateur* in the pay of a foreign embassy. His seedy shop in Soho, which announces Van Claben's pawnshop in Greenwich, is the meeting-place for a whole band of political activists, dominated by the 'ticket-of-leave apostle' Ossipon, known as 'the Doctor', and by the strange character 'the Professor', a bomb-maker who dreams only of the discovery of the perfect detonator. In order to provoke police repression against these characters, Verloc is charged with the mission of blowing up the Greenwich Observatory, a Western scientific and cultural fetish which, if destroyed, will shake the entire society based on time. The mission fails, however: Verloc entrusts the bomb to his wife's idiot brother Stevie, who contrives to blow himself up in Greenwich Park. When Verloc breaks the news to his wife Winnie, she kills him with a carving-knife and runs off, leaving the shop door open, just as Ferdinand will leave the pawnshop door open after Van Claben's death. She finally throws herself from a cross-Channel ferry and dies, like Nora Merrywin, the shape of a dress floating on the sea.

Conrad's London is clearly far closer to that depicted by Céline than, say, the image of the city which appears in Dickens's *Oliver Twist*, which nevertheless does present some similarities. Conrad establishes a dark, fogbound city, which extends from Soho to Greenwich and in which the activities of a shadowy group of pseudo-terrorists impinge tragically upon the lives of the protagonists, Verloc, Winnie and Stevie. Above all, in both novels, there is the mysterious and implacable function of retribution and detection in the form of a solitary policeman: Sergeant Matthew, in *Guignol's*

---

20. Joseph Conrad, *The Secret Agent*, Harmondsworth, Penguin, 1963, p. 196.

Band, and Inspector Heat, in *The Secret Agent*. Where the two novels differ crucially, however, is in their evaluation of the interaction between profundity and superficiality. Against all her instincts and a lifetime's conviction that things do not stand looking into, Winnie Verloc is forced by events to see the deep reality of existence which will lead her to murder and suicide. Céline, again uncharacteristically, chooses in *Guignol's Band* to remain on the surface of events in which comedy and pantomime dominate and to take his narrator, finally, out of the depths: when Ferdinand, Sosthène and Virginia cross the bridge at the end of the second volume, it is order to escape by omnibus and not by underground railway, and whilst they remain on the bridge, it is the corpse of Van Claben which is consigned to the deep.

It is this particular form of theatricality which introduces the most sustained and pervasive literary influence on the work, that of Shakespeare. Indeed, it is doubtful whether a more genuinely Shakespearian novel exists in modern French literature. This Shakespearian texture, obviously so appropriate to a novel set in London and particularly, in its last section, on the very site of Shakespeare's own theatre in Blackfriars, begins with what appears to be a purely random allusion. Castigating Denoël, his publisher, for being shocked at the violence of the novel, the author-narrator addresses the reader directly and comments ruefully: 'Je lui apporterais le Roi Lear qu'il n'y verrait que des massacres' (GB 1, 374). As the novel progresses, however, and increasingly in the final section, references to Shakespeare multiply: Prospero Jim's new tavern is called 'The Moor and Cheese', which combines the Fleet Street establishment 'The Cheshire Cheese' with a reference to *Othello, the Moor of Venice*. Through Delphine come references to *Macbeth*, *Romeo and Juliet*, a performance of which she interrupts, and *The Merry Wives of Windsor* (GB 2, 421). Yet, within this system of Shakespearian allusions, there are two plays which clearly dominate: *Macbeth* and *The Tempest*.

Of the two plays, it is *Macbeth* which, for the most part, has the less problematic relationship to Céline's novel, since it is used uniquely as an ironic, grand-tragic counterpoint to the story surrounding the death of Van Claben. It also forms part of a system of allusions which are conveyed solely by one character, Delphine, a character who is already mad and who ironically assumes the role of another mad woman: 'But I am Lady Macbeth!' (GB 1, 248). In Delphine's fantasy, Van Claben becomes the murdered king, Duncan, Ferdinand becomes Macbeth and Borokrom becomes Banquo. What is important about this calque, however, is not merely the comic and ironic reflection provided on events by a mad woman's ravings, but what it indicates about the role of Van Claben in the novel and the significance of his murder and final burial.[21]

It is *The Tempest*, however, Céline's favourite literary work, which informs the entire novel. The link is established in the first place through Prospero Jim, the landlord of the 'Croisière de Dingby' and, when that is destroyed, of 'The Moor and Cheese' south of the Thames, in Blackfriars. Through this character, Céline indulges in a certain amount of innocent word-play: 'Prospero', often shortened to 'Prosper', conveys the *prosperity* of the entire city; in addition, it provides a further link with Vallès: in *La Rue à Londres*, 'le old Jim' was the landlord of an opium den in Wapping.[22] It is, however, his role in relation to *The Tempest* which is crucial. In Shakespeare's last play, Prospero, Duke of Milan, through the treachery of his brother Antonio, has been exiled on a magic island. Here, he comes to understand the powers of magic and learns to dominate the spirits of the island, particularly the beast Caliban, through the manipulation of the occult. In the same way, the lugubrious landlord of the 'Croisière de Dingby' is an Italian exile, living in London, the capital of an island, and dominating his clientele through his *'vitriol du marin* qu'était un secret' (GB 1, 139). From Prospero Jim himself, however, the presence of *The Tempest* in *Guignol's Band* radiates out to dominate the whole work.

This presence is established first by the enchanted setting which Céline gives to his novel and which is a direct reflection of the magicality of Prospero's island. In *The Tempest*, Caliban reassures his fellow conspiritors with the words:

Be not afeard; the isle is full of noises,
Sounds and sweet airs, that give delight, and hurt not.
Sometimes a thousand twangling instruments
Will hum about mine ears; and sometimes voices,
That, if I had waked after a long sleep,
Will make me sleep again: and then, in dreaming,
The clouds methought would open, and show riches
Ready to drop upon me; that, when I waked,
I cried to dream again.[23]

In the same way, Céline's novel is punctuated by snatches of

21. A reference which carries forward the preoccupations of *L'Ecole des cadavres*.
22. Vallès, *La Rue à Londres*, pp. 270–1.
23. *The Tempest*, III, 2, 142–52.

magical children's songs and is bathed in an atmosphere of *féerie*, in which the 'lutins' (GB 1, 40), of the streets of London play the same role as the elves and spirits of Shakespearian comedy, from *A Midsummer Night's Dream* to *The Tempest* itself. In both cases, the aim is identical: to penetrate the heart of the dream-world. Similarly, both Shakespeare and Céline make use of naturalistic causes for the hallucinatory worlds which they create: the crew of the shipwrecked vessel in *The Tempest*, led by the steward Trinculo, accede to the *féerie* through drunkenness; in *Guignol's Band*, alcohol and taverns play an identical function, as do the narcotic cigarettes which lead to the death of Van Claben.

It is the use of the dream-world, 'When no man was his own',[24] which is intimately linked to a particular notion of exile, by which removal from normality, both social and rational, has an initiatory but also a rectificatory effect. Shakespeare's play is about exile: only Caliban is a native of the magic island; his master Prospero has been deliberately exiled there by his brother Antonio and, through Prospero's magic, all the characters of his past are brought back to share his exile and contribute, in spite of themselves, to his rehabilitation. *Guignol's Band* is equally a novel about exile: the only natives of London, significantly, are the sinister Matthew, and Virginia. The rest of the cast, Ferdinand, Sosthène, Cascade and his *bande*, Borokrom and Clodovitz, not to mention Prospero Jim himself, are foreign, and the entire action of the novel is played out amongst French and European characters who are far from home. *Guignol's Band*, therefore, quite as much as *The Tempest*, is a drama of exile in which things happen to the characters which would not happen when they were back in their normal setting. And this fact is reinforced by the way in which Céline follows the Shakespearian pattern of introducing and concluding the initiatory exile with a literal tempest: Prospero brings his victims to the island and finally shows his power over them through two magically contrived storms; Céline enters the magical exile of First World War London through associations produced by the bombing of Orléans in 1940, and the narrator Ferdinand only returns to normality after the extended zeppelin raid on London which concludes the second volume.

The purpose of the tempests in both works, however, is first to initiate, but ultimately to rectify. As Gonzalo concludes towards the end of Shakespeare's play:

24. Ibid., V, 1, 213.

Was Milan thrust from Milan, that his issue
Should become kings of Naples? O, rejoice,
Beyond a common joy! and set it down
With gold on lasting pillars; In one voyage
Did Claribel her husband find at Tunis,
And Ferdinand, her brother, found a wife
Where he himself was lost, Prospero his dukedom
In a poor isle, and all of us ourselves
When no man was his own.[25]

Not only does the magical experience of Prospero's island have the effect of revealing reality to all the characters, but it reestablishes a rightful normality: Prospero will return to his dukedom of Milan and his daughter Miranda will marry Ferdinand, the son of the King of Naples. In the same way, in *Guignol's Band*, the Prospero role switches from the landlord of the 'Croisière de Dingby' and 'The Moor and Cheese' to Sosthène, himself a magician, who accompanies another Ferdinand and his child-bride, Virginia, out of the novel to normality. The sea which takes Prospero and his family home to Milan is mirrored in Céline's novel by the bridge which takes Sosthène, Ferdinand and Virginia back to reality of the north bank of the river. In both cases, by the end the *voyage imaginaire* is finally over.

Guignol's Band, therefore, by being calqued upon *The Tempest*, brings to a close, not merely Céline's cycle of the evocation of the world prior to 1918, but a constant meditation on Shakespeare which is intimately connected with the progress of this cycle and which begins with the play *Progrès*, subtitled *Périclès*, of 1926. In this early work of Céline's, one obvious purpose of the Shakespearian title is to direct the reader's attention to the famous paradox of 'the virgin in the brothel' exploited by both authors and which looks forward in its turn to the name *Virginia* in *Guignol's Band*. More importantly, however, it coincides with *The Tempest* in emphasising one constant feature of Céline's work of the inter-war years, and one which continues in more dispersed form in *Féerie pour une autre fois* and the trilogy, the creation of an unreal space for the action, a limbo in which the protagonist and the fictional characters have the quality of ghosts. Both Shakespeare's *Pericles* and *The Tempest* are resurrection plays: in *Pericles*, Pericles himself and his daughter Marina are shipwrecked — literally, lost at sea — and the subsequent action takes place in a kind of afterlife from which they are ultimately brought back. Similarly, Prospero and

25. Ibid., V, 1, 205–13.

Miranda are not merely exiled from Milan, but from life itself, and they are joined in their spirit-world by the crew and passengers of the lost ship. In the same way, Céline will deploy in his fiction and polemic a setting which is the reflection of another and earlier reality and where his narrator is condemned to the role of phantom. In the two Shakespeare plays, however, the characters resurrect and return to life and normality, whereas the Célinian narrator, throughout the writings of the inter-war years, remains caught between past and present, 'mi-revenant lui-même'. Only at the end of *Guignol's Band* is a resurrection possible in Céline's work and that only after a complicated working-out of the role of London in the novel and the central figure of Titus Van Claben.

The use made by Céline of London in *Guignol's Band* goes far beyond mere transposition of autobiographical experience, to the extent that, in the same way that Prospero's island is one of the central ingredients of *The Tempest*, the particular qualities of the English capital are essential thematic concerns of the novel. The first and most significant of these characteristics is the fact that, simply, London is not Paris: within the novel, it constitutes an anti-Paris, and the fact that its inhabitants, Cascade, Borokrom, Clodovitz, Sosthène and Ferdinand, are exiles from Paris is by no means without importance. Throughout *Guignol's Band*, as a counterpoint to the main action in London, there are constant echoes of Ferdinand's life in the Passage des Vérododats which he is trying to escape: 'Je pense à mes vieux! ... ma mère en France dans sa boutique en train de rèparer des guipures ... et mon père à la "Coccinelle" en train de bien transcrire ses adresses ...' (GB 1, 288–9). And he recalls the sordid frailty and petty cruelty of 'les gens du Passage! les balecs! les voisins du Vérododat! t'en verras bien d'autres! Ils m'accusent! ils m'impliquent!' (GB 1, 289). Born into this situation, Ferdinand is a 'paumé' (GB 1, 23): one of society's natural and unalterable victims, just as Bardamu is a *miteux* in *Voyage au bout de la nuit*. Yet, whereas for Bardamu travel merely reinforces him in his status as a *miteux*, the journey from France to England has an ultimately liberating effect upon Ferdinand, and his liberation operates initially through Cascade and his nephew Raoul: 'Moi qu'étais petit cave de naissance, fils de mes parents, employés laborieux, soumis, gentils, bien serviables ... il m'avait fait l'instruction, ouvert les pupilles le Raoul' (GB 1, 309–10). Raoul, soon to be shot for malingering, and then his uncle, Cascade, a subversive version of the other uncle, Edouard, in *Mort à crédit*, succeed in diverting Ferdinand from the moral and social path of the *paumé* and in providing an alternative to the 'conseils des parents' which, announces the narrator, 'n'ont pas tenu devant l'existence' (GB 1, 23). The problem is that, until the end of the second volume, that liberation is only relative and hampered by guilt.

Yet, if the journey to London, which in the general context of Céline's inter-war writing constitutes a revenge upon Meanwell College and Brighton in *Mort à crédit*, brings a partial social and moral freedom, it also, and more importantly, takes Ferdinand to the world's centre of wealth and power, the world's centre of *féerie*. On one level, Céline's evocation of London as a symbol of strength in a declining world forms part of that well-established pattern in French literary and intellectual history into which he inserts himself in the anti-Semitic pamphlets. The London in which Ferdinand finds himself in *Guignol's Band* is that same London viewed as a symbol of political and metaphysical strength in the writings of Malraux and Drieu la Rochelle. Yet, whereas in *Bagatelles pour un massacre* and, particularly, *L'Ecole des cadavres*, Céline is willing to exploit the image of London as the repository of power, in *Guignol's Band* what fascinates Ferdinand is not so much the home of the Intelligence Service or the financial wealth of the City as the Port of London and its extraordinary accumulation of goods. For, it is this accumulation which guarantees two things: the wealth and vigour of the nation, certainly, but especially its privileged relation to *féerie*.

Thus, in his wide-eyed description of the docks at Wapping, Ferdinand, like Vallès but less censorious, is amazed at the quantity of goods shipped from all over the world to this island:

Après les maisons ribambelles, après les rues toutes analogues où je vous accompagne gentiment, les murailles s'élèvent . . . les Entrepôts, les géants remparts tout de briques . . . Falaises à trésors! . . . magasins monstres! . . . greniers fantasmagoriques, citadelles de marchandises, peaux de bouc quarries par montagnes, à puer jusqu'au Kamtchatka! . . . Forêts d'acajou en mille piles, liées telles asperges, en pyramides, des kilomètres de matériaux! . . . des tapis à recouvrir la Lune, le monde entier . . . tous les planchers de l'Univers! . . . Eponges à sécher la Tamise! de telles quantités . . . Des laines à étouffer l'Europe sous monceaux de chaleur choyante . . . Des harengs à combler les mers! Des Himalayas de sucre en poudre . . . Des allumettes à frire les poles! . . . Du poivre par énormes avalanches à faire éternuer Sept Déluges! . . . Mille bateaux d'oignons déversés, à pleurer pendant cinq cents guerres . . . Trois mille six cents trains d'haricots à sécher sous hangars couverts plus colossaux que les gares Charing, Nord et Saint-Lazare réunies . . . Du café pour toute la Plancte! à soutenir en leurs marches forcées les quatre cent mille conflits vengeurs des plus mordantes armées du monde . . . plus jamais assoyantes, ronflantes, exemptes de sommeil et bouffer, supertendues, fulminatrices, exaltées, crevantes à la charge, le coeur épanoui, emportées dans la super-mort par l'hyperpalpite super-gloire du café en poudre! . . . Le rêve des trois cent quinze empereurs! . . . (GB 1, 46–7).

Here, the wealth of London is centred on the sheer mass of its imports, a mass translated by the way in which the entire passage becomes an *exercice du style* in hyperbole, a frequent feature of Céline's style. More revealingly, however, Céline chooses to end his hyperbolic description of the wealth of the warehouses with a return to his major preoccupation, that of war: the mountain of powdered coffee is not there simply to impress, it is endowed with the precise and unusual connotations of keeping armies in a constant state of bellicose wakefulness. In other words, it is the anti-dream principle, which inevitably spells war. Yet it is not just the mass of products which impresses Ferdinand, it is also their exotic origins and the way in which they create a fairy-tale treasure-house: 'Voilà du travail sortilège, qu'existe, prenant, qu'au bord de l'eau' (GB 1, 46). London, in *Guignol's Band*, is the vigorous centre of the world's wealth, the storehouse of all its commodities, and, as a port, the meeting-place of land and sea, the conjuncture of reality and dreams, the capital of *féerie* itself.

Yet the historical coordinates of the novel are quite clear, and the mature narrator is writing in 1940 when that privileged role has been lost for ever. For, if London represents the principle of *féerie*, it is a principle which is already under threat, just as the world of the Parisian petite bourgeoisie is under threat at the time of the 1900 Exposition. Describing the patients at the London Hospital, Ferdinand remarks: 'C'est la population qui mue, si on réfléchit . . . Y a presque plus de marine à voile, c'est ça qu'amenait les vrais sauvages . . .' (GB 1, 121). Yet again Céline has chosen an historical moment in which the old world is being forced to give way to the new. Paris is condemned to modernity by the triumph of the Exposition; London will lose its role as the capital of *féerie* through the disappearance of its sailing-fleet, the last of which, the *Kong Hamsun*, leaves port without Ferdinand on board. It is this irreversible process which is conveyed, as in *Mort à crédit*, by the presence of the police: the ecstatic vision of the 'féeries des Mille et Une Nuits' (GB 1, 48) in the warehouses of Wapping is destroyed by the police: 'La police à cheval alors charge au triple galop . . .' (GB 1, 48), just as the Parisian police snuff out Ferdinand's delirium on the Place de la Concorde in *Mort à crédit*. In both cases, '[c'est] la fin d'un songe! . . .' (GB 1, 48). It is this function which accounts for the doubly sinister role of Sergeant Matthew, who is not only the embodiment of Ferdinand's guilt and paranoia after the death of Van Claben, but also that of the reality principle, locked in a struggle with the principle of *féerie*. As the narrator remarks of the police: 'Toute fantaisie les enrage'.

There is little doubt that, historically, it is Matthew, the tax-collector, who is the victor. London may be provisionally the anti-Paris, the embodiment of a fairy-tale world which Paris has ceased to be, but it is prey to the same forces which have conquered in France with the Exposition and the heavier-than-air machines which drive Courtial's *Zélé* from all the fairgrounds, and is well on its way to surrendering its wealth to the New World and the New York banks and its power to its own 'Jewish' bankers in the city. Between 1915 and 1940 the *féerie* and the port vanish, leaving the City and the Intelligence Service. That financial power is not absent from the novel's evocation of wartime London, however, but is presented in an oblique manner through the presence of the pawnbroker Titus Van Claben.

Van Claben, whose first name, Titus, provides yet another Shakespearian allusion: to *Titus Andronicus*, and whose 'allures Ali-Baba' (GB 1, 207) come from the vision of the *Thousand and One Nights* in the docks at Wapping, in addition to adding an oriental, racist dimension to his activities, is a '[prêteur] sur gages et sur parole' (GB 1, 207) in Greenwich, the home of the first meridian. He is therefore yet another junction of *mort* and *crédit* in Céline's fiction, in that his profession is that of the sale of credit and his place of work is at the centre of time. Moreover, he may be seen as a representative of London itself: the seat of world-time and the centre of world-credit and money-dealing.

It is his death, however, and the manner of his dying which are truly significant. His role as a literal and figurative tyrant is established by the close relationship of his name to that of the merchant Van Bagaden in the concluding ballet of *Bagatelles pour un massacre* and by Delphine's repeated reference to herself as Lady Macbeth after Van Claben's murder. In other words, through the Macbeth system of references, Van Claben is both tyrant and victim, both Duncan and Macbeth, but the essential point is that it is a monarch who has been extinguished in the person of the pawnbroker: the pinnacle of that system of financial, political and psychological domination which, for Jean-Joseph Goux, is contained in the trinity of gold, monarch and father. Van Claben is, therefore, not merely the personification of the tyranny of credit, he is also the return of the father-figure who dominates *Mort à crédit*, who is the implicit reader of *Bagatelles pour un massacre* and who reappears at the end of the first pamphlet in the form of the merchant Van Bagaden who persecutes the young Peter. It is highly significant, therefore, that Titus Van Claben should be killed by being forced to ingurgitate his own gold and then by being dropped on his head. The enforced ingurgitation of Van Claben's gold coins constitutes a refusal both of the gold principle and of the tyranny of the father: the oral excrement of the gold is returned to the body from whence it came. The links which bound Ferdinand to the world of credit, therefore, are substantially severed. It is for this reason that the act which finally kills Van Claben, the banging of his head on the stairs of his own shop, takes the form of an exact and direct inversion of Ferdinand's assault on Auguste in *Mort à crédit*. In the earlier novel, Ferdinand attempts to turn off the flow of words coming from his father by striking him on the head with an object, the typewriter, which symbolises Auguste's own social position, the modernity which threatens him and the language which the narrator will ultimately use against him. In the hallucinatory murder scene of *Guignol's Band*, Ferdinand and Borokrom stifle Van Claben with his own gold and then, in an attempt to recover the gold, turn him upside-down and drop him on his head. In both cases, it is the head, and particularly the speech organ which is aimed at, and in both cases it is the very principle of authority and meaning which is overthrown.

Yet, initially, if the death of Van Claben constitutes an inverted reflection of the assault on Auguste, it is no more successful. Auguste is not killed, and his presence remains to haunt Ferdinand through the successive works; Van Claben *is* killed, but only in an attempt to renege on the original project — the denial of the gold principle. He meets his death as Ferdinand and Borokrom are attempting to recover the gold they had returned to his body. It is for this reason that Van Claben's death gives rise to the underlying plot of the remainder of the first volume and all of the second volume of *Guignol's Band*, and that this should take the form of a sustained persecution complex on Ferdinand's part, a persecution complex given concrete form by the pervasive presence of the policeman Matthew and the informer Mille-Pattes. In other words, whilst in the general context of Céline's fiction, the form of the murder of Van Claben appears to announce a final resolution of the *mauvaise conscience* in the relationship between Ferdinand and Auguste, its incompleteness merely accentuates the guilt and the fear of detection.

Where *Guignol's Band* constitutes an advance on *Mort à crédit* and *Bagatelles pour un massacre*, however, is in the fact that, at the end of the novel, the ghost of Van Claben is finally laid. His corpse is abandoned by Delphine and Ferdinand when they take flight from the burning shop and it is the unresolved nature of the fate of Van Claben which constitutes the basis of the guilt and sense of persecution. It is for this reason that, until the fate of the pawn-broker is settled, Ferdinand is unable to take flight on the dreamlike sailing-ship, the *Kong Hamsun* and the novel is unable to end. Hence the importance of the final tableau in Prospero's 'The Moor and Cheese', which, as in Shakespearian comedy, groups together all the novel's characters for one final appearance: Ferdinand, Sosthène and Virginia, suddenly overwhelmed by the arrival of Cascade's *bande* and, even, of Borokrom and Clodovitz, another *fantôme burlesque* of bourgeois medicine. It is this sudden arrival of all the cast which prevents Ferdinand from slipping away to the *Kong Hamsun* before it sails with the evening tide and which is associated with the pretext that it is the Saint-Ferdinand, the nar-rator's name-day.[26] What is important about this information is not so much the allusion to the Saint himelf, although, as patron saint of engineers, he underlines the protective relationship of Ferdinand to Sosthène, the 'ingénieur initié' (GB 1, 314), and, behind him, to Courtial, as the fact that the novel ends with a celebration of Ferdinand's *name*. That celebration, and the ultimate liberation of the entire work, is finally only permitted by the way it encompasses the exorcism of the ghost of Van Claben. Céline establishes carefully the portentous nature of the scene as, through repeated messages, reminiscent of Shakespeare's history plays or the final act of *Macbeth* itself, news of the approach of Van Claben's body, brought by Borokrom and Clodovitz, is conveyed. Ferdinand's *fête*, then, is literally poisoned by the rotting corpse of Van Claben, stolen from the dissecting table of the London Hospital, just as Semmelweis's discovery comes from the dissecting room of the hospital in Vienna.

Yet, unnoticed at the time by anyone, through Cascade's agen-cies, the ghost of the pawnbroker is finally laid:

— Qu'est-ce qu'ils vont en foutre? à part les rillettes? . . . je redemande. C'etait la question.
— Ils vont le foutre au jus jolie bille! Si tu veux savoir! Les crabes le boufferont voila tout! . . . Vous êtes satisfait jeune homme? . . . Si tu veux connaître! On peut pas le brûler encore plus! Non? T'as pas vu sa tête? Tu veux pas la manger? Toi des fois? . . . Il faut que quelqu'un s'en

---

26. The 'Saint-Ferdinand' is 30 May.

occupe! . . . Si ça vous fait rien! . . . Monsieur la Belle Bise! . . . Monsieur finit pas son travail! Monsieur a d'autres idées! . . . Faut qu'on se magne . . . qu'on se démerde pour lui! . . . Faut faire disparaître ses ordures! Faut arranger ses petites choses! Voila Monsieur beau jeune homme! Héros magnifique et tout! Monsieur ne pense qu'à l'amour! (GB 2, 465).

It is Cascade, a counterpart to Edouard in *Mort à crédit*, who settles Ferdinand's unfinished business, his 'comptes en retard' (GB 2, 465–6) which, if left unpaid will, as the *exergue* to *L'Ecole des cadavres* reminds us, prevent him going to Heaven. Through Cascade, Van Claben is thrown into the sea and the threat which he represents is considerably diminished. As Ariel sings to Ferdinand in *The Tempest*:

> Full fathom five thy father lies;
>   Of his bones are coral made;
> Those are pearls that were his eyes:
>   Nothing of him that doth fade,
> But doth suffer a sea-change
> Into something rich and strange.
> Sea-nymphs hourly ring his knell. . . .[27]

The final burial of Van Claben's body in the waters of the Thames ushers in an ending of the novel which, in comparison with the earlier fiction, is more optimistic and more serene. For once in Céline's novels a bridge is crossed without effort and is no longer the barrier constituted by the bridges over the Seine in *Voyage au bout de la nuit* and *Les Beaux draps*; and its passage is made even easier by the fact that it goes from south to north, from Van Claben's territory to that of Virginia and the *féerie* of the docks. It is also the first time in Céline's fiction that a birth is envisaged which will be neither aborted nor diseased and which will not carry the shadow of death.

This is not to say that the ending of the novel is totally free from threat: Ferdinand, after all, has been liberated from the ghost of Van Claben and all he represents not through his own efforts, but through the mediation of Cascade, in exactly the same way that the narrator in *Mort à crédit* is saved at every turn through the intervention of *oncle* Edouard. Nor has the threat of Matthew entirely receded with the disposal of Van Claben's body: he still haunts the underground and forces Ferdinand and his companions to take the

27. *The Tempest*, I, 2, 396–402.

bus instead. Nevertheless, the contrast with the ending of *Mort à crédit* is striking. Whereas Céline's second novel ends in a grim search for protection, survival and non-being under Edouard's *pardessus*, there is a lightness and gaiety in the ending of *Guignol's Band* which indicates two things: in the magical evocation of London at the height of its economic power as the repository of the world's commodities, Céline has been able to exorcise the ghosts of gold and credit which are centred on the figure of the father and finally buried with the body of Van Claben; in addition, with his exorcism, he is able to look forward to a continued form of literary production. It is crucial that *Guignol's Band* be recognised as containing, not merely a personal awakening on the part of the narrator Ferdinand, but a self-confident *art poétique* which lays down the guidelines for subsequent fiction, which, for the first time, envisages a future:

> Le Jazz a renversé la valse, l'Impressionisme a tué le 'faux-jour', vous écrirez 'télégraphique' ou vous écrirez plus du tout!
>
> > *L'Emoi c'est tout dans la Vie!*
> > *Faut savoir en profiter!*
> > *L'Emoi c'est tout dans la Vie!*
> > *Quand on est mort c'est fini!*
>
> A vous de comprendre! Emouvez-vous! 'C'est que des bagarres tous vos chapitres!' Quelle objection! Quelle tourterie! Ah! attention! La niaise! En botte! Volent babillons! Emouvez bon Dieu! Ratata! Sautez! Vibrochez! Eclatez dans vos carapaces! fouillez-vous crabes! Eventrez! Trouvez la palpite nom de foutre! La fête est là! Enfin! Quelque chose! Réveil! Allez salut! Robots la crotte! Merde! Transposez ou c'est la mort (GB 1, 377).

Ferdinand's *fête*, therefore, which ends the novel, is both a personal 'réveil', a resurrection signalled by the novel's use of the model of *The Tempest*, and a stylistic renewal which breaks through the barrier encountered by *Casse-pipe* and guarantees continued creativity. The bridge over the Thames is also the bridge to *Féerie pour une autre fois*.

Conclusion

After *Guignol's Band*, Céline never again returned in extended form to the world of 1900. Doubtless, this is due in large part to the fact that the *belle époque* was now separated by two World Wars and that the Occupation and Liberation had provided Céline with other myths of more immediate concern. Yet, at the same time, it could be argued that Céline no longer needed to evoke that lost world, that, with the ending of *Guignol's Band*, a cycle quite naturally came to its end. Through this fiction, plays and pamphlets, he had dealt with most of the experiences he had undergone: childhood in Paris, the pre-war cavalry, the war itself, London in 1916, followed by the hallucinatory transposition of the world after the Armistice. More profoundly, in the course of his writing in the inter-war years, he had come to so understand the workings of the *belle époque* and its complex relationship with the present, that, as a ghost, it was finally exorcised with the burial in the waters of the Thames of Van Claben at the end of *Guignol's Band*.

In this process, however, Céline goes a long way. The modern world, investigated in the medical writings and *Mea culpa*, and symbolised by Ford, fills him with horror. Against it, he sets, not one Golden Age, but two, for the *belle époque* is, by itself, too ambiguous: it is a period of French history when the modern had not yet taken over, but, in Ferdinand's experience at least, it was an era dominated by the petite bourgeoisie. Moreover, it was an era which, with hindsight, was one of transition: the urban artisanal petite bourgeoisie was, even then, being driven out of Paris; the march of the modern, symbolised by the 1900 Exposition, that 'énorme brutalité', was already irreversible. What can Ferdinand do, however, except invent an additional Golden Age, this time situated in the unassailable, pre-industrial past — the Europe of Charlemagne or the High Middle Ages?

The problem, however, is that although this myth may be satisfying politically and, especially, aesthetically, it is constructed on one of the major aspects of gold in its symbolic form: not only its central role in the operation of credit, but its psychoanalytical implications in its connections with authority and, in particular, the father-figure. It is for this reason that, along with the extended reflection in Céline's work of the inter-war years on gold, credit, credibility and time, there is also the repeated and repetitive appearance, in various guises, not the least of which is the narrator himself, of Auguste, the father-monarch. And, in *Guignol's Band*, at the centre of time and the commodity fetish, it takes Ferdinand far longer to free himself from the weight of the murdered father, that *mauvaise conscience* which informs all of his writing of the period, than from the petit-bourgeois morality of his parents.

It is the role of the father-figure, however, which accounts for the complexity and ambiguity of the anti-Semitic pamphlets. Already, in the late 1920s, the writings on social medicine have demonstrated Céline's predilection for difficulty and obfuscation in what should be a simple polemical task, and this problematic aspect is immeasurably accentuated in the anti-Semitic texts. Ultimately, the inconsistencies in the medical writings and in the anti-Semitism of the works from 1937 to 1941 can be explained both by the author's distaste for the post-1918 world and by his recognition of social and economic vulnerability for which he finally holds the Jews responsible. His discovery, in the 'Hommage à Zola', however, that the truth can no longer be directly expressed leads him to explore a more oblique and sly means of 'tout dire', what Benjamin calls the 'culte de la blague'. At the same time, there is the combination, in all the polemical texts, of a personal *psychodrame* concentrated on the father who, in the anti-Semitic writing, is exaggeratedly imitated in order that he may be finally exorcised, and a half-serious suicidal attempt to provoke disaster, to call down upon the author all those forces of punishment and repression which are, again, of course, the prerogative of the father, and which he outlines in the Zola lecture: 'Alors ce sera fini et je serai bien content'.

Hence, cut off from his Golden Age forever, the narrator is both acutely aware of his presence in the modern world as a ghost and unconsciously striving to be one: for the ghost is at least beyond time and suffering, is no longer subject to the rules of credit and, in a most privileged way, is able to take revenge by haunting. Undoubtedly, by the end of *Guignol's Band*, Céline has largely resolved this complex role of the phantom in his work, by finally being allowed to make the transition to *féerie*. The strength of the concept in his imagination is amply demonstrated, however, by his return to it in one of the most celebrated episodes in *D'un château l'autre*, the scene in which the doctor-narrator on the quayside at Meudon encounters the mysterious 1900 *bateau-mouche*, *La Publique*, captained by Charon and with all his comrades from the Occupation on board. Not only is this one of Céline's last gestures to the world of the *belle époque*, it is also the clearest appearance of that image implicit through so much Céline's writing of the inter-war years, the *vaisseau-fantôme* with its ghostly navigator. And it is entirely in keeping with Céline's whole procedure of employing allusions, that this *vaisseau-fantôme* should be moored in Meudon, not just the home of the narrator, but the place where Wagner wrote his opera.

At the end of his preface to Albert Serouille's *Bezons à travers les âges*, Céline exhorts: 'Traqués, suppliciés, maudits, dans le passé tout notre coeur! Soyons jaloux de nos poussières!'[1] The whole of his writing in the inter-war years is an attempt to come to terms with the industrial suburbs of Paris, the persecution of which he and his class are the victims in the modern world, his apparent heartlessness in the present, and an abiding, though ambiguous, nostalgia for the *poussières* which, finally, constitute Céline's only Golden Age.

---

1. L.-F. Céline, 'Préface', Albert Serouille, *Bezons à travers les âges*, p. 14.

Bibliography

For a complete listing of works by Céline and secondary material on him, the reader is referred to the following bibliographies:

Dauphin, Jean-Pierre, *L.-F. Céline, Essai de bibliographie des études en langue française consacrées à Louis-Ferdinand Céline, Tome 1: 1914–1944* Paris, Minard, 1977
—, and Pascal Fouché, *Bibliographie des écrits de Louis-Ferdinand Céline*, Paris, Bibliothèque de littérature française contemporaine de l'université de Paris VII, 1985
Krance, Charles, 'Louis-Ferdinand Céline' in Douglas Alden and Richard A. Brooks, eds., *A Critical Bibliography of French Literature*, vol. 6, *The Twentieth Century*, Part I, Syracuse, NY, Syracuse University Press, 1980, pp. 743–65
Luce, Stanford and William Buckley, *A Half-Century of Céline. An Annotated Bibliography 1932–1982*, New York and London, Garland Publishers, 1983

Works by Céline

Collected Editions

Romans I (*Voyage au bout de la nuit*, *Mort à crédit*, introduction by Henri Mondor, chronology by Jean A. Ducourneau), Paris, Gallimard, coll. 'La Pléiade', 1962
Oeuvres de Louis-Ferdinand Céline ed. Jean A Ducourneau, Paris, André Balland, 1966–9, 5 vols
Romans II (*D'un château l'autre*, *Nord*, *Rigodon*), ed. Henri Godard, Paris, Gallimard, coll. 'La Pléiade', 1974
Romans I (*Voyage au bout de la nuit*, *Mort à crédit*), ed. Henri Godard, Paris, Gallimard, coll. 'La Pléide', 1981

Bibliography

Oeuvres de Céline, ed. Frédéric Vitoux, Paris, Aux Editions du Club de L'Honnête Homme, 1981, 9 vols

In addition, articles, correspondence and unpublished fragments by Céline may be found in the following collections:

Louis-Ferdinand Céline I, *Des témoins, correspondance, inédits, inter-férences, essais, études, photographies, bibliographie*, ed. Dominique de Roux and Michel Thélia (HER 3), 1962

Louis-Ferdinand Céline II, Paris, Minard, Lettres Modernes, 1965 (HER 5)

L.-F. Céline, ed. Dominique de Roux, Michel Beaujour and Michel Thélia, *Les Cahiers de l'Herne*, 1972 (a revised and composite edition of HER 3 and HER 5)

Cahiers Céline 1, Céline et l'actualité littéraire, 1932–1957, ed. Jean-Pierre Dauphin and Henri Godard, Paris, Gallimard, 1976 (CC 1)

Cahiers Céline 2, Céline et l'actualité littéraire, 1957–1961, ed. Jean-Pierre Dauphin and Henri Godard, Paris, Gallimard, 1976 (CC 2)

Cahiers Céline 3, Semmelweis et autres écrits médicaux, ed. Jean-Pierre Dauphin and Henri Godard, Paris, Gallimard, 1977 (CC 3)

Cahiers Céline 4, Lettres et premiers écrits d'Afrique, 1916–1917, ed. Jean-Pierre Dauphin, Paris, Gallimard, 1978 (CC 4)

Cahiers Céline 5, Lettres à des amies, ed. Colin W. Nettlebeck, Paris, Gallimard, 1979 (CC 5)

Cahiers Céline 6, Lettres à Albert Paraz, 1947–1957, ed. J.-P. Louis, Paris, Gallimard, 1980 (CC 6)

Céline. Textes et documents 1, Paris, Bibliothèque L.-F. Céline de l'université de Paris VII, 1979

Céline. Textes et documents 2, Paris, Bibliothèque de littérature française contemporaine de l'université de Paris VII, 1982

Céline. Textes et documents 3, Paris, Bibliothèque de littérature française contemporaine de l'université de Paris VII, 1985

Books

La Vie et l'oeuvre de Philippe-Ignace Semmelweis, Rennes, Imprimerie Francis-Simon, 1924 (subsequently published in Paris by Denoël et Steele, 1936, and Gallimard, 1952; included in CC 3)

La Quinine en thérapeutique, Paris, Doin, 1925

Voyage au bout de la nuit, Paris, Denoël et Steele, 1932

L'Eglise, Paris, Denoël et Steele, 1933

Mort à crédit, Paris, Denoël et Steele, 1936

Mea culpa, suivi de Semmelweis, Paris, Denoël et Steele, 1936

Bagatelles pour un massacre, Paris, Denoël, 1937

L'Ecole des cadavres, Paris, Denoël, 1938

Les Beaux draps, Paris, Nouvelles Editions Françaises, 1941

Bibliography

Guignol's Band, I, Paris, Denoël, 1944
Casse-pipe, Paris, Chambriand, 1949
Féerie pour une autre fois, I, Paris, Gallimard, 1952
Féerie pour une autre fois, II: *Normance*, Paris, Gallimard, 1954
Entretiens avec le Professeur Y, Paris, Gallimard, 1955
D'un Château l'autre, Paris, Gallimard, 1957
Ballets sans musique, sans personne, sans rien, Paris, Gallimard, 1959
Nord, Paris, Gallimard, 1960
Guignol's Band, II: *Le Pont de Londres*, Paris, Gallimard, 1964
Rigodon, Paris, Gallimard, 1969
Progrès, Paris, Mercure de France, 1978
Maudits soupirs pour une autre fois, Paris, Gallimard, 1985

Articles

'Observations physiologiques sur *Convoluta roscoffensis*', *Académie des Sciences*, 1920 (repr. in CC 3, 242–4)
'Prolongation de la vie chez les *Galleria mellonella*', *Académie des Sciences*, 1921 (repr. in CC 3, 245–6)
'Les Derniers jours de Semmelweis', *La Presse Médicale*, 25 June 1924, pp. 1067, 1072
'Note sur l'organisation sanitaire des usines Ford à Detroit', Internal memorandum for the League of Nations, 1925 (repr. in CC 3, 116–30)
'Notes sur le service sanitaire de la Compagnie Westinghouse à Pittsburgh', Internal memorandum for the League of Nations, 1925 (repr. in CC 3, 131–6)
'A propos du service sanitaire des usines Ford à Detroit', *Bulletins et mémoires de la Société de médecine de Paris*, 10, Session of 26 May 1928, pp. 303–12 (repr. in CC 3, 137–53)
'Les Assurances sociales et une politique économique de la santé publique', *La Presse Médicale*, 24 November 1928, pp. 1499, 1501 (repr. in CC 3, 154–66)
'L'infection puerpérale et les antivirus', *La Médecine*, April 1929, p. 309 (repr. in CC 3, 97–8)
'Note sur l'emploi des antivirus de Besredka en pansements humides', *Bulletins et mémoires de la Société de médecine de Paris*, Session of 10 May 1929, pp. 223–4 (repr. in CC 3, 98–100)
'L'Immunité dans les maladies infectieuses. A propos du livre récent de A. Besredka', *Paris médical*, June 1929, pp. 537–9 (repr. in CC 3, 101–9)
'Deux expériences de vaccination en masse et *per os* contre la typhoïde', *La Presse Médicale*, 11 September 1929, pp. 1193–4. (repr. in CC 3, 167–70)
'La Santé publique en France', *Monde*, 8 March 1930 (repr. in *Céline. Textes et documents*, 1, pp. 27–49)
'Essai de dignostique et de thérapeutique méthodiques "en série" sur certains malades d'un dispensaire', *Bulletins et mémoires de la Société de*

médecine de Paris, Session of 22 March 1930, pp. 163–8 (repr. in CC 3, 170–7)

'Les Hémorragies minimes des gencives en clientèle', *La Gazette médicale*, 1 November 1931, p. 614 (repr. in CC 3, 246–8)

'Mémoire pour le Cours des Hautes Etudes', unpublished memorandum, 1932 (repr. in CC 3, 178–214)

'Pour tuer le chômage tueront-ils les chômeurs?', *Le Mois*, 1 February–1 March 1933, pp. 57–60 (repr. in CC 3, 215–21)

'Hommage à Emile Zola' in Denoël, Robert, *Apologie de 'Mort à crédit'*, Paris, Denoël et Steele, 1936

'La Médecine chez Ford', *Lectures*, 40, 4, 1 August 1941, pp. 6–9; 5, 15 August 1941, p. 6

'Preface', Serouille, Albert, *Bezons a travers les ages*, Paris, Denoël, 1944

'A l'Agité du bocal' in Albert Paraz, *La Gala des vaches*, Paris, L'Elan, 1948

Secondary Works

Albums

Catalogue de l'Exposition Céline, Musée de l'Ancien Evêché de Lausanne, Lausanne, Edita SA, 1977

Dauphin, Jean-Pierre and Boudillet, Jacques, *Album Céline*, Paris, Gallimard, coll. 'La Pléïade', 1977

Books on Céline

Aebersold, Denise, *Céline. Un démystificateur mythomane*, Paris, Minard, coll. 'Archives des Lettres Modernes', 1977

Bellosta, Marie-Christine, *Le Capharnaüm célinien ou la place des objets dans 'Mort à crédit'*, Paris, Minard, coll. 'Archives des Lettres Modernes', 1976

Chesneau, Albert, *Essai de psychocritique de Louis-Ferdinand Céline*, Paris, Minard, coll. 'Archives des Lettres Modernes', 1971

Damour, A.-C. and J.-P., *L.-F. Céline. Voyage au bout de la nuit*, Paris, Presses Universitaires de France, 1985

Dauphin, Jean-Pierre, *Les Critiques de notre temps et Céline*, Paris, Garnier, 1976

Day, Philip Stephen, *Le Miroir allégorique de Louis-Ferdinand Céline*, Paris, Klincksieck, 1974

Debrie-Panel, Nicole, *Louis-Ferdinand Céline*, Lyon, Bitte, 1961

Della Torre, Renato, *Invito alla lettura di Céline*, Milan, Mursia, 1979

Flynn, James, ed., *Understanding Céline*, Seattle, Genitron Press, 1984

Fortier, Paul A., *Le Métro émotif de Céline*, Paris, Minard, 1981

Gibault, François, *Céline 1: 1894–1932: Le Temps des espérances*, Paris,

Mercure de France, 1977

—, *Céline*, 2: *1932–1944: Délires et persécutions*, Paris, Mercure de France, 1985

—, *Céline*, 3: *1944–1961: Cavalier de l'Apocalypse*, Paris, Mercure de France, 1981

Godard, Henri, *Poétique de Céline*, Paris, Gallimard, coll. Idées, 1985

Guénot, Jean, *Louis-Ferdinand Céline damné par l'écriture*, Paris, Jean Guenot, 1973

Hanrez, Marc, *Céline*, Paris, Gallimard, coll. 'La Bibliothèque idéale', 1961.

Hayman, David, *Louis-Ferdinand Céline*, New York, Columbia University Press, 'Columbia Essays on Modern Writers' 13, 1965

Hindus, Milton, *The Crippled Giant, A Bizarre Adventure in Contemporary Letters*, New York, Boar's Head Books, 1950 (reissued as: *The Crippled Giant. A Literary Relationship with Louis-Ferdinand Céline*, Hanover, NH, and London, University Press of New England, 1986; translated as: *Louis-Ferdinand Céline tel que je l'ai vu*, Paris, L'Herne, 1969)

Holthus, Gunther, *Untersuchungen zu Stil und Konzeption von Célines 'Voyage au bout de la nuit'*, Berne and Frankfurt, H. and P. Lang, 1972

Juilland, Alphonse, *Les Verbes de Céline: Première Partie: Étude d'ensemble*, Stanford, CA, Alma Libri, 1985

Kaminski, H.-E., *Céline en chemise brune*, Paris, Excelsior, 1938

Knapp, Bettina L., *Céline: Man of Hate*, Montgomery, AL, University of Alabama Press, 1974

Kristeva, Julia, *Pouvoirs de l'horreur. Essai sur l'abjection*, Paris, Le Seuil, 1980

Kunnas, Tarmo, *Drieu la Rochelle, Céline, Brasillach et la tentation fasciste*, Paris, Les Sept Couleurs, 1972

La Querière, Yves de, *Céline et les mots. Etude stylistique des effets de mots dans 'Voyage au bout de la nuit'*, Lexington, University Press of Kentucky, 1973

Lavoinne, Yves, *Voyage au bout de la nuit de Céline*, Paris, Hachette, coll. 'Poche critique', 1974.

Luce, Stanford, *A Glossary of Céline's Fiction*, Ann Arbor, MI, University Microfilms International, 1979

McCarthy, Patrick, *Céline*, Harmondsworth, Allen Lane, 1975

Mahé, Henri, *La Brinquebale avec Céline*, Paris, La Table Ronde, 1969

Matthews, J.H., *The Inner Dream. Céline as Novelist*, Syracuse, NY, Syracuse University Press, 1978

Monnier, Pierre, *Ferdinand furieux*, Lausanne, L'Age d'Homme, 1979

Morand, Jacqueline, *Les Idées politiques de Louis-Ferdinand Céline*, Paris, Librairie Générale de Droit et de Jurisprudence, 1972

Muray, Philippe, *Céline*, Paris, Le Seuil, coll. 'Tel quel', 1981

Noble, Ian, *Language and Narration in Céline's Novels. The Challenge of Disorder*, London, Macmillan, 1986

Bibliography

O'Connell, David, *Louis-Ferdinand Céline*, Boston, Twayne, 1976

Ostrovsky, Erika, *Céline and his Vision*, New York, New York University Press, 1967

—, *Voyeur voyant: a Portrait of Louis-Ferdinand Céline*, New York, Random House, 1971

Poulet, Robert, *Entretiens familiers avec Louis-Ferdinand Céline*, Paris, Plon, coll. 'Tribune Libre', 1958 (reprinted as: *Mon ami Bardamu*, Paris, Plon, 1971)

Richard, Jean-Pierre, *Nausée de Céline*, Montpellier, Fata Morgana, 1979

Roux, Dominique de, *La Mort de Louis-Ferdinand Céline*, Paris, Christian Bourgeois, 1966

Smith, André, *La Nuit de Louis-Ferdinand Céline*, Paris, Grasset, 1973

Szafran, Willi, *Louis-Ferdinand Céline. Essai psychologique*, Brussels, Editions de l'Université de Bruxelles, 1976

Thiher, Allen, *Céline: the Novel as Delirium*, Rutgers, NY, Rutgers University Press, 1972

Thomas, Merlin, *Louis-Ferdinand Céline*, London, Faber and Faber, 1979

Vandromme, Pol, *Céline*, Paris, Editions Universitaires, 1963

—, *Robert Le Vigan, compagnon et personnage de L.-F. Céline*, Kessel-Lô, La Revue Célinienne, 1980

—, *Du côté de Céline, Lili*, Kessel-Lô, La Revue Célinienne, 1983

—, *Marcel, Roger et Ferdinand*, Kessel-Lô, La Revue Célinienne, 1984

Vitoux, Frédéric, *Louis-Ferdinand Céline. Misère et parole*, Paris, Gallimard, 1973

—, *Bébert, le chat de Louis-Ferdinand Céline*, Paris, Grasset, 1976

—, *Céline*, Paris, Belfond, coll. 'Les Dossiers Belfond', 1978

Collections of Articles

Australian Journal of French Studies, XIII, 1–2, 1976: *Actes du colloque international d'Oxford, 1975.*

Bibliothèque L.-F. Céline de l'université de Paris VII, Bulletin no. 1, *Actes du Colloque International de Paris, 1976* (BLFC 1).

—, Bulletin no. 3, *Actes du Colloque International de Paris, 1979* (BLFC 3).

—, Bulletin no. 5, *Actes du Colloque International d'Oxford, 1981* (BLFC 5).

—, Bulletin no. 8, *Actes du Colloque International de la Haye, 1983* (BLFC 8).

Le Bulletin Célinien: nos. 1–46, 1982–6.

La Revue Célinienne, nos 1–3/4, 1979–81.

Revue des Lettres Modernes, Série L.-F. Céline.

Articles Cited in the Text

Alméras, Philippe, 'L'Amérique femelle ou les enfants de Colomb', *Aus-*

tralian Journal of French Studies, XIII, 1–2, 1976

Arland, Marcel, '*Bagatelles pour un massacre* par Louis-Ferdinand Céline', *Nouvelle Revue Française*, 293, February 1938

Bleton, Paul, 'Maximes, phrases et efficace d'un pamphlet', *Actes du Colloque International de Paris, 1979* (BLFC 3)

Forbes, Jill, 'Symbolique de l'espace: le "Londres" célinien', *Actes du Colloque International de Paris, 1976* (BLFC 1)

Fouché, Pascal, 'Féerie pour un autre Montmartre', *Quinzaine Littéraire*, June 1982

Gide, André, 'Céline, les Juifs et Maritain', *Nouvelle Revue Française*, April 1938

Hewitt, Nicholas, '*Mort à crédit* et la crise de la petite-bourgeoisie', *Australian Journal of French Studies*, XIII, 1–2, 1976

Kingston, Paul, 'Celine et l'antisémitisme de son époque: aspects de *Bagatelles pour un massacre*', *Actes du Colloque International d'Oxford, 1981* (BLFC 5)

Krance, Charles, '*Semmelweis* ou l'accouchement de la biographie célinienne', *Revue des Lettres Modernes, Serie Céline*, 2

Mancel, Yannik, 'De la Sémiotique textuelle à la théorie du "roman": Céline', *Dialectiques*, 8, 1975

Mounier, Emmanuel, '*Bagatelles pour un massacre*', *Esprit*, 66, March 1938

Muray, Philippe, 'Mort à crédo. *Celine, le positivisme et l'occultisme*', *Actes du Colloque International de La Haye, 1983* (BLFC 8)

—, 'Le Siècle de Céline', *L'Infini*, 8, Autumn 1984

Nettlebeck, Colin W., 'Céline devant l'an 40. *Les Beaux draps* et le debut de *Guignol's Band*', *Actes du Colloque International d'Oxford, 1981* (BLFC 5)

Out-Breut, Michèle, 'Une Analyse sémiotique de *Casse-pipe* (II)', *Actes du Colloque International de La Haye, 1983* (BLFC 8)

Poli, Jean-Dominique, 'Les Données de mentalité dans les romans et les pamphlets', *Actes du Colloque International de Paris 1976* (BLFC 1)

Richard, Jean-Pierre, 'Casque-pipe', *Littérature*, 29, 1978.

Robert, P.E., 'Marcel Proust et Louis-Ferdinand Céline: un contrepoint', *Bulletin des Amis de Marcel Proust*, 29, 1979

Roussin, Philippe, 'Tout dire', *Actes du Colloque International de la Haye, 1983* (BLFC 8)

Sautermeister, Christine, 'Quelques traits caractéristiques du comique de Céline à partir de *Casse-pipe*', *Actes du Colloque International de Paris, 1976* (BLFC 1)

—, 'Lecture théâtrale et cinématographique de *Casse-pipe*', *Actes du Colloque International de Paris, 1979* (BLFC 3)

Van Zoest, Aart, 'Une Analyse sémiotique de *Casse-pipe* (1)', *Actes du Colloque International de La Haye, 1983* (BLFC 8)

Bibliography

Other Works Cited in the Text

'Congrès de syndicats médicaux', *La Presse Médicale*, 8 February 1928

'Les Assurances Sociales', *La Presse Médicale*, 24 November 1928

'Les Méfaits des Assurances Sociales et les moyens d'y remédier. D'après Ervin Lick (de Dantzig)', *La Presse Médicale*, 24 November 1928

Adhémar, Jean, *Imagerie populaire française*, Milan, Electra, 1968

Arendt, Hannah, *Sur l'antisémitisme*, Paris, Calmann-Lévy, coll. 'Diaspora', 1973.

Ariès, Philippe, *Histoire des populations françaises et de leurs attitudes devant la vie depuis le XVIIIe siècle*, Paris, Self, 1948

Arland, Marcel, 'Sur un nouveau mal du siècle', *Nouvelle Revue Française*, 125, 1924

Aymé, Marcel, 'Avenue Junot', *Je suis partout*, 14 August 1943

Balzac, Honoré de, *La Cousine Bette*, Paris, Garnier, 1959

Baudelaire, Charles, *Oeuvres complètes*, Paris, Gallimard, 'Bibliothèque de la Pléiade', 1961

Benjamin, Walter, *Charles Baudelaire. A Lyric Poet in an Age of High Capitalism*, London, New Left Books, 1973

Bergonzi, Bernard, *The Early H.G. Wells. A Study of the Scientific Romances*, Manchester, Manchester University Press, 1961

Bernanos, Georges, *La France contre les robots*, Rio de Janeiro, 1944; Paris, Robert Laffont, 1947

Bloy, Léon, *Le Salut par les Juifs*, Paris, Librairie Adrien Demay, 1892

Briau, Eugène, 'Assurances Sociales et tuberculose', *La Presse Médicale*, 11 January 1928

—, 'Assurances Sociales et syphilis', *La Presse Médicale*, 8 February 1928

Camus, Albert, *Carnets*, Paris, Gallimard, 1962

Carco, Francis, *De Montmartre au Quartier Latin*, Paris, Albin Michel, 1927

Carroll, Lewis, *Through the Looking-Glass*, New York, New American Library, 1960

Cendrars, Blaise, *L'Or*, Paris, Denoël, 1960

Chevalier, J.-J., *Histoire des institutions et des régimes de la France moderne 1789–1958*, Paris, Dalloz, 1967

Chevalier, Louis, *Montmartre du plaisir et du crime*, Paris, Robert Laffont, coll. 'L'Homme et l'Histoire', 1980

Clarke-Kennedy, A.E., *London Pride. The Story of a Voluntary Hospital*, London, Hutchinson-Benham, 1979

Cohn, Norman, *Warrant for Genocide. The Myth of the Jewish World-Conspiracy and the Protocols of the Elders of Zion*, London, Eyre and Spottiswoode, 1967

Conrad, Joseph, *The Secret Agent*, Harmondsworth, Penguin, 1963

Daudet, Leon, *Le Stupide dix-neuvième siècle, exposé des insanités meurtrières qui se sont abbattues sur la France depuis 130 ans, 1789–1919*,

Paris, Nouvelles Editions de la Librairie Nationale, 1922

Defoe, Daniel, *The Shortest Way with the Dissenters and Other Pamphlets*, Oxford, Blackwell, 1927

Desfosses, P., 'Quelques réflexions sur les Assurances Sociales', *La Presse Médicale*, 29 October 1927

—, 'La Question des Assurances Sociales', *La Presse Médicale*, 11 January 1928

Dorgeles, Roland, *Au Beau temps de la Butte*, Paris, Albin Michel, 1963

Drumont, Edouard, *La Fin d'un monde*, Paris, Albert Savine, 1892

Duchartre, Pierre-Louis, and Saulnier, René, *L'Imagerie populaire. Les Images de tous les provinces français du XVe siècle au Second Empire. Les Complaintes, contes et chansons, légendes qui ont inspirè les images*, Paris, Librairies de France, 1925

Dumont, Jean-Marie, *La Vie et l'oeuvre de Jean-Charles Pellerin*, Epinal, Imagerie Pellerin, 1956

Eizig, Paul, *The Destiny of Gold*, London, Macmillan, 1972

Erikson, Erik H., *Childhood and Society*, Harmondsworth, Penguin, 1965

Fohlen, Claude, *La France de l'entre-deux-guerres (1917–1939)*, Paris, Castermann, 1966

Fontette, François de, 'Eléments pour une definition du Juif', *Annales du C.E.S.E.R.E.*, 5, 1982

Frank, Nino, *Les Années 30*, Paris, Horay, 1969

Gerbod, P., 'L'Union Soviétique dans l'opinion française 1917–1941', *Annales du C.E.S.E.R.E.*, 4, 1981

Goux, Jean-Joseph, *Freud, Marx. Economie et symbolique*, Paris, Le Seuil, 1973

Gove, Philip Babock, *The Imaginary Voyage in Prose Fiction*, London, The Holland Press, 1961

Gramsci, Antonio, *Selections from the Prison Notebooks*, ed. Quintin Hoare and Geoffrey Nowell Smith, London, Lawrence and Wishart, 1971

Guilloux, Louis, *Carnets 1921–1944*, Paris, Gallimard, 1978

Hesnard, A., *De Freud à Lacan*, Paris, Les Editions E.S.F., 1970

Hewitt, Nicholas, 'Looking for Annie: Sartre's *La Nausée* and the Interwar Years', *Journal of European Studies*, XII, 1982

Jayle, F., 'Le Congrès des Syndicats Médicaux de France', *La Presse Médicale*, 23 November 1927

Jouhandeau, Marcel, *Le Péril juif*, Paris, Fernand Sarlat, 1936

Jouin, Mgr., ed., *Le Péril Judeo-Maconnique*, 1: *Les 'Protocoles' de Sages de Sion*, Paris, Revue Internationale des Sociétés Secrètes/Emile Paul Frères, 1920

Julian, Philippe, *The Triumph of Art Nouveau. Paris Exhibition 1900*, London, Phaidon, 1974

Kargalitsky, J., *The Life of H.G. Wells*, New York, Barnes and Noble, 1966

Kochan, Lionel, *The Jew and his History*, London, Macmilllan, 1977

Kupferman, Fred, *Au Pays des Soviets. Le Voyage français en Union Soviétique 1917–1939*, Paris, Julliard, coll. 'Archives', 1979

Laing, R.D., *The Divided Self*, Harmondsworth, Penguin, 1965

Lanoux, Armand, 'Trois personnages en quête d'une bohème', *Quinzaine Littéraire*, June 1982

Laurent, Jacques, *Les Bêtises*, Paris, Grasset, 1971

Le Goff, Jacques, 'Au Moyen Age, Temps de l'Eglise et Temps du Marchand', *Annales*, 15, 1960

Lorrain, Jean, *Poussières de Paris*, Paris, Ollendorf, 1902

Macaulay, Lord, *The History of England from the Accession of James the Second*, Volume II, ed. Charles Harding Firth, London, Macmillan, 1913–15

Mac Orlan, Pierre, '*La Folie-Almayer* et les aventuriers dans la littérature', *Nouvelle Revue Française*, 81, 1920

—, *Le Petit manuel du parfait aventurier*, Paris, Editions de la Sirène, 1920

Magraw, Roger, *France 1815–1914. The Bourgeois Century*, London, Fontana, 1983

Maier, Charles S., 'Between Taylorism and Technocracy', *Journal of Contemporary History*, V, 2, 1970

Malraux, André, *La Tentation de l'Occident*, Paris, Grasset, 1926

—, *Les Conquérants* in *Romans*, Paris, Gallimard, coll. 'La Pléïade', 1947

Mandel, Arnold, *Nous autres Juifs*, Paris, Hachette, 1978

Manoni, Maud, *The Child, his 'Illness' and the Others*, Harmondsworth, Penguin, 1973

Mercier, Ernest, *Réflexions 1936*, Paris, Editions du Centre Polytechnique d'Etudes Economiques, 1936

Morand, Paul, *1900*, Paris, Editions de France, 1931

Orwell, George, *The Road to Wigan Pier*, Harmondsworth, Penguin, 1962

Ory, E., 'Courtes réflexions d'un solitaire sur les Assurances Sociales', *La Presse Médicale*, 8 February 1928

Ory, Pascal, *Les Collaborateurs 1940–1945*, Paris, Le Seuil, coll. 'Points', 1980

—, *Les Expositions Universelles de Paris*, Paris, Ramsay, 1982

Palmade, Guy P., *Capitalisme et capitalistes francais au XIXe siècle*, Paris, Armand Colin, 1961

Parrinder, Patrick, *H.G. Wells*, Edinburgh, Oliver and Boyd, coll. 'Writers and Critics', 1970

Poliakov, Léon, *Histoire de l'antisémitisme*, 2: *De Voltaire à Wagner*, Paris, Calmann-Lévy, 1968

Portes, Jacques, 'Les Etats-Unis dans les manuels d'Histoire et de Géographie de la IIIe République (1871–1914)', *Revue d'Histoire Moderne et Contemporaine*, 1981

Roman, Jean, *Paris 1890s*, London, Prentice Hall International, 1961

Sadoul, Georges, *Histoire générale du cinéma*, 5: *Le Cinéma muet*, Paris, Denoël, 1975

Bibliography

Sartre, Jean-Paul, *Réflexions sur la question juive*, Paris, Gallimard, coll. 'Idées', n.d.

—, *Situations*, IV, Paris, Gallimard, 1964

Saulnier, R., and H. Van der Zee, 'La Mort de crédit', *Downa Sztuka Lwów*, II, 1939

Serouille, Albert, *Bezons à travers les âges*, Paris, Denoël, 1944

Singer, Charles, and E. Ashworth Underwood, *A Short History of Medicine*, Oxford, Clarendon Press, 1962

Singer-Kérel, Jeanne, *Le Coût de la vie à Paris de 1840 à 1954*, Paris, Armand Colin, 1961

Soucy, Robert, *Fascism in France. The Case of Maurice Barrès*, Berkely, Los Angeles and London, University of California Press, 1972

Specklin, P., 'Les Répercussions des Assurances Sociales sur l'exercice de la médecine', *La Presse Médicale*, 16 January 1929

—, 'Considérations critiques sur les Assurances Sociales. Une solution nouvelle: l'épargne individuelle obligatoire', *La Presse Médicale*, 6 March 1929

Stern, Bernhard J., *Social Factors in Medical Progress*, New York, AMS Press, 1968

Swift, Jonathan, 'A Modest Proposal' in *Irish Tracts 1728–1733*, Oxford, Blackwell, 1964

Targowla, Olivier, *Les Médecins aux main sales*, Paris, Belfond, coll. 'L'Echappée', 1976

Thibaudet, Albert, 'Le Roman de l'aventure', *Nouvelle Revue Française*, 1919

Thuillier, G., 'Hygiène corporelle aux XIXe et XXe siècles, *Annales de Démographie Historique*, 1975

Troyat, Henri, *Un si long chemin*, Paris, Stock, 1976

Vallès, Jules, *La Rue à Londres*, Paris, Les Editeurs Français Réunis, 1951

Vallière, P. de, *Honneur et fidélité. Histoire des Suisses au service étranger*, Laussanne, Les Editions d'Art Suisse Ancien, 1940

Nesta Helen Webster, *Britain's Call to Arms: an Appeal to our Women*, London, 1914

—, *The Surrender of an Empire*, London, 1931

Wells, H.G., *An Experiment in Autobiography*, 1, London, Gollancz, 1934

—, *Kipps*, London, Fontana, 1961

—, *The New Machiavelli*, London, Odhams, 1911

—, *Tono-Bungay*, London, Pan Books, 1964

Wilson, Edmund, *Axel's Castle*, London, Fontana, 1961

Zeldin, Theodore, *France 1848–1945*, 1, *Ambition, Love and Politics*, London, Oxford University Press, 1973

Index

Index

Marx, Karl, 53, 115
Massis, Henri, 193
Maurras, Charles, 176, 193, 198
Maurron, Charles, 81, 117
Mercier, Ernest, 35, 143
Metternich, Prince Klemens von, 42, 53
Michelet, E., 107, 184
Miller, Henry, 74
Millet, Jean-François, 108
Mirabeau, Comte Honoré Gabriel, 51, 52
Moncey, Maréchal Bon Adrien Jeannot de, 70, 81
Monmouth, Duke of, 39, 78–9
Montaigne, Michel de, 83, 184
Montandon, Georges, 171, 184
Montmartre, 68–9, 70, 71–5, 93, 99, 154, 155
Morand, Paul, 33, 94, 156, 184, 193, 206
Moreau-Vautier, 90
Mounier, Emmanuel, 39, 150, 151, 153, 157
Muray, Philippe, 4, 9, 85, 191, 193
Musset, Alfred de, 43
Mussolini, Benito, 35, 171

Napoleon I, 12, 51, 52, 54, 70, 71, 76, 79, 81, 83
Napoleon III, 7, 94, 111, 195
Nettlebeck, Colin W., 152
Nietzsche, Friedrich, 48, 53, 146, 160, 172, 178, 183, 185, 192
Nimier, Roger, 132, 135
nouveau mal du siècle, 6, 12, 51, 54

Offenbach, Jacques, 65–6
Orwell, George, 69
Ory, E., 24
Ory, Pascal, 88, 89, 93, 152, 153, 158, 180, 196
Out-Breut, Michèle, 125
Overbeck, Frantz, 53

Palmade, Guy, 100, 108, 111
Parrinder, Patrick, 104
Pascin, Jules, 71
Pasteur, Louis, 8, 41, 45, 171
Pereire, Isaac and Emile, 111
Pétain, Philippe, 179
Petitjean, Dr, 23
Philip, André, 34
Picasso, Pablo, 5, 72
Poincaré, Raymond, 20, 58, 134, 151, 179
Poli, Jean-Dominique, 152
Poliakov, Leon, 198
Pollet, Eveline, 7
Portes, Jacques, 34
Poulet, Robert, 5, 119, 126, 131
Protocols of the Elders of Zion, The, 155, 167, 174, 195, 196
Proust, Marcel, 9, 13, 58, 66, 67, 77, 78, 84, 85, 97–8, 119, 120, 122, 197
Psichari, Ernest, 128

Queneau, Raymond, 72

Rabelais, François, 115
Ravachol (François Claudius Koenigstein), 5
Rebatet, Lucien, 26, 150, 151, 153, 159, 172, 173, 179, 193
Rémy, Dr, 23
Renan, Ernest, 95
Renard, Jules, 42
Revel, Jean-François, 124
Richard, Jean-Pierre, 125, 129
Richepin, Jean, 72
Rimailho, Emile, 34
Robert, P.-E., 67
Robinsonade, 65–7
Romains, Jules, 25
Roman, Jean, 127
Roosevelt, Franklin D., 166
Roussin, Philippe, 4–5, 9, 174, 197
Roux, Dominique de, 126

Sadoul, Georges, 62
Saint-Exupéry, Antoine de, 83, 145
Saint-Simon, Comte Claude Henri de, 34, 91, 111
Sand, George, 120
Sartre, Jean-Paul, 6, 122, 146–7, 169
Saulnier, René, 107
Saunders, Kim, 30, 81
Sautermeister, Christine, 125, 126, 127
Serge, Victor, 74
Shakespeare, William, 11, 192, 210–14, 217, 219, 220, 221
Simenon, Georges, 156
Singer, Charles, 45
Singer-Kérel, Jeanne, 19
Soucy, Robert, 198
Soupault, Ralph, 71
Specklin, P., 25
Stalin, Joseph, 35
Stavisky, Alexandre, 90, 108, 111